Modern Critical Views

Modern Critical Views

Modern Critical Views

ALICE WALKER

Edited and with an introduction by
Harold Bloom
Sterling Professor of the Humanities
Yale University

CHELSEA HOUSE PUBLISHERS
New York ◊ Philadelphia

© 1989 by Chelsea House Publishers, a division of Main Line Book Co.

Introduction © 1988 by Harold Bloom

Printed and bound in the United States of America

10   9

∞ The paper used in this publication meets the minimum requirements of the American National Standard for Permanence of Paper for Printed Library Materials, Z39.48–1984.

Library of Congress Cataloging-in-Publication Data
Alice Walker.
    (Modern critical views)
    Bibliography: p.
    Includes index.
    1. Walker, Alice, 1944–   —Criticism and interpretation. I. Bloom, Harold. II. Series.
PS3573.A425Z53   1988   813'.54   87–25668
ISBN 1–55546–314–2

Contents

Editor's Note

This book gathers together a representative selection of the best criticism available upon the writings of Alice Walker. The critical essays are reprinted here in the chronological order of their original publication. I am deeply indebted to Henry Finder for his customary erudition and judgment in helping me to edit this volume.

My introduction gently intimates that the critics of Alice Walker somewhat idealize the influence-relation between women writers, and black women writers in particular, following Walker herself in this regard. Peter Erickson begins the chronological sequence of criticism with a discussion of the family dynamic in Alice Walker's work, with an emphasis upon a daughter's guilt-obsessed relation to her mother.

Celebration of individual responsibility throughout Walker's writing is the subject of the study by Thadious M. Davis, while Barbara Christian, in contrast, commends Walker for teaching black women the absolute necessity of self-love.

In Keith Byerman's reading, there is an evolution from artistic celebration of folk-ways to very explicit polemic in Walker's work, an evolution that necessarily has in it elements of artistic loss. But in Mae G. Henderson's perspective, *The Color Purple* strongly "subverts the traditional Eurocentric male code which dominates the literary conventions of the epistolary novel." Whether this polemical assertion redefines and extends literary forms and traditions, as Henderson asserts, may not be the same matter as the redefinition of male-female relationships, but Henderson identifies the two.

Susan Willis relates the quest of returning to community in Walker's writings to the Southern Civil Rights movement, and suggests that Walker must be taken seriously as a revolutionary activist as well as a revolutionary writer. The emphasis moves back from politics to psychology in W. Lawrence Hogue's analysis of *The Third Life of Grange Copeland*.

Both Dianne F. Sadoff and Deborah E. McDowell center their discussions

where I venture also in my introduction, upon the nature of the influence process in Walker's work. Tracing the influence of Zora Neale Hurston upon
Walker, Sadoff shrewdly affirms that misprision, or strong misreading, is
necessary even in the relations of women writers to one another, though these
relations are different from those prevailing between male writers. McDowell,
more idealizing than Sadoff, credits Walker with having helped to create a
purely female aesthetic and even a black female aesthetic.

Voice, as my introduction suggests, is the crucial element in Walker's
literary polemic, and the issue of voice is dominant in John F. Callahan's
exegesis of *Meridian,* which he sees as the start "of the restoration of the
reciprocal sense of language and experience that is essential if America is to
resume a revolutionary course." Equally commendatory, Tamar Katz celebrates
the risk-taking didacticism of *The Color Purple.*

Two of Walker's essays—"In Search of Our Mothers' Gardens" and "*One
Child of One's Own*"—and her short story, "Everyday Use"—are read by
Marianne Hirsch as materials for our reimagining of "the conjunction of anger
and love" in maternal subjectivity. The volume concludes with a searching
appraisal of *The Color Purple* by Bell Hooks, who remarks on the conservatism of its narrative universe but recommends to us "those crucial moments
in the text where the imagination works to liberate."

Introduction

A contemporary writer who calls herself "author and medium" is by no means idiosyncratic, and Alice Walker certainly seems to me a wholly representative writer of and for our current era. The success of *The Color Purple* is deserved; Walker's sensibility is very close to the Spirit of the Age. Rather than seek to analyze verse and fictional prose that is of a kind I am not yet competent to judge, or a speculative essay such as "In Search of Our Mothers' Gardens" which eludes me, I will center here upon Walker's meditations upon her acknowledged precursor, Zora Neale Hurston. "There is no book more important to me than this one," Walker wrote of Hurston's masterwork, *Their Eyes Were Watching God*. Perhaps the only literary enthusiasm I share with Walker is my own deep esteem for that admirable narrative, about which I have written elsewhere.

Walker associated her feeling for Hurston with her similar veneration for famous black women singers, Billie Holiday and Bessie Smith. That association is a moving trope or defense, since Hurston, like Walker, was a writer and not a vocalist. Here is another tribute by Walker to Hurston:

> We live in a society, as blacks, women, and artists, whose contests we do not design and with whose insistence on ranking us we are permanently at war. To know that second place, in such a society, has often required more work and innate genius than first, a longer, grimmer struggle over greater odds that first—and to be able to fling your scarf about dramatically while you demonstrate that you know—is to trust your own self-evaluation in the face of the Great White Western Commercial of white and male supremacy, which is virtually everything we see, outside and often inside our own homes. That Hurston held her own, literally, against the flood of whiteness and maleness that diluted so much other black art of the period in which she worked is a testimony to her genius and her faith.

1

As black women and as artists, we are prepared, I think, to keep that faith. There are other choices, but they are despicable.

Zora Neale Hurston, who went forth into the world with one dress to her name, and who was permitted, at other times in her life, only a single pair of shoes, rescued and recreated a world which she labored to hand us whole, never underestimating the value of her gift, if at times doubting the good sense of its recipients. She appreciated us, in any case, *as we fashioned ourselves.* That is something. And of all the people in the world to be, she chose to be herself, *and more and more herself.* That, too, is something.

The strength of this rhetoric is considerable, and has the literary force of a medium. Walker's tribute to Hurston bears an eloquent title: "On Refusing to Be Humbled by Second Place in a Contest You Did Not Design." To write a novel indeed is to enter a contest you did not design, and to *fashion yourself* certainly is the ambition of every novelist or poet aspiring to permanence. To write *The Third Life of Grange Copeland, Meridian,* and *The Color Purple* is to have entered a contest Walker did not design, an agon with *Their Eyes Were Watching God.* No feminist critic will agree with that statement, which for them reflects my purely male view of literature. Yet we do not live forever. Do we reread *Their Eyes Were Watching God* or do we reread *The Color Purple?* And if we choose to reread both, do we repress the comparisons that the two novels provoke in regard to one another?

Walker's most poignant paragraphs on Hurston come at the end of her superbly personal essay, "Looking for Zora":

> There are times—and finding Zora Hurston's grave was one of them—when normal responses of grief, horror, and so on, do not make sense because they bear no real relation to the depth of the emotion one feels. It was impossible for me to cry when I saw the field full of weeds where Zora is. Partly this is because I have come to know Zora through her books and she was not a teary sort of person herself; but partly, too, it is because there is a point at which even grief feels absurd. And at this point, laughter gushes up to retrieve sanity.
>
> It is only later, when the pain is not so direct a threat to one's own existence that what was learned in that moment of comical lunacy is understood. Such moments rob us of both youth and vanity. But perhaps they are also times when greater disciplines are born.

This may not be Browning at the grave of Shelley, but it is close enough. The pain is familial, since the literary mother, like the poetic father, evokes in the ephebe all the terrible poignance of Freud's "family romances." Michael G. Cooke, writing on Hurston, states the particular dilemma of the black writer's quest for a voice:

> What gives singularity to the black writer's burden in searching for a voice is the twofold factor of frequency and context. Either directly or in projection through a central character, black writer after black writer, generation upon generation, from Frederick Douglass to Alice Walker, evinces the problem of voice. And it is appropriate to regard the most outspoken black writers of the protest movement as bearers of the burden in another guise. Theirs is not so much a free voice as the forced voice of reaction and resentment.

The School of Resentment, which has many factions both critical and creative, does not regard voice as a problem, since the celebration of community necessarily decries individuated subjectivity while exalting collective roarings (or murmurings) as the more moral mode. I fear that influence and its anxieties do not vanish even in the presence of the most self-abnegating of ideologies or idealisms. Our most distinguished critics of Hurston evade this burden, but it is there nevertheless. Here is Elizabeth Meese on "Orality and Textuality in *Their Eyes Were Watching God*":

> By extricating herself from cultural control, Janie/Hurston creates culture. Through the retelling of Janie's story, orality becomes textuality. Textuality is produced by Janie's learned orality, her participation in the oral tradition of the culture. She learns to be one of the people; thus, this is a story of her acculturation into black womanhood and her artistic entitlement to language. By chronicling Janie's development, Hurston transforms the status of narrative from the temporality characteristic of oral tradition to the more enduring textuality required to outwit time's effect on memory. In doing so, she presents feminist readers with a map of a woman's personal resistance to patriarchy, and feminist writers—in particular Alice Walker—with the intertext for later feminist works.

If one is presented with an intertext, does one pay nothing for the gift? Janie/Hurston creates culture but does Meridian/Walker? Again, here is that dynamic deconstructive duo, Barbara Johnson and H. L. Gates, Jr., rightly praising *Their Eyes Were Watching God* for giving us (and Walker) "A Black and Idiomatic Free Indirect Discourse":

> Janie, in effect, has *rewritten* Joe's text of himself, and liberated herself in the process. Janie "writes" herself into being by *naming,* by speaking herself free. In *The Color Purple,* Alice Walker takes this moment in Hurston's text as the moment of revision, and creates a character whom we witness literally writing herself into being, but writing herself into being in a language that imitates that idiom *spoken* by Janie and Hurston's black community generally. This scene and this transformation or reversal of status is truly the first feminist critique of the fiction of the authority of the male voice, and its sexism, in the Afro-American tradition.

That is admirably precise and accurate; *The Color Purple's* Celie indeed writes "herself into being in a language that imitates that idiom *spoken* by Janie and Hurston's black community generally." The authority of the male voice, and its sexism, may well be subverted by Hurston (she herself would have disowned any such intention or accomplishment). But what has Walker subverted by imitating and so repeating a revisionist moment that she has not originated? No feminist critic will admit the legitimacy of that question, but it abides and will require an answer.

PETER ERICKSON

"Cast Out Alone/to Heal/and Re-create/ Ourselves": Family-based Identity in the Work of Alice Walker

One of the major concerns of Alice Walker's art is the exploration of intra-family relationships. For a group of poems gathered under the heading "Surrounding Ground and Autobiography," Walker supplies the following preface: "To acknowledge our ancestors means we are aware that we did not make ourselves . . . . The grace with which we embrace life, in spite of the pain, the sorrows, is always a measure of what has gone before." The family dynamic in Alice Walker's work is a key part of the formative influence of "what has gone before." In Walker's first novel, the family configuration is defined by the child's special relationship to her grandfather and by the tension between father and grandfather. The use of the family as an imaginative structure—as a way of organizing experience—then undergoes an important change: the prominence of the grandfather as against the father in the first novel gives way in the second to an emphasis on a daughter's guilt-laden relation to her mother.

I. "I COULDN'T EVER EVEN *EXPRESS* MY *LOVE!*"

The Third Life of Grange Copeland (1970), a novel which concerns three generations of a rural Southern black family, begins by demonstrating with a vivid matter-of-factness the family's entrapment in a vicious cycle of poverty. Permanently indebted to the white owner of the cotton fields in which he works, Grange Copeland seeks release in drinking, in violence against his wife, and in being "devoid of any emotion." Particularly convincing is the

From *CLA Journal* 23, no. 1 (September 1979). © 1980 by the College Language Association.

picture of Grange's submission as seen from the point of view of his son
Brownfield, who has begun to work in the fields at the age of six:

> While he stared at the hair one of the workers—not his father who
> was standing beside him as if he didn't know he was there—said
> to him softly, "Say 'Yessir' to Mr. Shipley," and Brownfield looked
> up before he said anything and scanned his father's face. The mask
> was as tight and still as if his father had coated himself with wax.
> And Brownfield smelled for the first time an odor of sweat, fear,
> and something indefinite. Something smothered and tense (which
> was of his father and of the other workers and not of mint) that
> came from his father's body. His father said nothing. Brownfield,
> trembling, said "Yessir," filled with terror of this man who could,
> by his presence alone, turn his father into something that might
> as well have been a pebble or a post or a piece of dirt, except for
> the sharp bitter odor of something whose source was forcibly con-
> tained in flesh.

To compensate for his emotionally absent parents, Brownfield dwells in
the fantasy created by his "favorite daydream":

> Brownfield's wife and children—two children, a girl and a boy—
> waited anxiously for him just inside the door in the foyer. They
> jumped all over him, showering him with kisses. While he told
> his wife of the big deals he'd pushed through that day she fixed
> him a mint julep. After a splendid dinner, presided over by the
> cook, dressed in black uniform and white starched cap, he and
> his wife, their arms around each other, tucked the children in bed
> and spent the rest of the evening discussing her day (which she
> had spent walking in her garden), and making love.

We are made to feel that Brownfield's vision is impossibly idyllic and that
the gap between the actual family and the fantasy family is absolute. By the
end of the first two masterfully compressed chapters, the family has
disintegrated: his father disappears, his mother commits suicide, and
Brownfield is left alone. Himself trapped in the vicious cycle, Brownfield never
succeeds in establishing the secure family of his original daydream. Yet, at
the conclusion of the novel, the cycle has been broken. Brownfield's futile
dream of family happiness has become a more real possibility for his daughter
Ruth. This possibility is supported by the historical change which the Civil
Rights movement represents and is exemplified specifically by a black couple,
the Civil Rights worker and his pregnant wife:

Quincy put his arm around his wife, his hand moving up and down her side. He held her loosely yet completely, as if she meant everything to him, and the glow in her eyes was pure worship when she looked up at him. Grange was touched almost to tears by the simplicity and directness of their love.

Ruth's potential for a positive version of family has previously been encouraged by her grandfather, Grange, who ultimately makes possible her escape from the negative family syndrome:"You're special to me because you're a part of me; a part of me I didn't even used to want. I want you to go on a long time, have a heap of children." Much of the interest lies in seeing how the novel makes the leap from the pattern of destructive family relationships to the positive image of family at the end—how, for instance, the novel moves from the hopelessness of Brownfield's "favorite daydream" to the hope embodied in Quincy and Helen.

It is difficult to keep in full view the novel as a whole. The style of narration is deceptively simple. Each element is in itself simple, but the steady accumulation of detail creates a complicated effect of density and generational depth. The novel's forward movement is swift, inexorable, and yet—paradoxically—casual and imperceptible. The numerous shifts of situation through the course of the novel give it an epic-like sweep which makes it seem hard to maintain one's bearings and to keep track of developments as an entire sequence. One crucial event, however, clearly defines the shape of the novel by dividing it in two. This key turning point occurs when Brownfield murders his wife Mem and his father Grange takes away his daughter Ruth. Grange's intervention is briefly foreshadowed in part 4, chapter 17, where his return from the North coincides with the birth of Ruth; but the relationship between Grange and Ruth does not begin until part 7, chapter 31, at the approximate center of the novel. Only with the gradual growth of their relationship does a firm basis for hope emerge. Prior to this decisive midpoint of the novel, we witness a series of false escapes from despair. Tantalizing hopes are raised to be regularly and cruelly punctured. The narrative logic of alternating hope and despair requires the reader to "Expect nothing. Live frugally / On surprise" (*Revolutionary Petunias*) in a less optimistic sense than the second half of the novel permits.

After his father has abandoned the family and his mother has died, Brownfield sees that the cycle which destroyed his parents is in danger of repeating itself in his own life: "He knew too that the minute he accepted money from Shipley he was done for. If he borrowed from Shipley, Shipley would make sure he never finished paying it back." However, he avoids one trap only to fall into another. His journey to "new freedom" leads to a "local Negro bar and grill": "His mother and father had come to such places, perhaps this same one, and when they had fought and argued in public it was usually among the kind of people who would frequent such a place." It is later made clear that Brownfield's parents had fought in this very same place and that Brownfield has inherited the prostitute/lover whom his father had visited every Saturday as part of his weekly binge. A renewal of hope follows when Brownfield meets and marries Mem, who is educated and "life-giving." But family history is soon destined to repeat itself:

> That was the year he first saw how his own life was becoming a repetition of his father's. . . . His crushed pride, his battered ego, made him drag Mem away from school-teaching. Her knowledge reflected badly on a husband who could scarcely read and write. It was his great ignorance that sent her into white homes as a domestic, his need to bring her down to his level! . . . His rage could and did blame everything, *everything* on her.

The next revival of hope occurs when Mem asserts herself against Brownfield. "Her big dream" has been "to buy a house," to escape "moving from one sharecropper's cabin to another." Initially, she is "unable to comprehend that all her moves upward and toward something of their own would be checked by him." Parts 5 and 6 deal with Mem's successful efforts to find a house and a job, and with her loss of them. It is impossible not to feel the elation of Mem's announcement:" 'We got us a new house,' she said, as if she were dropping something precious that would send up delightful bright explosions. 'We got us a new house in town!' she whispered joyously." Her determination in opposing Brownfield's resistance to her plan is also exhilarating. Though desperate and painful, her threatening Brownfield with the shotgun in chapter 25 is seen as a necessary step. Her ultimatum gives the feeling that a new start is possible: "If you intend to come along I done made out me some rules for you, for make no mistake it's going to be my house and in my house what the white man expects us to act like ain't going to git no consideration." This fresh start is nevertheless immediately undercut by Brownfield's desire for revenge. He gloats when they lose the house and are forced to move to a dilapidated cabin. However, Mem's determination persists: "I'm going to git well again, and git work again, and when I do I'm going to leave you," she announces. Consequently, Brownfield shoots her. This climactic destruction of hope paradoxically signals the beginning of the first substantial hope in the novel. Although the process of revenge is once again set in motion—Brownfield "was thinking of his father's attachment to Ruth

and of how perfect a revenge it would be if he could break it"—this time
Brownfield's plot fails. In the final chapter, Grange protects Ruth by shooting
Brownfield, as if to cancel Brownfield's shooting of Mem. The relentless con-
version of hope into hopelessness is ended.

Though it is reserved for the second half of the novel, the relationship
between Grange and Ruth constitutes the emotional heart of *The Third Life
of Grange Copeland*. This relationship, the most fully developed in the book,
is lovingly and often humorously described. Grange's association of Ruth with
"innocence" and "miracle," the sanctity of family bonds rescued from the threat
of degradation, and the air of improbability are reminiscent of Shakespeare's
late romance, with the grandfather-daughter tie substituted for father-daughter
pairing. In Walker's novel, the relationship between grandfather and daughter
is strongly redemptive. Ruth saves Grange; Grange, in turn, saves her. Ruth
is the source of Grange's "third life": "[H]e had wanted her so much he could
not believe himself capable of such strong emotion" " '[H]ere is a reason to
get yourself together and hold on.' " Grange nurtures Ruth and, in the end,
defends her independence at the cost of his life. The sense of redemption is
qualified by the price which has to be paid for it. The novel's conclusion is
compelling because it lies somewhere between a happy ending and a
melodramatic catastrophe. We cannot help feeling joyful about the fact that
Ruth's future is assured, but this emotion is mixed with the realization that
her future is based on a sacrifice of whose complexity she is not fully aware.

Beyond suspense about the outcome in terms of plot, there is the drama
of Grange's moral predicament. His problem is to coordinate and reconcile
his past with his present devotion to Ruth. Thus he summarizes the three
stages in his life: "The white folks hated me and I hated myself until I started
hating them in return and loving myself. Then I tried just loving me, and then
you, and *ignoring* them much as I could." His first life culminates in the
"murder" of his wife as he admits to his son: "[Y]our ma'd be alive today
if I hadn't just as good as shot her to death, same as you done your wife."
His second life opens with the "murder" of a pregnant white woman who
has just been deserted by her male companion (the murder is not a literal
one in that it consists of the woman's choosing to drown rather than be saved
by a black person):

> . . . in a strange way, a bizarre way, it liberated him. He felt in some
> way repaid for his own unfortunate life. It was the taking of that
> white woman's life—and the denying of the life of her child—the
> taking of her life, not the taking of her money, that forced him
> to want to try to live again. He believed that, against his will, he

had stumbled on the necessary act that black men must commit
to regain, or to manufacture their manhood, their self-respect.

Grange moves beyond this position when he finds a more positive source of
identity in his relationship to Ruth. His third life begins with his commitment
to her and ends with the murder of his own son.

Grange is unable to explain himself fully to Ruth because he cannot communicate the whole story of his life:

> And Grange knew he would never tell her of his past, of the
> pregnant woman and his lectures of hate. . . .
>
> She was not to know until another time, that her grandfather,
> as she knew him, was a reborn man. She did not know fully, even
> after he was dead, what cruelties and blood fostered his tolerance
> and his strength. And his love.
>
> What could he tell his granddaughter about her sadly loving,
> bravely raging and revengeful grandmother? . . .
>
> The strangely calm eyes of the old man looked across the fence
> to rest on his granddaughter. He marveled that, knowing him so
> well, she knew nothing of that other life. Or even of the dismal
> birth of her own father.

In the end, Ruth is sheltered from the suffering of Grange's sacrificial death:
"He had been shot and felt the blood spreading under his shirt. He did not
want Ruth to see. Other than that he was not afraid." The reader is forced
to recognize that Ruth's awareness and the reader's awareness diverge. Ruth's
experience of Grange and of Brownfield is restricted to a relatively simple
dichotomy of good and evil. The reader's wider perspective includes some
sympathy for Brownfield and the knowledge of Grange's guilt in, for example,
exploiting Josie for Ruth's salvation.

The issue of justice in the novel turns on one's evaluation of the distinction between Grange and Brownfield. Brownfield's effort to regain his daughter
makes a forceful claim on our sympathy: " 'But *you was no daddy to me!'*
he said to Grange, 'and I ain't going to let you keep my child to make up
for it!' " This partially valid (though also twisted) logic is reinforced when
we recall the moment early in the novel when Grange abandons his family:

> Brownfield pretended to be asleep. . . . He saw Grange bend over
> him to inspect his head and face. He was him reach down to touch
> him. He saw his hand stop, just before it reached his cheek.
> Brownfield was crying silently and wanted his father to touch the

tears. . . . He saw his father's hand draw back, without touching him. He saw him turn sharply and leave the room. He heard him leave the house.

The difference between the two men as it emerges in their confrontation over Ruth is that, unlike Brownfield, Grange has been capable of change due to his acceptance of responsibility. As Grange puts it: "I *know* the danger of putting all the blame on somebody else for the mess you make out of your life. I fell into the trap myself!" This distinction is legitimate, but it is also "unfair" in the sense that Grange has learned about the personal responsibility—which he argues Brownfield doesn't have—from Ruth:

> "You put it *all* on them!" she said starting up. . . .
> "The white folks didn't kill my mother," she said at last. "He did!"
>
> "And I could parade Shipleys before her from now till doomsday and she'd still want to know what's done happened to her granddaddy's love!"

Brownfield is partly defeated by circumstance: he is not allowed a second chance; there is no granddaughter available to act as a catalyst to help him change. Grange's murder of Brownfield at the conclusion of the novel is not, then, a simple expression of justice. It is rather a tragic resolution of an insoluble conflict between Grange and Brownfield.

Ruth participates in the tragedy which leads to her freedom when she and Brownfield meet alone. Using the same argument Brownfield had tried to use against Grange, Ruth rejects her father's one genuine effort to respond to her:

> "You never cared for us," said Ruth. . . . "I don't want any of your damn changes now," she thought, and hated and liked herself for this lack of charity.
>
> "I couldn't ever even *express* my love!" he said. . . .
> "I loved my childrens," said Brownfield, sweating now. "I loved your mama."
>
> These tortured words, and they did sound as if they escaped from a close dungeon in his soul, hung on the air as a kind of passionate gibberish. Ruth shook her head once more to clear it; truly she could not even understand him when he spoke of loving.

This moment in the novel which seals Brownfield's doom is illuminated by

Alice Walker's commentary in *Interviews with Black Writers* (edited by John O'Brien [hereafter cited as *Interviews*]): "Because all along I wanted to explore the relationship between parents and children: specifically between daughters and their father . . . , and I wanted to learn, myself, how it happens that the hatred a child can have for a parent become inflexible." Seen from the perspective of Ruth's hatred of her father, the sense of her triumph at the end is marked by "unforgiveness."

II. "COULD HE DISAVOW HIS FATHER AND LIVE?"

"A Sudden Trip Home in the Spring" (1971) provides a striking clarification of the familial themes of *The Third Life of Grange Copeland*. The reader who approaches the short story by way of the novel recognizes a substantial overlapping. The two works share (1) the sense of a family on the move— "And go they would. Who knew exactly where, before they moved? Another soundless place, walks falling down, roofing gone"; (2) the image of a father who has been defeated by his life as a sharecropper and whose anger has turned inward against his own family—"Did it matter now that often he had threatened their lives with the rage of his despair?"; and (3) the primacy of the relationship between the daughter and a grandfather who has transcended defeat—"He was the first person Sarah wanted to see when she got home."

In *The Third Life of Grange Copeland,* the point of view is evenly distributed among Brownfield, Ruth, and Grange, while the short story is told exclusively from the daughter's perspective. This centering on the daughter sharpens the conflict in her respective attitudes towards the grandfather and the father. Unlike Ruth in *The Third Life of Grange Copeland,* Sarah Davis must face in a more sustained way her problematic relationship to her father. Because Sarah is returning to the home she has already left and because she is an artist, the project of recovering her family as a key to her identity is more explicitly formulated. Sarah's school friends "had no idea what made her," "had no idea from where she came," and Sarah herself is in danger of losing the sustenance which precise knowledge of her origins could provide.

The crucial image for identity in the story is the face—as an important passage, prior to Sarah's return home, suggests:

> There was a full wall of her own drawings, all of black women. She found black men impossible to draw or to paint; she could not bear to trace defeat onto blank pages. Her women figures were matronly, massive of arm, with a weary victory showing in their eyes. Surrounded by Sarah's drawing was a red SNCC poster of

an old man holding a small girl whose face nestled in his shoulder. Sarah often felt she was the little girl whose face no one could see.

As the story unfolds, the generalization about black men is transformed: the image of defeat is attached specifically to Sarah's father, while her grandfather and her brother provide models of victory. Once home, Sarah explains to her brother the impasse in her art in terms of the face: "Sarah shook her head, a frown coming between her eyes. 'I sometimes spend weeks,' she said, 'trying to sketch or paint a facet that is unlike every other face around me, except, vaguely for one.' " The scene in the SNCC poster in Sarah's room at school is enacted at her father's funeral when Sarah sits beside her grandfather: she "briefly leaned her cheek against his shoulder and felt like a child again." Her grandfather's face becomes a touchstone in the search for her own:

> The defeat that had frightened her in the faces of black men was the defeat of black forever defined by white. But that defeat was nowhere on her grandfather's face. . . .
>
> "One day I will paint you, Grandpa," she said as they turned to go. "Just as you stand here now, with just," she moved closer and touched his face with her hand, "just the right stubborn tenseness of your cheek. Just that look of Yes and No in your eyes."

Sarah repeats the gesture with her brother: "She leaned peacefully into her brother's arms." He, too, provides a shape for the elusive face she has been trying to form: "She watched her brother from a window in the bus; her eyes did not leave his face until the little station was out of sight." The physical contact with her grandfather and brother, and the perception of their faces are seen as the precondition for the development of Sarah's art. These family faces provide a necessary context and a direction; through them, Sarah sees her way to continuing the search for her own face, her own identity. At the beginning of the story, there is a disparity between Sarah's face and her identity:

> Her eyes enchanted her friends because they always seemed to know more, and to find more of life amusing, or sad, than Sarah cared to tell. . . . She was gentle with her friends, and her outrage at their tactlessness did not show. . . . Embarrassment sometimes drove her to fraudulent expression.

Upon her return to school at the end, her face is given back to her:

> "How was it?" She watched her reflection in a pair of smiling hazel eyes.

"It was fine," she said slowly, returning the smile, thinking of her grandfather.

The burden of "A Sudden Trip Home in the Spring" is that one must go back to one's family in order to go forward, that the family background must be experienced as a resource rather than a liability. Yet the powerful impact of the story does not come only from Sarah's resolve at the end. Equally engaging is the way this affirmation is complicated by the pressure of un-resolved issues concerning the father. To say—without a bitterness which con-founds love—"I am my father's daughter" as one of the answers to the ques-tion "Who am I?" has not been entirely possible for Sarah.

The difficulty of reclaiming the father is introduced through the analogue of Richard Wright and his father. Sarah explains with poignant succinctness: "He was a man who wrote, a man who had trouble with his father." As Sarah proceeds to elaborate, the urgency of her questions makes it clear that, in talking about Richard Wright, she is thinking about herself: "Who was Wright without his father? . . . Was he, in fact, still her father's son? Or was he freed by his father's desertion to be nobody's son, to be his own father? Could he disavow his father and live?" The rhetorical implication is that Sarah cannot deny the connection between her father and herself. But to give the reason why this is so is also to state the problem: "Wright's father was one faulty door in a house of many ancient rooms. Was that one faulty door to shut him off forever from the rest of the house? . . . I see him as a door that refused to open, a hand that was always closed. A fist."

The "closed" quality of Wright's father has its counterpart in Sarah's father, whose opacity is not simply a function of his being literally dead:

> Sarah looked for a long time into the face, as if to find some answer
> to her questions written there. It was the same face, a dark,
> Shakespearean head framed by gray, woolly hair and split almost
> in half by a short gray mustache. It was a completely silent face,
> a shut face.

To some extent, her father's "shutness" does not matter since, continuing the metaphor, Sarah finds an alternative in her brother. " 'You are my door to all rooms,' she said; 'don't ever close.'" Nonetheless, her inability to establish direct contact with her father remains a limitation. The loss is not simply that her father is dead, but that their failed relationship leaves a psychological void, a gap in her identity. Sarah acknowledges her own "stony silence"; she has been a closed door to her father as much as he had been to her:

> When he was alive she had avoided him.

"Where's that girl at?" her father would ask. "Done closed herself up in her room again," he would answer himself.

For Sarah's mother had died in her sleep one night. . . . And Sarah had blamed her father.

Sarah's closedness with respect to her father ("but [she] still had not spoken the language they both knew. Not to him.") is enacted in the present through the reserve in her mourning: "Tears started behind her shoulder blades but did not reach her eyes." The bond with her grandfather rather than her father is emphasized at the funeral, "a short and eminently dignified service, during which Sarah and her grandfather alone did not cry."

There is some release from the contempt in which Sarah has held her father: *"Perhaps it doesn't matter whether I misunderstood or never understood"*; *"Whatever had made her think she knew what love was or was not?"* Yet the precariousness of the release is registered in the phrase "Stare the rat down," a refrain which enters into Sarah's expression of determination in the final paragraph. There has been an actual rat under her father's coffin, but it serves "more as a symbol of something." What the rat symbolizes is overdetermined. The act of staring it down suggests a combination of acknowledging, controlling, and suppressing the pain of their emotional separateness during her father's life—painful feelings which threaten to overwhelm her now unless tightly held in.

The utter seriousness of Alice Walker's treatment of one's relation to one's family is exemplified by the personal testimony of her second volume of poetry, *Revolutionary Petunias & Other Poems* (1973). The poem "For My Sister Molly Who in the Fifties," which ends abruptly with the report that she "Left us," can be juxtaposed with "Burial," in which Walker pays homage to the family by going back to "the old, unalterable / roots": "Today I bring my own child here; / to this place where my father's / grandmother rests undisturbed." To see "from the angle of her death" is presented as an indispensable orientation.

To see from the perspective of Molly's refusal to conserve and cherish the memory of the family is disturbing:

> As saw my brothers cloddish
> And me destined to be
> Wayward
> My mother remote   My father
> A wearisome farmer
> With heartbreaking
> Nails.

The refrain "For My Sister Molly Who in the Fifties" tries to call Molly back within the family sphere by claiming her as "sister," but the effort fails in face of the resounding final line: "Left us." Alice Walker's commentary provides a rich context for the poem:

> I loved her so much it came as a great shock—and a shock I don't expect to recover from—to learn she was ashamed of us. We were so poor, so dusty and sunburnt. We talked wrong. We didn't know how to dress, or use the right eating utensils. And so, she drifted away, and I did not understand it. Only later, I realized that sometimes (perhaps), it becomes too painful to bear: seeing your home and family— shabby and seemingly without hope—through the eyes of your new friends and strangers. She had felt—for her own mental health—that the gap that separated us from the rest of the world was too wide for her to keep trying to bridge.
>
> (*Interviews*)

This divide between family origin and later life is the one which Sarah Davis attempts to cross in "A Sudden Trip Home in the Spring." Molly's view of the father as "A wearisome farmer / With heartbreaking / Nails" corresponds in the short story to Richard Wright's rediscovery of his father as "an old, watery-eyed field hand, bent from plowing, his teeth gone, smelling of manure." Sarah Davis's detached attitude resonates with Molly's lack of generosity: "Her father would be holding, most likely, the wide brim of hat in his nervously twisting fingers."

One of the central motifs of *Revolutionary Petunias* is the successful search for the mother who presides over the poems by virtue of her inspiration of the master image of the flower. Alice Walker has explained the importance to her of her mother's genius for growing flowers toward the end of "In Search of Our Mothers' Gardens." The title *Revolutionary Petunias* is discussed specifically in terms of her mother's petunias in the interview with John O'Brien. The grandfather's presence also makes itself felt through the image of flowers:

> My grandfather, at eighty-five, never been out of Georgia, looks at me with the glad eyes of a three-year-old. The pressures on his life have been unspeakable. How can he look at me this way? "Your eyes are widely open flowers / Only their centers are darkly clenched / To conceal / Mysteries That / lure me to a keener blooming / Than I know / And promise a secret/I must have."
>
> (*Interviews; Revolutionary Petunias*)

The father is relatively absent from the family portrait in *Revolutionary Petunias*. He is a missing figure to a greater degree than Molly, who is linked to the family constellation by her association with flowers: she "walked among the flowers / And brought them inside the house" / (*Interviews; Revolutionary Petunias*).

If the mother is symbolized by the flower which blooms and opens, then the father is implicitly seen as the opposite: "a door that refused to open, a hand that was always closed. A fist" ("A Sudden Trip Home in the Spring"). Alice Walker's nonfiction contains frequent references to her mother. As early as the dedication in *The Third Life of Grange Copeland*, she is the one "who made a way out of no way." It is not until recently that Alice Walker has spoken in detail about her father. The essay "My Father's Country is the Poor" is especially moving when placed in the context of her writing up to this point. The relationship to the father depicted in the essay has a resemblance to that in "A Sudden Trip Home in the Spring." Like Sarah Davis, Alice Walker feels cut off from her father by her education, by his lack of opportunity to grow. Yet the spirit of the short story and that informing the essay written six years later are entirely different. In the latter piece, the father blossoms as he does not in the former. He is firmly located by his facial image: "a fine large nose and immense dark and intelligent eyes." As Alice Walker recalls that her going to college marked "the end of my always tenuous relationship with my father," she breaks the silence which has enshrouded "the pain in his beautiful eyes" at the moment of parting.

The constriction in Sarah Davis's mourning for her father in the short story stands in sharp contrast to the open, celebratory grieving in this essay. The emotional tone of Alice Walker's elegy for her own father can perhaps best be described in the words of the extraordinary recent poem, "on crying in public," in which the poet discovers "the freedom of tears." In the poem's last stanza, the final line is crucial:

> now i think it is just time for me to thaw
> completely—*and it's okay*
> for i am coming back to the world for the last time
> crying from sadness
> but crying toward joy.

A companion poem describes the "stripping" away of a symmetrical family composite to reveal "naked" individual identity:

> No. I am finished with living
> for what my mother believes

for what my brother and father defend
for what my lover elevates
for what my sister, blushing, denies or rushes
to embrace.
I find my own
small person
a standing self
against the world.

III. "IT IS DEATH NOT TO LOVE ONE'S MOTHER"

Alice Walker's second novel, *Meridian* (1976), consists of extended mourning, the importance of which had been asserted in her first novel where a white woman is criticized for making herself impervious to her own sufferings:

> Her face became one that refused to mark itself with suffering. He knew, even before he saw them, that her eyes would be without vital expression. . . .
>
> Somehow this settling into impenetrability, into a sanctuary from further pain, seemed more pathetic to him than her tears. At the same time her icy fortitude in the face of love's desertion struck him as peculiarly white American. No blues would ever come from such a saving of face.
>
> (*The Third Life of Grange Copeland*)

Meridian's face, by contrast, is characterized by its sadness:

> When she was thoughtful or when she was unaware of being observed, her face seemed deeply sad, as if she knew there was no hope, in the long run, for anyone in the world. . . .
>
> . . . she was considered *approaching beautiful* only when she looked sad. When she laughed, this beauty broke; and people, captivated by the sad quality of her face, seemed compelled to joke with her just enough to cause her to laugh and lose it. Then, freed of their interest in her, they walked away.
>
> (*Meridian*)

In the end, Meridian's openness to grieving and to personal suffering is seen to have been a vital resource which allows a sudden Lazarus-like "Release." Yet, throughout the novel, Meridian's sadness is linked to her being "sick." Whether sadness will lead to survival or to collapse has been an open question until the very end: "Meridian would return to the world cleansed of sickness."

This way of ending has had to compete with a compulsive alternative:

> She dreamed she was a character in a novel and that her existence presented an insoluble problem, one that could be solved only by her death.
>
> Even when she gave up reading novels that encouraged such a solution—and nearly all of them did—the dream did not cease.

The final tentative affirmation—"crying from sadness / but crying toward joy"—is harder to achieve in the second novel. At the conclusion of *The Third Life of Grange Copeland,* Ruth is alone, but a future which is wholly potential lies before her; Meridian's isolation is based on the experience of relationships (with Eddie and with Truman Held) which do not work out. Ruth sees the Civil Rights movement as promise while Meridian sees it in retrospect, its momentum apparently lost. Upon Meridian falls the burden of assessment and of continuation: "But don't you think the basic questions raised by King and Malcolm and the rest still exist? Don't you think people, somewhere deep inside, are still attempting to deal with them?"

Meridian surveys the sixties from the funeral of John Kennedy to the funeral of Martin Luther King: "It was a decade marked by death. . . . Funerals became engraved on the brain." The painful memories are revived, the losses relived, the sacred names recorded and preserved anew. The difficulty as well as the necessity of achieving satisfactory mourning is indicated:

> . . . the thrill of being able, once again, to endure unendurable loss produced so profound an ecstasy in mourners that they strutted, without noticing their feet, along the thin backs of benches: their piercing shouts of anguish and joy never interrupted by an inglorious fall. They shared rituals for the dead to be remembered.
>
> But now television became the repository of memory, and each onlooker grieved alone.

> . . . the mourners removed their coats and loosened girdles and ties. Those who had never known it anyway dropped the favorite song, and there was a feeling of relief in the air, of liberation, that was repulsive.
>
> Meridian turned, in shame, as if to the dead man himself.

The novel mourns not only those individuals killed in the struggle, but also the loss of the struggle itself. One meaning of the title is perhaps that the Civil Rights movement of the sixties is a high point from which it may not be possible to recover:

> The posters had fallen away from the walls or rotted, but when she [Lynne] held her candle up to one she saw the grayed outline of hundreds of marching forms, though underneath this faded picture the words had been completely eroded away. It was as if the marchers moved through some ghostly, unreal place, specters themselves and not in the least afraid, apprehensive about what would happen when they floated off the picture, off the wall, into a place even more dead, more final.

The difficulty of carrying on the movement is displayed at the outset in Meridian's ghostlike ritual of a nonviolent demonstration. "Burnt out" herself, she leads a line of poor black children past a tank and policemen with rifles to a circus wagon containing a "mummified white woman" who turns out to be made of plastic and thus "a fake." Meridian completes this mock-mourning by collapsing into the paralysis which is a symptom of her sickness; she is carried home "exactly as they would carry a coffin." It is as if the dead figures of the Civil Rights movement are now reflected in her own body.

The novel is strewn with incidents which demand mourning. An account is kept of the casualties of ordinary people to parallel the series of famous names from Kennedy to King: The Wild Child; Louvinie; the victims of fire-bombing; "a gentle drama student from Ohio"; Camara; the five-year-old boy who needlessly drowns; the son who is "a slain martyr in the Civil Rights struggle"; Agnes; the woman who kills her baby. One explanation of Meridian's illness is the steady accumulation of anguish with which the process of healing cannot keep pace. She suffers from a permanent "battle fatigue":

> She was as weary as anyone, so that she spent a good part of her time in tears. At first she had burst into tears whenever something went wrong or someone spoke unkindly or even sometimes if they spoke, period. But now she was always in a state of constant tears.

However, Meridian's anxiety is shown to have an additional source in the family nexus.

The dialectic between father and mother is more evenly balanced here than in Walker's earlier fiction. Although "unambitious," and in the end broken, Meridian's father is nonetheless a sympathetic character. In the long-standing argument with Meridian's mother over the status of Indians, he is the more imaginative and attractive of the two. His sensitivity makes him "a mourner":

> As she tiptoed closer to the bookshelves and reached to touch a photograph of a frozen Indian child (whose mother lay beside her

in a bloody heap) her father looked up from his map ["that showed the ancient settlements of the Indians in North America"], his face wet with tears, which she mistook, for a moment, for sweat. Shocked and frightened, she ran away.

The focal point of his vision is the Indian burial mound on the land which he farms and which is taken by the government for a park "not open to Colored": "Meridian grieved with her father for the loss of the farm." Before the farm is appropriated, Meridian has inherited through her father the experience, within the Sacred Serpent burial mound, of ecstasy (which later becomes intertwined with her paralysis).

A core of permanent grief of a different kind attaches to Meridian's mother. Like Ruth in *The Third Life of Grange Copeland*, Meridian "loses" her mother. The difference is that Ruth's mother is murdered, while Meridian "loses" her mother when she is unable to comply with her mother's desire that she "accept Christ":

> But her mother moved away, tears of anger and sadness coursing down her face. Her mother's love was gone, withdrawn, and there were conditions to be met before it would be returned. Conditions Meridian was never able to meet.

Ruth's memory of her mother is minimal and relatively straightforward: Grange calls her "a saint" and gives Ruth a locket picture of Mem as a birthday present. Meridian's interaction with her mother receives, by contrast, much closer and more sustained scrutiny. It is as if Meridian's mother is a Mem who survives: we now see the difficulties of being the child of a heroic mother.

The exploration of the relationship between Meridian and her mother is an instance of Alice Walker's ruminative style. A meandering, yet disciplined meditation is effected by continually dropping the subject and later returning to it for a fresh look; intricacy and intensity are built up by this circling back to take up another facet of the mother-daughter relationship, to press the analysis further. Walker establishes a frame of reference in the present from which she can delve into the past. Meridian's mother is introduced in a flashback within a flashback as "that past" which cannot be ignored.

Meridian's troubled feelings about her mother revolve around the conflict between the need to love her mother—"it is death not to love one's mother"—and the need to be different from her. Meridian is unable to break away easily from her mother because "an almost primeval guilt" prevents her from criticizing her mother:

> She imagined her mother in church, in which she had invested all

> that was still energetic in her life, praying for her daughter's soul, and yet, having no concern, no understanding of her daughter's *life* whatsoever; but Meridian did not condemn her for this.
>
> To Meridian, her mother *was* a giant. . . . That her mother was deliberately obtuse about what had happened meant nothing beside her own feelings of inadequacy and guilt. Besides, she had already forgiven her mother for anything she had ever done to her or might do.
>
> It seemed to Meridian that her legacy from her mother's endurance . . . was one she would never be able to match. It never occurred to her that her mother's and her grandmother's extreme purity of life was compelled by necessity. They had not lived in an age of choice.

The lives of mother and daughter are similar in that the crucial event is pregnancy. As Meridian perceives it, her mother "could never forgive her community, her family, his family, the whole world, for not warning her against children." By her existence, Meridian spoils her mother's life: "It was for stealing her mother's serenity, for shattering her mother's emerging self, that Meridian felt guilty from the very first." Meridian's own pregnancy—for which her mother had not prepared her—"came as a total shock" and compounds her guilt. After her husband abandons her, she has an opportunity to go to college, which she is unwilling to give up. To pursue her education, she decides to give away her child despite the opposition of her mother: " 'I have six children,' she continued self-righteously, 'though I never wanted to have any, and I have raised every one myself.' " Meridian follows the courage of her conviction, but her mother's disapproval takes its toll: "[S]he felt condemned, consigned to penitence, for life. . . . She thought of her mother as being worthy of this maternal history, and of herself as belonging to an unworthy minority." A second pregnancy, about which Meridian confides to no one, is ended by abortion. In the culminating chapter of the first part (entitled "Meridian"), a teacher at Saxon College grants Meridian the forgiveness she would like to have received from her mother: "Instinctively, as if Meridian were her own child, Miss Winter answered, close to her ear on the pillow, 'I forgive you.' Ultimately Meridian extends this forgiveness to Truman Held: "know i wish to forgive you" (compare Ruth's "unforgiveness" toward Brownfield).

A chapter later in the novel ("Camara") involves a reconsideration of two issues posed in the very first chapter—Meridian's inability to commit herself either to revolutionary violence or to the church. She is now caught by surprise by the church's reorientation:

And what was Meridian, who had always thought of the black church as mainly a reactionary power, to make of this? . . . Perhaps it was, after all, the only place left for black people to congregate, where the problems of life were not discussed fraudulently and the approach to the future was considered communally, and moral questions were taken seriously.

In Meridian's rediscovery of the church, there is perhaps an implicit reconciliation with her mother. In seeing the church (which had originally divided mother and daughter) as a positive force, Meridian accepts a legacy—however transformed—of her mother. Through her experience of the church, Meridian envisions herself as an artist:

> . . . perhaps it will be my part to walk behind the real revolutionaries—those who know they must spill blood in order to help the poor and the black and therefore go right ahead and when they stop to wash off the blood and find their throats too choked with the smell of murdered flesh to sing, I will come forward and sing from memory songs they will need once more to hear. For it is the song of the people, transformed by the experience of each generation, that holds them together, and if any part of it is lost the people suffer and are without soul. If I can only do that, my role will not have been a useless one after all.

Though Meridian remains apart, she retains the religious feeling of "communal spirit, togetherness, righteous convergence." It is this sense of relatedness which qualifies her isolation at the hymn-like end of the novel: "[A]ll the people who are as alone as I am will one day gather at the river. We will watch the evening sun go down. And in the darkness maybe we will know the truth."

THADIOUS M. DAVIS

Walker's Celebration of Self in Southern Generations

Perhaps Alice Walker alone of her generation of black women Southern writers persistently identifies herself and her concerns with her native region —the deep South of Georgia and Mississippi. "No one," she has concluded, "could wish for a more advantageous heritage than that bequeathed to the black writer in the South: a compassion for the earth, a trust in humanity beyond our knowledge of evil, an abiding love of justice. We inherit a great responsibility . . . for we must give voice to centuries not only of silent bitterness and hate but also of neighborly kindness and sustaining love" ("Black Writer"). Her heritage is complex; nevertheless, like Louisiana native Ernest Gaines, Walker grounds her fiction and poetry primarily in the experiences of the South and Southern blacks. Her three volumes of poetry, three novels, and two collections of stories, all depend upon what black life is, has been, and can be in a specified landscape that becomes emblematic of American life.

While Walker's paradigm communities are nearly always black, rural, and Southern, they become viable emblems by means of her creation of familial and social generations that underscore her concerns with familial identity, continuity and rupture, and with social roles, order and change. In shaping her fiction and much of her poetry according to patterns of generations, she has established a concrete means of portraying who her people are and what their lives mean.

Though her dominant themes (spiritual survival and individual identity, as well as freedom, power, and community) link her to the literary heritages of both Southern and black writers, her structures and forms address most

From *The Southern Quarterly* 21, no. 4 (Summer 1983). © 1983 by the University of Southern Mississippi.

clearly the uniqueness of her particular vision within these traditions. Walker
weds her intellectual themes to the life experiences of "just plain folk" who
are also black and mainly poor; she has said of them, "their experience as
ordinary human beings" is "valuable," and should not be "misrepresented,
distorted, or lost" ("Saving the Life"). In her literary works, she stresses her
own history and by extension the cultural history of Southern blacks and
American blacks. "It is," Walker asserts in the novel *Meridian,* "the song of
the people, transformed by the experiences of each generation, that holds them
together, and if any part of it is lost the people suffer and are without soul."
Her own works are, in a sense, "the song of the people" celebrating and pre-
serving each generation.

Walker's heritage and history provide a vehicle for understanding the
modern world in which her characters live. "Because I'm black and I'm a
woman and because I was brought up poor and because I'm a Southerner,
. . . the way I see the world is quite different from the way many people see
it," she has observed to Krista Brewer: "I could not help but have a radical
vision of society . . . the way I see things can help people see what needs
to be changed" ("Writing to Survive"). Her vision, however, is a disturbing
one to share. Walker relies upon sexual violence and physical abuse to portray
breaches in black generations. Typically, she brings to her work a terrible
observance of black self-hatred and destruction. While Walker does not negate
the impact of a deleterious past, she rarely incorporates white characters as
perpetrators of crimes against blacks. Her works simply presume, as she states,
that "all history is current; all injustice continues on some level" ("One Child").
Her images of people destroyed or destroying others originate in a vision of
cultural reality expressed matter-of-factly, such as in the poem from *Revolutionary Petunias,* "You Had to Go to Funerals": "At six and seven / The face
in the gray box / Is nearly always your daddy's / Old schoolmate / Mowed
down before his / Time." Walker's racial memory of a tangible, harsh reality
succeeds in focusing experience, holding it fixed, and illuminating some
aspects of brutality that might well be overlooked or obscured.

Walker's fiction expresses the outrage that she feels about the injustices
of society; "I think," she has stated, "that growing up in the South, I have
a very keen sense of injustice—a very prompt response to it" ("Writing to
Survive"). It may well be that some of the brutal depictions of life in her
writings are ways of responding to both particular and general injustices
suffered by blacks throughout their history in the United States. Gloria
Steinem, for instance, has concluded after interviewing Walker that "the rage
and the imaginings of righteous murders that are in her writing are also in
her. You just have to know her long enough to see the anger flash" ("Do You

Know"). There are hidden layers in Walker's handling of injustice, so that it is not so easy to follow the logic behind it in her fiction. She herself has confessed, "It's true that I fantasize revenge for injustices, big and small. . . . I imagine how wonderful it must feel to kill the white man who oppresses you. . . . Lately . . . I've come to believe that you have some help when you fight. If a country or a person oppresses folks, it or he will pay for it. That happens more often than not. Years after the Indians died in the Trail of Tears, Andrew Jackson, who had been President at the time, had to be wrapped like a mummy to keep the flesh on his bones" ("Do You Know"). Her fictional use of rage, however, is more often than not contained within a family environment and directed toward self or kin, rather than towards outsiders.

One scene in *Meridian* delineates the everyday quality of familial rage in Walker's fiction. A woman who believes that her family and community, as well as the racial barriers and social order of the South, have all combined to rob her of a full life irons into her children's and husband's clothes her frustrations and her creativity. Instead of loving her family openly or accusing anyone explicitly, she uses her ordinary domestic chore to enclose her children in "the starch of her anger," as Walker labels it. This character, Mrs. Hill, includes her children in her victimization, and in the process she excludes them from any meaningful, close relationship with her. The result is a tension- and guilt-ridden existence, both for Mrs. Hill and for her family. The scene suggests how personal outrage and anger stemming from social and historical forces (particularly ignorance, discrimination, racism, exploitation, and sexism) become warped and distorted in Walker's world.

In fact, Walker has discussed her writing, and need to write, in terms that articulate her deflection of rage and her reconciliation with it. After the birth of her daughter, she put her frustrations and her energy into her work: "Write I did, night and day, *something,* and it was not even a choice, . . . but a necessity. When I didn't write I thought of making bombs and throwing them. . . . Writing saved me from the sin and *inconvenience* of violence—as it saves most writers who live in 'interesting' oppressive times and are not afflicted by personal immunity" ("One Child"). She does not have to add that her writing absorbed the violence, especially emotional violence, in the lives of her characters. Walker's recollection and the scene from *Meridian* add a situational context to the prevalent violence and excessive pain found in all of her fiction, but they do not fully address the motivational context for the choice of family as the expressive vehicle.

Walker creates a multiplicity of permanently maimed and damaged souls within the family structure who feel no pressure for responsible living or assume exemption from the demands of responsibility. There may be occasions of optimism or hope; for example, when Sarah, a Southern black art student in "A Sudden Trip Home in the Spring," returns from New York for her father's funeral, she comes, with the help of her brother, to understand her father's life after years of resenting his flaws, and she resolves to learn how to make her grandfather's face in stone. But more pervasive in Walker's fiction is despair: women who commit suicide, such as the wife in "Her Sweet Jerome," who sets fire to herself and her marriage bed; men who maim or kill, such as the father in "The Child Who Favored Daughter," who cuts off his daughter's breasts; people who allow themselves to become animals, such as Brownfield in *The Third Life of Grange Copeland,* who, accepting a "nothingness" in himself, shoots his wife in the face while his children watch; and people who simply give up on life, such as Myrna in "Really Doesn't Crime Pay?" who spends her days softening her hands and thwarting her husband's desire for a child.

Walker assumes that by revealing negative actions and violent encounters, she may be able to repair the damage done by unreflective people who are unable to recognize that their actions have more than personal consequences, that they may rend bonds between generations and thus affect all members of a family, community, race, or society. In her depictions of abuse and violence, Walker takes the risk of misrepresenting the very people whom she seeks to change. Yet her unrelenting portraits of human weaknesses convey her message that art should "make us better"; "if [it] doesn't . . . then what on earth is it for?" ("Do You Know"). Her message, postulated in her novels, is that the breaches and violations must be mended for health and continuity, for "survival *whole,*" as her character Grange Copeland declares.

Reparation or redemption may be undertaken by a single individual in whom Walker vests the responsibility for survival, because it is the action of a single individual that has caused the breakdown of experience or identity in private lives, and ultimately in the public or social life of the group. Individual characters acting alone become repositories of decent behavior, as well as harbingers that the messages embedded in the lives of generations of blacks will not be lost. One example is Elethia, a young woman who masterminds the retrieval of "Uncle Albert," a mummified black man who is all teeth, smiles, and servitude as a decoration in the window of a "whites only" restaurant, despite the reality of his having been a rebellious slave whose teeth were knocked out for his efforts to remain human. Elethia knows that Uncle Albert's denigration to a subservient happy waiter cannot be allowed. She and her cohorts break the plate glass, reclaim the mummy, burn it, and save the ashes. She aims to rid the world of all false, stereotypical images of blacks, especially men, and to recover the past, rectify its misrepresentations, and preserve the truth for future generations. Elethia realizes that the work will not end with rescuing Uncle Albert, but that it will extend over her lifetime. Walker's individual Elethias understand that breaches may have occurred between succeeding generations, but that progress in the present and towards the future depends upon reconstruction of the bridges that, as Carolyn Rodgers says in her poem "It Is Deep," one generation has "crossed over on." Although "Elethia" is not one of Walker's most successful stories, it adheres to her belief that the world, her reality, is filled with connections, oftentimes unsuspected connections, which she as an artist can illuminate.

Walker believes that as a writer she must work towards a larger perspective, which she describes as "connections made, or at least attempted, where none existed before, the straining to encompass in one's glance at the varied world the common thread, the unifying theme through immense diversity, a fearlessness of growth, of search, of look, that enlarges the private and the public world" ("Saving the Life"). For her, one way of structuring "the common thread" is by means of generations; she values the strength and purpose black generations have given to her writing, but she refuses to reduce their meanings to platitudes or to ignore the complexities of their lives.

"It is not," Walker stresses "my child who has purged my face from history and herstory and left mystory . . . a mystery; my child loves my face . . . as I have loved my own parents' faces . . . and have refused to let them be denied, or myself to let them go" ("One Child"). Repeatedly, she uses the image of her mother's face "radiant," "ordering the universe in her personal conception of beauty. Her face . . . is a legacy . . . she leaves to me" ("In Search"). Walker treasures and preserves in her works not merely her parents' faces and her own, but those of her grandparents and great-grandparents and all her blood and social relatives as well. For instance, in the poem from *Goodnight Willie Lee* entitled "talking to my grandmother who died poor (while hearing Richard Nixon declare 'I am not a crook')," she concludes: "i must train myself to want / not one bit more / than i need to keep me alive / working / and recognizing beauty / in your so nearly undefeated face." It is in her grandmother's "so nearly undefeated face" that Walker reads at what cost her people have survived.

Her conception of the black writer and herself is inextricably linked to survival. She has said, "Only recently did I fully realize . . . that through the years of listening to my mother's stories of her life, I have absorbed not only the stories themselves, but something of the manner in which she spoke, something of the urgency that involves the knowledge that her stories like her life must be recorded" ("In Search"). Derived partly from the urge to retain her parents' faces and their stories, her sense of black writers is that they are involved in a moral and physical struggle "the result of which," as she points out, "is expected to be some kind of larger freedom" ("Saving the Life"). Walker attributes this search for freedom to a black literary tradition based upon slave narratives which foster the belief in escape from the body along with freedom for the soul. Indeed, while the oral tradition, essential to even the most literary of slave narratives, such as Frederick Douglass's, is a prominent part of Walker's writing, its strength as a mode of telling in her work may be more immediately linked to her mother's voice. "Do you actually speak with your mother's voice?" Mary Helen Washington has asked Walker. The response is forthright: "Just as you have certain physical characteristics of your mother's—her laughter or her toes or her grade of hair—you also internalize certain emotional characteristics that are like hers. That is part of the legacy. They are internalized, merged with your own, transformed through the stories. When you're compelled to write her stories, it's because you recognize and prize those qualities of her in yourself" ("Her Mother's Gifts").

Because of her conception of art and the artist, as well as her recognition of the value of her mother's stories and her family's faces, Walker displays an enormous sympathy for the older generation of Southern women ("Head-ragged Generals") and men ("billy club scar[red]"), whose lives were sacrifice. As she has revealed in "The Women" from *Revolutionary Petunias:* "They were women then / My mama's generation / . . . How they battered down / Doors / . . . To discover books / Desks / A place for us / How they knew what we / Must know / Without knowing a page / Of it / Themselves. The poem celebrates the generation that preceded Walker's own, those men and women who opened doors through which they themselves would never pass and who were unafraid to attempt personal and social change in order to restructure subsequent generations. Walker acknowledges their achievement, but also their adversities.

Her older men, in particular, have experienced troubled, difficult lives, such as those of Grange Copeland and Albert in *The Color Purple.* These men have been abusive in their youths, but they come to an essential under-standing of their own lives and their families' as they learn to be reflective, responsible, and expressive individuals. Although they may seem to reflect her anti-male bias, they are more significant as portrayals of Walker's truth-telling from a particular perspective that is conscious of their weaknesses— weaknesses that they distort into violence against other blacks, especially women and children—and conscious, too, of their potential for regeneration. Walker's men to whom sexuality is no longer an issue are redeemed by learning to love and assume responsibility for their actions. In presenting these men, Walker first depicts what has come to be the stereotypes of blacks, essentially those set destructive patterns of emotional and psychological responses of black men to black life, their women, children, friends, whites, and themselves. Then she loosens the confines of the stereotype and attempts to penetrate the nexus of feelings that make these lives valuable in themselves and for others.

Much of the redemption, nevertheless, is only potential as Walker portrays it. The nameless husband in *The Color Purple* becomes "Albert" in his later years, because, like Grange Copeland in Walker's first novel, he discovers reflection which makes him a defined person who can accept the responsibility for his mistakes and the suffering he has caused, especially his abusive treatment of his wife whom he had denigrated ("You a woman . . . you nothing at all"). Despite his contemplative demeanor at the end of the novel, Albert remains in the realm of potential. His apparent psychological return to roots, though inadequately motivated, is primarily a portent of a healing process.

Walker names this healing a "wholeness" in her essay, "Beyond the Peacock: The Reconstruction of Flannery O'Connor," in which she, like her characters, returns to her roots in order to regenerate herself and to comprehend the pervasive impact of social environment. Her attitude is clear in the poem from *Once,* "South: The Name of Home," which opens: "when I am here again / the years of ease between / fall away / The smell of one / magnolia / sends my heart running / through the swamps. / the earth is red / here— / the trees bent, weeping / what secrets will not / the ravished land / reveal / of its abuse." It is an environment that is not without a history of pain, but it nonetheless connects generations of blacks to one another, to a "wholeness" of self, and to "the old unalterable roots," as in "Burial": "Today I bring my own child here; / to this place where my father's / grandmother rests undisturbed beneath the Georgia sun / . . . Forgetful of geographical resolutions as birds / the farflung young fly South to bury / the old dead"(*Revolutionary Petunias*). One key to "wholeness," even if it is rarely achieved, is the development of self-perception by means of generational ties to the land.

The achievements and dreams that emerge from the connected experience of generations are expressions of freedom and beauty, of power and community. The primary dream, usually voiced in terms of the creation of art, is that of freedom to be one's own self, specifically to be one's own black self and to claim, as do Walker's blues singers Shug Avery in *The Color Purple* and Gracie Mae Still in "Nineteen Fifty-five," one's own life for one's self and for future generations.

Walker transforms the individual, so much a part of the special characteristics used to define the white South, into a person who is black and most often female. In the one-page story "Petunias" from *You Can't Keep a Good Woman Down,* she individualizes an unnamed woman with a history and a sense of herself. The woman writes in her diary just before her death in an explosion of a bomb her son intends for the revolution: "my daddy's grandmama was a slave on the Tearslee Plantation. They dug up her grave when I started agitating in the Movement. One morning I found her dust dumped over my verbena bed, a splinery leg bone had fell among my petunias." This woman and others in Walker's canon are the stereotyped, the maimed, the distorted blacks who still rise, as Maya Angelou entitles one of her works, "Still I Rise." These characters become redeemed as individuals with an indelible sense of self. But that act of rising out of the depths of degradation or depression is accomplished by means of the person's coming to terms with the truth of his or her community, with his or her social and historical place among others who have suffered, grieved, laughed, and lusted, but who miraculously have held on to dignity and selfhood. Characters, such as Sammy Lou, a woman on her way to the electric chair for killing her husband's murderer, pass on a powerful legacy of individual identity; Sammy Lou leaves her children the instructions: "Always respect the word of God," and "Don't yall forget to *water* my purple petunias" (*Revolutionary Petunias*).

Walker operates within this legacy. She keeps before her the vision of her own mother, who cultivated magnificent flower gardens, despite her work from sun up to dark either in the fields or as a domestic for less than twenty dollars a week. Walker refers to her mother's gardens as her "art," "her ability to hold on, even in simple ways" ("In Search"). That garden is her recurrent metaphor for both art and beauty, endurance and survival; it is essentially, too, Walker's articulation of the process by which individuals find selfhood through examining the experiences of others who have preceded them. As she has stated, "Guided by my heritage of a love of beauty and a respect for strength, in search of my mother's garden, I found my own" ("In Search"). In fact, her very first novel, *The Third Life of Grange Copeland,* directly involves the gardens of the character Mem as emblems of her tenacious will to survive in beauty and in love.

In celebrating her people (characters, mediums, models, and family), Walker demonstrates a deeply-rooted consciousness of her role as an artist in a socially and politically complex world. "To acknowledge ancestors means," she states, "we are aware that we did not make ourselves. . . . The grace with which we embrace life, in spite of the pain, the sorrows, is always a measure of what has gone before" (*Revolutionary Petunias,* preface). By acknowledging ancestors, she acknowledges that she is part of a black tradition of artists, particularly that strain stemming from Southern slave narrators, folk tellers of tales, and literary artists. These include Zora Neale Hurston, one of her major influences, and Margaret Walker, her fellow poet and novelist who in the 1940s paid tribute to blacks in "For My People" and in the process celebrated her roots "deep in Southern life" and her "grandmothers . . . strong . . . full of memories." Similarly, Alice Walker derives meaning from the historical experiences of her foremothers, because she insists, "nothing is ever a product of the immediate present" (O'Brien, *Interviews*).

She takes into account the dynamics of collective identity along with the demands that social codes place upon the group, and she considers the structure of personal identity with its unreflected social relations, especially family. She shapes her fiction so that both collective and personal identities become keys to character, theme, and plot. At the same time, she structures the experience of identity in terms of social and familial generations that have the potential to transform black life.

In her first novel, *The Third Life of Grange Copeland,* three generations of Copelands converge to create Ruth's identity, and three generations form the stages or lives of the patriarch and title character, Grange Copeland. When any one member of the Copeland family or of a particular social generation of blacks (from 1920 to 1960) ignores the dynamics of family structures or forgets the historical perspective that the structures are maintained through necessity and love, he or she loses the capacity for primary identifications with race, family, and community, and loses as well the major basis for defining one's self and one's humanity. The most detailed illustration presented in the novel is Brownfield, the son of Grange and a member of the middle generation in the work.

Brownfield Copeland becomes one of "the living dead, one of the many who had lost their souls in the American wideness." He reduces his murder of his wife to a simple theorem: *"He liked plump women. . . . Ergo,* he had murdered his wife because she had become skinny." Because of his twisted logic, Brownfield "could forget [his wife's] basic reality, convert it into comparisons. She had been like good pie, or good whiskey, but there had never been a self to her." Not only by means of the murder itself, but also by the process of his reasoning about it, he strips himself of his humanity when he negates his culpability with the negation of his wife's existence as a human being.

Brownfield's physical death sadly, though appropriately in Walker's construction, comes at the hands of his father Grange and over the future of his daughter Ruth. But his spiritual death occurs much earlier "as he lay thrashing about, knowing the rigidity of his belief in misery, knowing he could never renew or change himself, for this changelessness was now all he had, he could not clarify what was the duty of love." He compounds one of the greatest sins in Walker's works, the refusal or inability to change, with his dismissal of meaning in family bonds. Ironically, his death makes possible the completion of change in his daughter's life that had been fostered by his father, who late in his life understood the necessity of moving beyond the perverted emotions constricting the lives of the Copelands.

In *Meridian,* Walker's second novel, the heroine divests herself of immediate blood relations—her child and her parents—in order to align herself completely with the larger racial and social generations of blacks. Meridian Hill insists that although seemingly alone in the world, she has created a fusion with her generation of activist blacks and older generations of oppressed blacks. The form of the work, developed in flashbacks, follows a pattern of Meridian's casting off the demands made by authority and responsibility within the conventional family and traditional institutions. Unlike Brownfield's rejection of responsibility, the rupture in this novel is ultimately positive, despite its being the most radical and mysterious instance of change and acceptance in Walker's fiction. It is positive because the novel creates a new basis for defining Meridian's self and for accepting responsibility for one's actions. In fact, the controlling metaphor is resurrection and rebirth, an acting out of the renewal impossible for Brownfield. By the end of the novel, Meridian's personal identity has become a collective identity. "There is water in the world for us / brought by our friends," she writes in one of her two poems, "though the rock of mother and god / vanishes into sand / and we, cast out alone / to heal / and re-create / ourselves." In spite of her painful private experiences, Meridian is born anew into a pluralistic cultural self, a "we" that is and must be selfless and without ordinary prerequisites for personal identity. And significantly, because she exemplifies Walker's recurrent statement of women as leaders and models, Meridian leaves her male disciple Truman Held to follow her and to await the arrival of others from their social group.

Truman's search, structurally a duplication of Meridian's, is part of personal change that is more necessary for men than for women in Walker's fiction and that becomes social change through the consequences of actions taken by individuals who must face constraints, as well as opportunities, in their lives, but must also know why they act and what the consequences will be. Truman resolves to live the life of an ascetic so that he might one day be worthy to join Meridian and others "at the river," where they "will watch the evening sun go down. And in the darkness maybe [they] will know the truth." The search for truth leads Truman, like Meridian, to a commitment to the social generation of blacks to which he belongs. He follows Meridian's rationale for his action: "i want to put an end to guilt / i want to put an end to shame /

whatever you have done my sister / (my brother) / know i wish to forgive you / love you." By so doing, Truman accepts his personal duty towards all blacks, discovers his own meaning, and commits his life in love to both present and future generations.

Perhaps Walker's third novel most effectively conveys her messages and evidences her heritage as a black southern writer. In *The Color Purple,* which won the Pulitzer Prize for fiction in 1983, she takes a perspectivistic or "emic" approach to character delineation and cultural reality. She sees and portrays a world from the inside outward; she uses the eyes of Celie, a surnameless, male-dominated and abused woman, who records her experiences in letters. Celie is not a "new" character in Walker's fiction; she is similar to one of the sisters in "Everyday Use," the bride in "Roselily," and the daughter in "The Child Who Favored Daughter," but unlike these other silent, suffering women characters, Celie writes her story in her own voice. She tells her life as only she has known it: a girl, merely a child, raped by her stepfather whom she believes is her natural father; that same girl bearing his two children only to have them stolen by him and to be told that they are dead; the denial and suppression of that girl's actual background and history, as well as her letters from her sister.

In Celie's epistles, Walker makes her strongest effort so far to confront the patterns in a specified world and to order and articulate the codes creating those patterns. In effect, she uses the uncovered patterns to connect, assimilate, and structure the content of one human being's world and relationship to that world. Celie writes letters—her story, history—to God and to her sister Nettie. She writes out of desperation and in order to preserve some core of her existence. In love and hope, she writes to save herself, just as Walker has said of her own writing: "I have written to stay alive . . . I've written to survive"; "writing poetry is my way of celebrating with the world that I have not committed suicide the evening before" ("Writing to Survive"; *Interviews*). Celie writes from the heart, and grows stronger, more defined, more fluent, while simultaneously her intensely private, almost cryptic style develops into a still personal, subjective style, but one which encompasses much more of the lives surrounding her.

While social interactions and institutions typically define human reality, these do not ultimately define Celie's. She is isolated and alone, despite the numbers of family members and others impinging upon her world. Slowly and cautiously, she builds a reality that is different, one based upon her singular position and the abstractions she herself conceives in the course of her everyday life. Her inner life is unperverted by the abuse and violence she suffers. Only when she has formulated the outlines of her private identity in writing does her interaction with others become a significant factor in making sense of social codes in the public world. When she reaches her conclusions, she has rejected most of the available social models for personal identity; she is neither Shug Avery, the hardliving blues singer who gives and takes what she wants in being herself, nor is she Nettie, her sister who can experience the wider world outside the social environment of her childhood. Yet, Celie passionately loves both of these women, and has tried at different stages to emulate them. Celie's own subjective probings lead her to confirm her individual interpretation of herself and of her situational contexts. Nonetheless, she does arrive, as invariably a Walker bearer of responsibility must, at her place in the spectrum of life, her relationship to others, and her own continuity.

Celie affirms herself: "I'm pore, I'm black, I may be ugly and can't cook, a voice say to everything listening. But I'm here." Her words echo those of Langston Hughes's folk philosopher, Jesse B. Semple (Simple): "I'm still here. . . . I've been underfed, underpaid. . . . I've been abused, confused, misused. . . . I done had everything from flat feet to a flat head . . . but I am still here. . . . I'm still here." Celie's verbal connection to Hughes's black everyman and the black oral tradition extends her affirmation of self, so that it becomes racial, as well as personal, and is an actualization, rather than the potentiality that most often appears in Walker's work. Celie *is,* or in her own black folk English, she *be's* her own black, nappy-haired, ordinary self in all the power and pain that combine in her writing to reveal the girl, the female becoming totally a woman-person who survives and belies the weak, passive exterior her family and community presume to be her whole self. Her act of writing and affirming is magnificent. It is an achievement deserving of celebration, and perhaps not coincidentally, it is Walker's first "happy ending," not only for her character Celie, but for most of her fictional family as well.

Celie's progeny will make the present and future generations. Her two children—Adam, who takes the African name "Omatangu" and marries an African woman, and Olivia, who promises to be a sister to her brother's bride Tashi—exist without the blight affecting their mother and their aunt, even though their lives as children of missionaries in Africa have not been without the problems of colonialization and oppression. Adam's and Olivia's return to America, to the South, and to Celie at the end of the novel may be contrived, but it signals the continuity of generations, the return (ironically perhaps) to the "old, unalterable roots." Their return is cause for a larger hope for the race, and for celebration within the family and community, because they have survived "whole," literally since they miraculously survive a shipwreck and symbolically since they have acquired definite life-affirming attitudes.

Near the end of the novel, Celie's stepson comments on a fourth of July barbecue, and in the process provides a commentary on the letters Celie has written and the novel Walker has produced; he says, "White folks busy celebrating they independence from England. . . . Us can spend the day celebrating each other." *The Color Purple,* with its reiteration of "purple" as the motif symbolizing the miracle of color and life apparent in all of Walker's works, is a celebration of "each other," individual selves inextricably linked in social and familial generations. In the celebration is an inexplicable strength, which Walker attributes to her own optimism, "based," she states, "on what I saw of the courage and magnificence of people in Mississippi and in Georgia. . . . I saw that the human spirit can be so much more incredible and beautiful than most people ever dream . . . that people who have very little, . . . who have been treated abominably by society, can still do incredible things . . . not only *do* things, but can be great human beings" ("Writing to Survive").

Despite her concentration on the brutal treatment of black women and the unmitigated abuse of children, Walker believes in the beauty and the power of the individual, and ultimately of the group. And because she does, she is willing to gamble on ways of articulating her unique vision. She is not always successful; the experimental stories of *You Can't Keep a Good Woman Down* are an example, as are the unconvincing letters from Celie's sister Nettie in Africa. However, even in the less effective works, Walker validates the necessity of struggling out of external constrictions to find meaning in one's own life. It seems quite appropriate that both her dedication and statement at the end of *The Color Purple* reaffirm and invoke the spirits of people who fill her head and her work with their voices and their presence, with the selves that come to *be* within the pages of her writing.

Certainly, in the composition of much of her work so far, Alice Walker must have felt as she did while writing "The Revenge of Hannah Kemhuff," a work inspired by one of her mother's own stories: "I gathered up the historical and psychological threads of the life my ancestors lived, and in the writing . . . I felt joy and strength and my own continuity. I had that wonderful feeling that writers get sometimes . . . of being with a great many people, ancient spirits, all very happy to see me consulting and acknowledging them, and eager to let me know through the joy of their presence, that indeed, I am not alone" ("Saving the Life"). Perhaps this consoling vision of interconnections is one reason why Alice Walker can capture the deep layers of affirmative and destructive feelings in human beings who must live and make their lives known, and why she can compel readers to heed their messages.

BARBARA CHRISTIAN

The Black Woman Artist as Wayward

I find my own
small person
a standing self
against the world
an equality of wills
I finally understand
        —"On Stripping
            Bark from
            Myself"

Alice Walker has produced a significant body of work since 1968, when *Once,* her first volume of poetry, was published. Prolific, albeit a young writer, she is already acclaimed by many to be one of America's finest novelists, having captured both the American Book Award and the coveted Pulitzer in 1983.

Her substantial body of writing, though it varies, is characterized by specific recurrent motifs. Most obvious is Walker's attention to the black woman as creator, and to how her attempt to be whole relates to the health of her community. This theme is certainly focal to Walker's two collections of short stories, *In Love and Trouble* and *You Can't Keep a Good Woman Down,* to her classic essay, "In Search of Our Mothers' Gardens," and to *Meridian* and *The Color Purple,* her second and third novels. And it reverberates in her personal efforts to help rescue the works of Zora Neale Hurston from a threatening oblivion. Increasingly, as indicated by her last collection of poems, *Good Night, Willie Lee,* Walker's work is black women-centered.

Another recurrent motif in Walker's work is her insistence on probing

---

From *Black Women Writers (1950-1980)*, edited by Mari Evans. © 1983 by Mari Evans. Doubleday (Anchor Books), 1984.

the relationship between struggle and change, a probing that encompasses the pain of black people's lives, against which the writer protests but which she will not ignore. Paradoxically such pain sometimes results in growth, precisely because of the nature of the struggle that must be borne, if there is to be change. Presented primarily through three generations of one family in Walker's first novel, *The Third Life of Grange Copeland,* the struggle to change takes on overt societal dimensions in *Meridian,* her second novel. Characteristically this theme is presented in her poetry, fiction, and essays, as a spiritual legacy of black people in the South.

One might also characterize Walker's work as organically spare rather than elaborate, ascetic rather than lush, a process of stripping off layers, honing down to the core. This pattern, impressionistic in *Once,* is refined in her subsequent volumes of poetry and clearly marks the structure of her fiction and essays. There is a concentrated distillation of language which, ironically, allows her to expand rather than constrict. Few contemporary American writers have examined so many facets of sex and race, love and societal changes, as has Walker, without abandoning the personal grace that distinguishes her voice.

These elements—the focus on the struggle of black people, especially black women, to claim their own lives, and the contention that this struggle emanates from a deepening of self-knowledge and love—are characteristics of Walker's work. Yet it seems they are not really the essential quality that distinguishes her work, for these characteristics might be said to apply to any number of contemporary black women writers—e.g., Toni Morrison, Paule Marshall, June Jordan. Walker's peculiar sound, the specific mode through which her deepening of self-knowledge and self-love comes, seems to have much to do with her contrariness, her willingness at all turns to challenge the fashionable belief of the day, to reexamine it in the light of her own experiences and of dearly won principles which she has previously challenged and absorbed. There is a sense in which the "forbidden" in the society is consistently approached by Walker as a possible route to truth. At the core of this contrariness is an unwavering honesty about what she sees. Thus in *Once,* her first volume of poems, the then twenty-three-year-old Walker wrote, during the heyday of Afro-Americans' romanticizing of their motherland, about her stay in Africa, in images that were not always complimentary. In her poem "Karamojans" Walker demystified Africa:

> A tall man
> Without clothes
> Beautiful
> Like a statue

> Up close
> His eyes
> Are running
> Sores

Such a perception was, at that time, practically blasphemy among a progressive element of black thinkers and activists. Yet, seemingly impervious to the risk of rebuke, the young Walker challenged the idealistic view of Africa as an image, a beautiful artifact to be used by Afro-Americans in their pursuit of racial pride. The poet does not flinch from what she sees—does not romanticize or inflate it ("His eyes / Are running / Sores"). Yet her words acknowledge that she knows the ideal African image as others project it: "Beautiful / Like a statue." It is the "Up close" that sets up the tension in the lines between appearance and reality, mystification and the real, and provides Walker's peculiar sound, her insistence on honesty as if there were no other way to be. The lines, then, do not scream at the reader or harp on the distinction between the image and the man she sees. The lines *are* that distinction. They embody the tension, stripping its dimensions down to the essentials. "Karamojans" ends:

> The Karamojans
> Never civilized
> A proud people
> I think there
> Are
> A hundred left.

So much for the concept of pride without question.

At the cutting edge of much of Walker's early work is an intense examination of those ideas advocated by the most visible of recent Afro-American spokespersons. In 1970, at the height of cultural nationalism, the substance of most black literary activity was focused on the rebellious urban black in confrontation with white society. In that year Walker's first novel, *The Third Life of Grange Copeland,* was published. By tracing the history of the Copeland family through three generations, Walker demonstrated the relationship between the racist sharecropping system and the violence that the men, women, and children of that family inflict on each other. The novel is most emphatically located in the rural South, rather than the Northern urban ghetto; its characters are Southern peasants rather than Northern lumpen, reminding us that much of Afro-American population is still under the yoke of a feudal sharecropping system. And the novel is written more from the angle of the tentative survival of a black family than from an overt confrontation between black and white.

Also, Walker's first novel, like Marshall's *The Chosen Place, the Timeless People* (1969) and Morrison's *The Bluest Eye* (1970), seemed out of step with the end-of-the-decade work of such writers as Imamu Baraka, or Ishmael Reed—black writers on opposing sides of the spectrum—in that the struggle her major characters wage against racism is located in, sometimes veiled by, a network of family and community. The impact of racism is felt primarily through the characters' mistaken definitions of themselves as men and women. Grange Copeland first hates himself because he is powerless, as opposed to powerful, the definition of maleness for him. His reaction is to prove his power by inflicting violence on the women around him. His brief sojourn in the North where he feels invisible, a step below powerlessness, causes him to hate whites as his oppressors. That, however, for Walker, does not precipitate meaningful struggle. It is only when he learns to love himself, through his commitment to his granddaughter, Ruth, that Grange Copeland is able to confront the white racist system. And in so doing, he must also destroy his son, the fruit of his initial self-hatred.

The Third Life of Grange Copeland, then, is based on the principle that societal change is invariably linked to personal change, that the struggle must be inner- as well as outer-directed. Walker's insistence on locating the motivation for struggle within the self led her to examine the definition of nigger, that oft-used word in the literature of the late sixties. Her definition, however is not generalized but precise: a nigger is a black person who believes he or she is incapable of being responsible for his or her actions, that the white folks are to blame for everything, including his or her behavior. As Grange says to his son, Brownfield, in their one meaningful exchange in the novel: " 'When they get you thinking they're to blame for everything they have you thinking they're some kind of gods. . . . Shit, nobody's as powerful as we make them out to be. We got our own souls, don't we?' "

The question lingering at the end of this novel—whether the psychological impact of oppression is so great that it precludes one's overcoming of it—is also a major undercurrent of the literature of this period. There is a tension in the militant literature of the late sixties between a need to *assert* the love of black people for black people and an anger that black people have somehow allowed themselves to be oppressed. The ambivalence caused by a desire for self-love and an expression of shame is seldom clearly articulated in the literature but implied in the militant black writer's exhortation to their people to stop being niggers and start becoming black men and women. What Walker did, in her first novel, was to give voice to this tension and to graph the development of one man in his journey toward its resolution.

Grange Copeland's journey toward this resolution is not, however, an idea that Walker imposes on the novel. A characteristic of hers is her attempt to use the essence of a complex dilemma organically in the composing of her work. So the structure of *The Third Life of Grange Copeland* is based on the dramatic tension between the pervasive racism of the society and the need for her characters, if they are to hold on to self-love, to accept responsibility for their own lives. The novel is divided into two parts, the first analyzing the degeneration of Grange's and then his son Brownfield's respective families, the second focusing on the regeneration of the Copelands, as Grange, against all odds, takes responsibility for Brownfield's daughter, Ruth. Within these two larger pieces, Walker created a quilt of recurring motifs which are arranged, examined, and rearranged so that the reader might understand the complex nature of the tension between the power of oppressive societal forces and the possibility for change. Walker's use of recurring economical patterns, much like a quilting process, gives the novel much of its force and uniqueness. Her insistence on critically examining the ideas of the time led her not only to analysis but also to a synthesis that increasingly marks her work.

Walker is drawn to the integral and economical process of quilt-making as a model for her own craft. For through it, one can create out of seemingly disparate everyday materials patterns of clarity, imagination, and beauty. Two of her works especially emphasize the idea of this process: her classic essay "In Search of Our Mothers' Gardens" and her short story "Everyday Use." Each piece complements the other and articulates the precise meaning of the quilt as idea and process for this writer.

In "In Search of Our Mothers' Gardens," Walker directly asks the question that every writer must: From whence do I, as a writer, come? What is my tradition? In pursuing the question she focuses most intensely on her female heritage, in itself a point of departure from the route most writers have taken. Walker traces the images of black women in the literature as well as those few of them who were able to be writers. However, as significant as the tracing of that literary history is, Walker's major insight in the essay is her illumination of the creative legacy of "ordinary" black women of the South, a focus which complements but finally transcends literary history. In her insistence on honesty, on examining the roots of *her own* creativity, she invokes not so much the literature of black women, which was probably unknown to her as a budding child writer, but the creativity known to her of her mother, her grandmother, the women around her.

What did some slave women or black women of this century do with the creativity that might have, in a less restrictive society, expressed itself in paint, words, clay? Walker reflects on a truth so obvious it is seldom acknowledged: they used the few media left them by a society that labeled them lowly, menial. Some, like Walker's mother, expressed it in the growing of magnificent gardens; some in cooking; others in quilts of imagination and passion like the one Walker saw at the Smithsonian Institution. Walker's description of that quilt's impact on her brings together essential elements of her more recent work: the theme of the black woman's creativity—her transformation despite opposition of the bits and pieces allowed her by society into a work of functional beauty.

But Walker does not merely acknowledge quilts (or the art black women created out of "low" media) as high art, a tendency now fostered by many women who have discovered the works of their maternal ancestors. She is also impressed by their *functional* beauty and by the process that produced them. Her short story "Everyday Use" is in some ways a conclusion in fiction to her essay. Just as she juxtaposed the history of black women writers with the creative legacy of ordinary black women, so she complemented her own essay, a search for the roots of her own creativity, with a story that embodies the idea itself.

In "Everyday Use," Walker again scrutinized a popular premise of the times. The story which is dedicated to "your grandmama" is about the use and misuse of the concept of heritage. The mother of two daughters, one selfish and stylish, the other scarred and caring, passes on to us its true definition. Dee, the sister who has always despised the backward ways of her Southern rural family comes back to visit her old home. She has returned to her black roots because now they are fashionable. So she glibly delights in the artifacts of her heritage: the rough benches her father made, the hand-made butter churn which she intends to use for a decorative centerpiece, the quilts made by her grandma Dee after whom she was named—the *things* that have passed on. Ironically, in keeping with the times, Dee has changed her name to Wangero, denying the existence of her namesake, even as she covets the quilts she made.

On the other hand, her sister Maggie is not aware of the word *heritage*. But she loves her grandma and cherishes her memory in the quilts she made. Maggie has accepted the *spirit* that was passed on to her. The contrast between the two sisters is aptly summarized in Dee's focal line in the story: " 'Maggie can't appreciate these quilts!' she [Dee] said. 'She'd probably be backward enough to put them to everyday use.' " Which her mother counters with: " 'She can always make some more. Maggie knows how to quilt.' "

The mother affirms the functional nature of their heritage and insists that it must continually be renewed rather than fixed in the past. The mother's succinct phrasing of the meaning of *heritage* is underscored by Dee's lack of knowledge about the bits and pieces that make up these quilts, the process of quilting that Maggie knows. For Maggie appreciates the people who made them while Dee can only possess the "priceless" products. Dee's final words, ironically, exemplify her misuse of the concept of heritage, of what is passed on:

> "What don't I understand?" I wanted to know.
> "Your heritage," she said. And then she turned to Maggie, kissed her and said. "You ought to try to make something of yourself, too, Maggie. It's a new day for us. But from the way you and mama still live you'd never know it."

In critically analyzing the uses of the concept of heritage, Walker arrived at important distinctions. As an abstraction rather than a living idea, its misuse can subordinate people to artifact, can elevate culture above the community. And because she used, as the artifact, quilts which were made by Southern black women, focused attention on those supposedly backward folk who never heard the word heritage but fashioned a functional tradition out of little matter and much spirit.

In "Everyday Use," the mother, seemingly in a fit of contrariness, snatches the beautiful quilts out of the hands of the "black" Wangero and gives them to the "backward" Maggie. This story is one of eleven in Walker's first collection of short stories, *In Love and Trouble.* Though written over a period of some five years, the volume is unified by two of Walker's most persistent characteristics: her use of a Southern black woman character as protagonist, and that character's insistence on challenging convention, on being herself, sometimes in spite of herself.

Walker sets the tone for this volume by introducing the stories with two excerpts, one from *The Concubine,* a novel by the contemporary West African writer Elechi Amadi, the other from *Letters to a Young Poet* by the early-twentieth-century German poet Rainer Maria Rilke. The first excerpt emphasizes the rigidity of West African convention in relation to women. Such convention results in a young girl's contrariness, which her society explains away by saying she is unduly influenced by *agwu,* her personal spirit. The second excerpt from Rilke summarizes a philosophy of life that permeates the work of Alice Walker:

> People have (with the help of conventions) oriented all their solutions towards the easy and towards the easiest of the easy; but it is clear that we must hold to what is difficult; everything in nature grows and defines itself in its own way, and is characteristically

and spontaneously itself, seeks at all costs to be so against all opposition.

The protagonists in this volume embody this philosophy. They seek at all costs to be characteristically and spontaneously themselves. But because the conventions which gravely affect relationships between male and female, black and white, young and old, are so rigid, the heroines of *In Love and Trouble* seem backward, contrary, mad. Depending on their degree of freedom within the society, they express their *agwu* in dream, word, or act.

Roselily, the poor mother of illegitimate children, can express her *agwu* only through dreaming, during her wedding to a Northern Black Muslim. Though her marriage is seen by most as a triumphant delivery from her poor backward condition, she sees that, as a woman, whether single or married, Christian or Muslim, she is confined. She can only dream that "She wants to live for once. But doesn't quite know what that means. Wonders if she ever has done it. If she ever will."

In contrast to Roselily, Myrna, the protagonist of "Really, Doesn't Crime Pay" is the wife of a middle-class Southern black man. Still, she too is trapped by her husband and society's view of woman, though her confinement is not within a black veil but in the decorative mythology of the Southern Lady. However, unlike Roselily, Myrna does more than dream, she writes. In a series of journal entries, she tells us how the restrictions imposed upon her creativity lead her to attempt to noisily murder her husband, an act certainly perceived by her society as madness.

Most of the young heroines in this volume struggle through dream or word, against age-old as well as new manifestations of societal conventions imposed upon them. In contrast, the older women act. Like the mother in "Everyday Use," the old woman in "The Welcome Table" totally ignores convention when she enters the white church from which she is barred. The contrary act of this backward woman challenges all the conventions—"God, mother, country, earth, church. It involved all that and well they knew it."

Again, through juxtaposing the restrictions imposed on her protagonists with their subsequent responses, Walker illuminates the tension as she did in *The Third Life of Grange Copeland* between convention and the struggle to be whole. Only this time, the focus is very much on the unique vortex of restrictions imposed on black women by their community and white society. Her protagonists' dreams, words, acts, often explained away by society as the expressions of a contrary nature, a troubled *agwu,* are the price all beings, against opposition, would pay to be spontaneously and characteristically themselves. In *In Love and Trouble,* Walker emphasized the impact of sexism as well as racism on black communities. Her insistence on honesty, on the validity of her own experience as well as the experience of other Southern black women, ran counter to the popular notion of the early seventies that racism was the only evil that affected black women. Her first collection of short stories specifically demonstrated the interconnectedness of American sexism and racism, for they are both based on the notion of dominance and on unnatural hierarchical distinctions.

Walker does not choose Southern black women to be her major protagonists only because she is one, but also, I believe, because she has discovered in the tradition and history they collectively experience an understanding of oppression which has elicited from them a willingness to reject convention and to hold to what is difficult. Meridian, her most developed character, is a person who allows "an idea—no matter where it came from—to penetrate her life." The idea that penetrates Meridian's life, the idea of nonviolent resistance, is really rooted in a question: when is it necessary, when is it right, to kill? And the intensity with which Meridian pursues that question is due to her view of herself as a mother, a creator rather than a destroyer of life. The source to which she goes for the answer to that question is her people, especially the heritage that has been passed on to her by her maternal ancestors. She is thrilled by the fact that black women were "always imitating Harriet Tubman escaping to become something unheard of. Outrageous." And that "even in more conventional things black women struck out for the unknown." Like Walker in *In Search of Our Mothers' Gardens*, Meridian seeks her identity through the legacy passed on to her by Southern black women.

Yet Walker did not rest easy even with this idea, an idea which glorifies the black woman. For in *Meridian* she scrutinized that tradition which is based on the monumental myth of black motherhood, a myth based on the true stories of sacrifice black mothers performed for their children. But the myth is also restrictive, for it imposes a stereotype of black women, a stereotype of strength which denies them choice, and hardly admits of the many who were destroyed. In her characterization of Margaret and Mem Copeland in *The Third Life of Grange Copeland* Walker acknowledged the abused black women who, unlike Faulkner's Dilsey, did not endure. She went a step further in *Meridian*. Meridian's quest for wholeness and her involvement in the Civil Rights movement is initiated by her feelings of inadequacy in living up to the standards of black motherhood. Meridian gives up her son because she believes she will poison his growth with the thorns of guilt and she has her tubes tied after a painful abortion. In this novel, then, Walker probed the idea of black motherhood, as she developed a character who so elevates it that she at first believes she can not properly fulfill it. Again, Walker approaches the forbidden as a possible route to another truth.

Not only did Walker challenge the monument of black motherhood in *Meridian,* she also entered the fray about the efficacy of motherhood in which American feminists were then, as they are now, engaged. As many radical feminists blamed motherhood for the waste in women's lives and saw it as a dead end for a woman, Walker insisted on a deeper analysis: she did not present motherhood in itself as restrictive. It is so because of the little value society places on children, especially black children, on mothers, especially black mothers, on life itself. In the novel, Walker acknowledged that a mother in this society is often "buried alive, walled away from her own life, brick by brick." Yet the novel is based on Meridian's insistence on the sacredness of life. Throughout her quest she is surrounded by children whose lives she tries to preserve. In seeking the children she can no longer have she takes responsibility for the life of all the people. Her aborted motherhood yields to her a perspective on life—that of "expanding her mind with action." In keeping with this principle, Walker tells us in her essay "*One* Child of One's Own":

> It is not my child who has purged my face from history and herstory and left mystory just that, a mystery; my child loves my face and would have it on every page, if she could, as I have loved my own parents' faces above all others, and refused to let them be denied, or myself to let them go.

In fact, *Meridian* is based on this idea, the sacredness and continuity of life—and on another, that it might be necessary to take life in order to preserve it and make it possible for future generations. Perhaps the most difficult paradox that Walker has examined to date is the relationship between violence and revolution, a relationship that so many take for granted that such scrutiny seems outlandish. Like her heroine, Meridian, who holds on to the idea of nonviolent resistance after it has been discarded as a viable means to change, Walker persists in struggling with this age-old dilemma—that of death giving life. What the novel *Meridian* suggests is that unless such a struggle is taken on by those who would change society, their revolution will not be integral. For they may destroy that which they abhor only to resurrect it in themselves. Meridian discovers, only through personal struggle in conjunction with her involvement with the everyday lives of her people,

> that the respect she owed her life was to continue, against whatever obstacles, to live it, and not to give up any particle of it without

a fight to the death, preferably *not* her own. And that this existence extended beyond herself to those around her because, in fact, the years in America had created them One Life.

But though the concept of One Life motivates Meridian in her quest toward physical and spiritual health, the societal evils which subordinate one class to another, one race to another, one sex to another, fragment and ultimately threaten life. So that the novel *Meridian,* like *The Third Life of Grange Copeland,* is built on the tension between the African concept of animism, "that spirit inhabits all life," and the societal forces that inhibit the growth of the living toward their natural state of freedom.

Because of her analysis of sexism in the novel as well as in *In Love and Trouble,* Walker is often labeled a feminist writer. Yet she also challenges this definition as it is formulated by most white American feminists. In "*One* Child of One's Own" (1978), Walker insisted on the twin "afflictions" of her life. That white feminists as well as some black people deny the black woman her womanhood—that they define issues in terms of blacks on one hand, women (meaning white women) on the other. They miss the obvious fact—that black people come in both sexes. Walker put it strongly:

> It occurred to me that perhaps white women feminists, no less than white women generally, cannot imagine that black women have vaginas. Or if they can, where imagination leads them is too far to go.
>
> Perhaps it is the black woman's children, whom the white woman—having more to offer her own children, and certainly not having to offer them slavery or a slave heritage or poverty or hatred, generally speaking: segregated schools, slum neighborhoods, the worst of everything —resents. For they must always make her feel guilty. She fears knowing that black women want the best for their children just as she does. But she also knows black children are to have less in this world so that her children, white children, will have more. (In some countries, all.)
>
> Better then to deny that the black woman has a vagina. Is capable of motherhood. Is a woman.

And Walker *also* writes of the unwillingness of many black women to acknowledge or address the problems of sexism that affect them because they feel they must protect black men. To this she asserts that if black women turn away from the women's movement, they turn away from women moving all over the world, not just in America. They betray their own tradition, which includes women such as Sojourner Truth and Ida B. Wells, and abandon their responsibility to their own people as well as to women everywhere.

In refusing to elevate sex above race, on insisting on the black woman's responsibility to herself and to other women of color, Walker aligns herself neither with prevailing white feminist groups nor with blacks who refuse to acknowledge male dominance in the world. Because her analysis does not yield to easy generalizations and nicely packaged clichés, she continues to resist the trends of the times without discarding the truths upon which they are based.

Walker's second collection of short stories, *You Can't Keep a Good Woman Down* (1981), delves even more emphatically into the "twin afflictions" of black women's lives. Like *In Love and Trouble,* this book probes the extent to which black women have the freedom to pursue their selfhood within the confines of a sexist and racist society. However, these two collections, published eight years apart, demonstrate a clear progression of theme. While the protagonists of *In Love and Trouble* wage their struggle in spite of themselves, the heroines of *You Can't Keep a Good Woman Down* consciously insist upon their right to challenge any societal chains that bind them. The titles of the two collections succinctly indicate the shift in tone, the first emphasizing trouble, the second the self-assertiveness of the black woman so bodaciously celebrated in the blues tradition. The name of a famous blues song, "You Can't Keep a Good Woman Down," is dedicated to those who "*insist* on the value and beauty of the authentic." Walker's intention in this volume is clearly a celebration of the black woman's insistence on living. From whence does this insistence come, Walker asks? How does it fare in these contemporary times?

The stories in this collection are blatantly topical in their subject matter, as Walker focuses on societal attitudes and mores that women have, in the last decade, challenged—pornography and male sexual fantasies in "Porn," and "Coming Apart," abortion in "The Abortion," sadomasochism in "A Letter of the Times," interracial rape in "Luna Advancing." And the forms Walker invents to illuminate these issues are as unconventional as her subject matter. Many of the stories are process rather than product. Feminist thinkers of the seventies asserted a link between process (the unraveling of thought and feeling) and the way women have perceived the world. In keeping with this theory, Walker often gives us the story as it comes into being, rather than delivering the product, classic and clean. The author then not only breaks the rules by writing about "womanist" issues (Walker defines a womanist as a "black feminist"), she also employs a womanist process. For many of these stories reflect the present, when the process of confusion, resistance to the established order, and the discovery of a freeing order is, especially for women, a pre-requisite for growth.

Such a story is "Luna Advancing," in which a young Southern black woman's development is reflected through her growing understanding of the complexity of interracial rape. At the beginning of the story, practically everything she tells us is tinged with an air of taking things for granted. She lightly assumes that black people are superior. This generalization, however, is tested when Luna, a white friend of hers, tells her that during the "move-ment," she was raped by a black man they both know. Our narrator naturally is opposed to rape; yet she had not believed black men actually raped white women. And she knows what happens if a black man is even accused of such an act. Her earlier sense of clarity is shattered. Doubts, questions, push her to unravel her own feelings: "Who knows what the black woman thinks of rape? Who has asked her? Who *cares?*"

Again Walker writes about a forbidden topic and again she resists an easy solution. For although she speaks from the point of view of sisterhood with all women she also insists, as she did in "*One* Child of One's Own," that all women must understand that sexism and racism in America are critically related. Like all her previous fiction, this blatantly contemporary story is rooted in and illuminated by history, in this instance, the work of the great anti-lynching crusader Ida B. Wells. The dialogue between our narrator and this nineteenth-century black womanist focuses on the convoluted connection be-tween rape and lynchings, sex and race, that continues to this day. As a result, "Luna Advancing" cannot end conclusively. There are two endings, After-thoughts, Discarded Notes, and a Postscript as the narrator and writer mesh. Walker shows us her writing process, which cannot be neatly resolved since the questions she posed cannot be satisfactorily answered. The many endings prod the reader, insisting on the complexity of the issue and the characters.

> Dear God,
>   Me and Sophie work on the quilt. Got it frame up on the porch.
> Shug Avery donate her old yellow dress for scrap, and I work in
> a piece every chance I get. It's a nice pattern call Sister's Choice.
>
>   (*The Color Purple*)

The form of *The Color Purple* (1982), Walker's most recent novel, is a further development in the womanist process she is evolving. The entire novel is written in a series of letters. Along with diaries, letters were the dominant mode of expression allowed women in the West. Feminist historians find letters to be a principal source of information, of facts about the everyday lives of women *and* their own perceptions about their lives, that is of both "objective" and "subjective" information. In using the epistolary style, Walker is able to have her major character Celie express the impact of oppression on her spirit as well as her growing internal strength and final victory.

Like Walker's other two novels, this work spans generations of one poor rural Southern black family, interweaving the personal with the flow of history; and, like her essays and fiction, the image of quilting is central to its concept and form. But in *The Color Purple,* the emphases are the oppression black women experience in their relationships with black men (fathers, brothers, husbands, lovers) and the sisterhood they must share with each other in order to liberate themselves. As an image for these themes two sisters, Celie and Nettie, are the novel's focal characters. Their letters, Celie's to God, Nettie's to Celie, and finally Celie's to Nettie, are the novel's form.

Again, Walker approaches the forbidden in content as well as form. Just as the novel's form is radical, so are its themes, for she focuses on incest in a black family and portrays a black lesbian relationship as natural and freeing. The novel begins with Celie, a fourteen-year-old who is sexually abused by her presumed father and who manages to save her sister Nettie from the same fate. Celie is so cut off from everyone and her experience is so horrifying, even to herself, that she can only write it in letters to God. Her letters take us through her awful pregnancies, her children being taken away from her, and the abuses of a loveless marriage. She liberates herself, that is, she comes to value herself, through the sensuous love bond she shares with Shug, her husband's mistress, her appreciation of her sister-in-law Sophie's resistant spirit, and the letters from her sister Nettie which her husband had hidden from her for many years. We feel Celie's transformation intensely since she tells her story in her own rural idiomatic language, a discrete black speech. Few writers since Zora Neale Hurston have so successfully expressed the essence of the folk's speech as Walker does in *The Color Purple.*

In contrast to Celie's letters, Nettie's letters to Celie from Africa, where she is a missionary, are written in standard English. These letters not only provide a contrast in style, they expand the novel's scope. The comparison-contrast between male-female relationships in Africa and the black South suggest that sexism for black women in America does not derive from racism, though it is qualitatively affected by it. And Nettie's community of missionaries graphically demonstrates Afro-Americans' knowledge of their ancestral link to Africa, which, contrary to American myth, predates the Black Power Movement of the 1960s.

Though different in form and language, *The Color Purple* is inextricably linked to Walker's previous works. In *In Search of Our Mothers' Gardens,* Walker speaks about three types of black women: the physically and psychologically abused black women (Mem and Margaret Copeland in *The Third Life of Grange Copeland),* the black woman who is torn by contrary instincts (Meridian in her youth and college years), and the new black woman who re-creates herself out of the creative legacy of her maternal ancestors. Meridian begins that journey of transformation. But it is Celie, even more than her predecessor, who completes Walker's cycle. For Celie is a "Mem" who survives and liberates herself through her sisters' strength and wisdom, qualities which are, like the color purple, derived from nature. To be free is the natural state of the living. And Celie's attainment of freedom affects not only others of her sisters, but her brothers as well.

Both Walker's prose and her poetry probe the continuum between the inner self and the outer world. Her volumes of poetry, like her fiction and essays, focus on the self as part of a community of changers, whether it is the Civil Rights movement in *Once,* the struggle toward liberation in *Revolutionary Petunias,* the community of women who would be free in *Good Night, Willie Lee.* Yet her poems are distinguished from her prose in that they are a graph of that self which is specifically Alice Walker. They are perhaps even more than her prose rooted in her desire to resist the easiest of the easy. In her poetry, Walker the wayward child challenges not only the world but herself. And in exposing herself, she challenges us to accept her as she is. Perhaps it is the stripping of bark from herself that enables us to feel that sound of the genuine in her scrutiny of easy positions advocated by progressive blacks or women.

Her first volume, *Once,* includes a section / "Mornings / of an Impossible Love," in which Walker scrutinizes herself not through her reflections on the outer world as she does in the other sections, but through self-exposure. In the poem "Johann," Walker expresses feelings forbidden by the world of the 1960s.

In "So We've Come at Last to Freud," she arrogantly insists on the validity of her own emotions as opposed to prescriptives:

> Don't label my love with slogans;
> My father can't be blamed
> > for my affection
>
> Or lack of it.
> Ask him
> He won't understand you.

She resists her own attempt of self-pity in "Suicide":

> Thirdly if it is the thought
> of rest that
> fascinates
> laziness should be admitted
> in the clearest terms

Yet in "The Ballad of the Brown Girl," she acknowledges the pain of loss, the anguish of a forbidden love.

As these excerpts show, Walker refuses to embellish or camouflage her emotions with erudite metaphor or phrase. Instead she communicates them through her emphasis on single-word lines, her selection of the essential word, not only for content but for cadence. The result is a graceful directness that is not easily arrived at.

The overriding theme of *Once,* its feel of unwavering honesty in evoking the forbidden, either in political stances or in love, persists in *Revolutionary Petunias.* Walker, however, expands from the almost quixotic texture of her first volume to philosophical though intensely personal probings in her second. For *Revolutionary Petunias* examines the relationship between the nature of love and that of revolution. In these poems she celebrates the openness to the genuine in people, an essential quality, for her, in those who would be revolutionaries. And she castigates the false conventions constructed by many so-called revolutionaries. As a result, those who are committed to more life rather than less are often outcasts and seem to walk forbidden paths.

The volume is arranged in five sections, each one evoking a particular stage in the movement forward. In the first section, "In These Dissenting Times," Walker asserts that while many label their ancestors as backward, true revolutionaries understand that the common folk who precede them are the source of their strength. She reminds us that we "are not the first to suffer, rebel fight love and die. The grace with which we embrace life, in spite of the pain, the sorrows, is always a measure of what has gone before."

The second section, "Revolutionary Petunias, The Living Through," is about those who know that the need for beauty is essential to a desire for revolution, that the most rebellious of folk are those who feel so intensely the potential beauty of life that they would struggle to that end without ceasing. Yet because the narrow-minded scream that "poems of / love and flowers are / a luxury the Revolution / cannot afford," those so human as to be committed to beauty and love are often seen as "incorrect." Walker warns that in living through it one must "Expect nothing / Live frugally on surprise . . . wish for nothing larger / than your own small heart / Or greater than a star ("Expect nothing"). And in words that reverberate throughout her works, she exposes herself as one who must question, feel, pursue the mysteries of life. The title of the poem "Reassurance" affirms for us her need to sustain herself in her persistent questionings.

> I must love the questions
> themselves
> as Rilke said
> like locked rooms
> full of treasure
> to which my blind
> and groping key
> does not yet fit.

Flowing out of the second section, the third, "Crucifixion," further underscores the sufferings of those who would see the urge to revolution as emanating from a love for people rather than empty proscriptive forms. In it the ideologues drive out the lovers, "forcing . . . the very sun / to mangled perfection / for your cause" ("Lonely Particular"). And many like the "girl who would not lie; and was not born 'correct,' " or those who "wove a life / of stunning contradiction" are driven mad or die ("The Girl Who Died #2").

Yet some endured. The fourth section, "Mysteries . . . the Living Beyond," affirms the eventual triumph of those who would change the world because:

> the purpose of being
> here, wherever we are, is to increase
> the durability and the occasions of
> love among and between peoples.
> (June Jordan)

Love poems dominate this section, though always there is Walker's resistance to preordained form:

> In me there is a rage to defy
> the order of the stars
> despite their pretty patterns.
> "Rage"

And in "New Face," Walker combines the philosophical urge to penetrate the mysteries of life with the personal renewal which for her is love. From this renewal comes her energy to dig deeper, push further.

A single poem, "The Nature of This Flower Is to Bloom," is the last movement in the five-part collection, as Walker combines through capitalized short phrases ("Rebellious. Living. / Against the Elemental crush") the major elements of *Revolutionary Petunias*. In choosing a flower as the symbol for revolution, she suggests that beauty, love, and revolution exist in a necessary relationship. And in selecting the petunia as the specific flower, she emphasizes the qualities of color, exuberance, and commonness rather than blandness, rigidity, or delicacy.

In completing the volume with this succinct and graceful poem, Walker also reiterates her own stylistic tendencies. Most of her poems are so cohesive they can hardly be divided into parts. I have found it almost impossible to separate out a few lines from any of her poems without quoting it fully, so seamless are they in construction. This quality is even more pronounced in her most recent volume of poetry, *Good Night, Willie Lee, I'll See You in the Morning*. As in Walker's collections, though there are a few long poems, most are compact. In general, the voice in her poem is so finely distilled that each line, each word is so necessary it cannot be omitted, replaced, or separated out.

Like *Revolutionary Petunias*, *Good Night, Willie Lee* is concerned with the relationship between love and change, only now the emphasis is even more on personal change, on change in the nature of relationships between women and men. This volume is very much about the demystification of love itself; yet it is also about the past, especially the pain left over from the "Crucifixion" of *Revolutionary Petunias*.

Good Night, Willie Lee, I'll See You in the Morning is a five-part journey from night into morning, the name of each movement being an indication of the route this writer takes in her urge to understand love, without its illusions or veils. In the first movement, "Confession," Walker focuses on a love that declines into suffering. In letting go of it, she must go through the process of "stripping bark from herself" and must go deeper to an understanding of her past in "Early Losses, a Requiem." Having finally let the past rest in peace, she can then move to "Facing the Way," and finally to a "Forgiveness" that frees her.

The first poem of "Confession" is entitled "Did This Happen to Your Mother? Did Your Sister Throw Up a Lot?," while the last poem of this section ends "Other / women have already done this / sort of suffering for you / or so I thought." Between these two points, Walker confesses that "I Love a man who is not worth / my love" and that "Love has made me sick." She sees that her lover is afraid "he may fail me . . . it is this fear / that now devours / desire." She is astute enough to understand that his fear of love caused him to hold "his soul / so tightly / it shrank / to fit his hand.' In tracing the decline of love she understands the pull of pain: "At first I did not fight it / I *loved* the suffering / It was being alive!" "I savored my grief like chilled wine."

From this immersion in self-pity, she is saved by a woman, a friend who reminds her that other women have already done this for her and brings her back to herself. The steps of this first movement are particularly instructive for the rest of this volume, since Walker does not pretend, as so much feminist poetry does, that she is above passion, or the need or the desire for sharing love with a man. What she does is to communicate the peaks and pitfalls of such an experience, pointing always to the absolute necessity for self-love. Only through self-love can the self who can love be preserved. And for Walker, self-love comes from "On Stripping Bark from Myself." In one of the finest poems of this volume, Walker chants her song of independence. Her wayward lines are a response to a worldwide challenge:

> because women are expected to keep silent about
> their close escapes I will not keep silent
>
> . . . .
> No I am finished with living
> for what my mother believes
> for what my brother and father defend
> for what my lover elevates
> for what my sister, blushing, denies or rushes
> to embrace

for she has discovered some part of her self:

> Besides
>
> my struggle was always against
> an inner darkness: I carry with myself
> the only known keys
> to my death.

So she is

> happy to fight
> all outside murderers
> as I see I must.

Such stripping of bark from herself enables her to face the way, to ask questions about her own commitment to revolution, whether she can give up the comforts of life especially "the art that transcends time," "whose sale would patch a roof / heat the cold rooms of children, replace an eye / feed a life" ("Facing the Way"). And it is the stripping of bark from herself that helps her to understand that:

the healing
of all our wounds
is forgiveness
that permits a promise
of our return
at the end.
                ("Good Night, Willie
                Lee, I'll See You in
                the Morning")

It is telling, I believe, that Walker's discovery of the healing power of forgiveness comes from her mother's last greeting to her father at his burial. In this volume so permeated by the relationship of woman to man, her mother heads the list of a long line of women—some writers, like Zora Neale Hurston, others personal friends of Alice Walker—who pass unto her the knowledge they have garnered on the essence of love. Such knowledge helps Walker to demystify love and enables her to write about the tension between the giving of herself and the desire to remain herself.

In her dedication to the volume she edited of Zora Neale Hurston's work (*I Love Myself: A Zora Neale Hurston Reader*), Walker says of her literary ancestor: "Implicit in Hurston's determination to 'make it' in a career was her need to express 'the folk' and herself. Someone who knew her has said: 'Zora would have been Zora even if she'd been an Eskimo.' That is what it means to be yourself; it is surely what it means to be an artist." These words, it seems to me, apply as well to Alice Walker.

KEITH BYERMAN

Walker's Blues

*T*he *Color Purple,* Walker's award-winning and much-praised novel, has achieved immense popularity. In part, this success can be explained because the book is, in essence, a "womanist" fairy tale. Like Snow White, Celie is poisoned (psychologically in the novel) by an evil step-parent; like Cinderella, she is the ugly, abused daughter who ultimately becomes the princess; like Sleeping Beauty, she is awakened from her death-in-life by the kiss of a beloved; and like them all, she and her companions, after great travails, live happily ever after. Moreover, the fairy-tale quality is more than metaphoric, since major plot elements are worked out with fairy-tale devices. The story is generated out of what Vladimir Propp calls interdiction and violation of interdiction. Celie is told by her evil stepfather, after he rapes her, that she must tell no one but God what he has done; she chooses to write her story, which, as shall be seen below, makes it a public text. Transformation from a life of shame to one of self-esteem occurs when Celie receives the physical embrace of the regal Shug Avery. Finally, the plot is resolved and the characters reunited through the exposure of villainy and the death of the primary villain, an event which reverses the dispossession of Celie and her sister Nettie.

Since the fairy tale itself is a folk form, albeit a European one, there is no obvious contradiction between it and the Afro-American and African materials that enrich the narrative. In fact, such materials enhance the sense of a faerie world where curses, coincidences, and transformations are possible. The power for healing and change latent in folk arts and practices important to black women—quilting, mothering, blues singing, "craziness," and conjure—fit the pattern of the female character in the fairy tale who is

---

From *Fingering the Jagged Grain.* © 1985 by the University of Georgia Press.

victimized but then saved through love and magic. One of the things that mark
Walker's text as womanist is her insistence that these female capacities are
a superior way of bringing about change. One trait that distinguishes *The
Color Purple* from her earlier work is her setting up of an opposition between male and female folk wisdom; the former wisdom, passed from father
to son, claims, in Walker's view, the natural inferiority of women and the
need to keep them under control, through violence if necessary. What was
implicit in *Grange Copeland* becomes explicit here as part of the oral tradition.

The dominating male voice is present as the first words of the narrative:
"You better not never tell nobody but God. It'd kill your mammy." These
statements simultaneously demand female silence and place the responsibility for illicit behavior on the woman. They are spoken by the man Celie believes
to be her father after he has raped her. In effect, he makes her voice rather
than his action the fatal force in the family. By his definition, it is not his
violation of taboo but Celie's violation of his command that will kill the
mother. He presumes that his rules of order transcend those of the social order.
But silence does not protect the women; the mother dies anyway, and Celie
continues to be sexually assaulted. In fact, the father uses the silence as
evidence of acquiescence to his desires. Neither Celie nor her mother exists
for him except as ciphers to which he can arbitrarily assign meanings.

Appropriately, in this context, Celie chooses to write rather than speak
to God. At one point, Nettie recalls a comment by her sister: "I remember
one time you said your life made you feel so ashamed you couldn't even talk
about it to God, you had to write it, bad as you thought your writing was."
On the one hand, the statement suggests the effectiveness of the father's threat;
one so degraded as Celie denies herself even the most private speech act.
Nonetheless, she can write. In this sense, the process of writing is itself
associated with shame; it is the expression of those beyond salvation, those
who have been dehumanized. Writing, then, takes on those characteristics
of the disreputable that, as indicated earlier, are linked with the folk culture.
In entering the culture, it becomes dialectical. For example, the act of writing,
though apparently motivated by Celie's desire to obey the original interdiction
against speech, is clearly a violation of the command. Spoken words are tran-
sient; writing lasts as long as ink and paper. By putting down her thoughts,
Celie makes possible discovery of her pain and victimization. The fundamental
violation here is that she writes herself into humanity and thereby contradicts
the stipulation that she be a mere cipher. She gives herself an inner life and
a concrete history and thus an otherness that the patriarchal order denies her.
In the folk tradition, then, her letters subvert oppression in the process of
affirming it.

Celie's story concentrates first on the tyrannies exemplified by the initial interdiction. The first letter makes clear the source of her troubles: "He never had a kine word to say to me. Just say You gonna do what your mammy wouldn't. First he put his thing up gainst my hip and sort of wiggle it around. Then he grab hold my titties. Then he push his thing inside my pussy. When that hurt, I cry. He start to choke me, saying You better shut up and git used to it." When she becomes pregnant, her dying mother blames her for bringing shame to the family. The father steals the baby and apparently kills it. Celie fears for the life of the second one. Then he marries again, casting her aside as waste material, but this does not end the threat to the family: "I see him looking at my little sister. She scared." When Nettie attracts the interest of a widower, Celie advises her to take advantage of the opportunity: "I say Marry him, Nettie, an try to have one good year out your life. After that, I know she be big." But the father has other ideas; he offers the older sister to Mr. ——— instead, arguing that she will make a better wife because she is ugly and not "fresh." The discussions between the two men take the form of negotiations over livestock; the deal is closed when a cow is included with the woman. Celie literally has become a commodity, one with a low exchange value.

Life with Mr. ——— (the designation Celie uses through most of the book) is no better. He continually beats and berates her, and he allows his children to treat her like a servant. He goes into periods of melancholy during which he leaves the arduous tasks of the farm to Celie and his son Harpo. Moreover, he does not consider marriage a deterrent to his desires. He pursues Nettie when she comes to live with them, eventually forcing her to run away to avoid rape. His true love has always been Shug Avery, a blues singer with whom he lived years earlier. His affection for her produces the central irony of the book: though it initially damages Celie's self-esteem and their marriage, it eventually is the means of revitalization and rehumanization for both of them.

But the role of the blues singer, to be discussed in more detail below, is only one of the folk images in the book. Quilting, for example, functions as a way of creating female community in a world that represses female expression. Early in the story, Celie, who has largely accepted the male definition of woman's place, advises Harpo to beat his new wife into submission. She does this in part because she has trouble with the concept of an independent woman, since such a figure implicitly calls into question her own submissiveness. When Sofie confronts her with the consequences of her advice, she cannot adequately explain her action, but faces for the first time her hatred of her own womanhood. This awareness enables the two of them to establish

rapport through the folk arts of the dozens and quilt-making. The exchange
of insults allows them to vent any remaining hostility:

> I'm *so* shame of myself, I say. And the Lord he done whip me
> little bit too.
> The Lord don't like ugly, she say.
> And he ain't stuck on pretty.
> This open the way for our talk to turn another way.

This ritual, usually associated with males, creates an equality and intimacy
between them that guilt and anger had previously made impossible. It leads
to the quilting, which has a healing influence: "Let's make quilt pieces out
of these messed up curtains, she say. And I run git my pattern book. I sleeps
like a baby now." Later on, sewing on the quilt occasions opportunities to
discuss various problems; moreover, the process itself is a way of literally keeping one's history. The yellow stars Celie makes out of Shug's dress recall the
designs she used to make for her daughter Olivia's diapers. And in Africa,
Nettie uses a quilt to force that daughter's adoptive mother to remember Celie,
a recollection that absolves Nettie of accusations against her and that allows
Corrine to die in peace.

The African traditions, made available through the device of Nettie's letters, suggest the universality of oppression. The African male order, just like
its American counterpart, denies the validity of female expression; girl children
are not permitted to participate in the education provided by the missionaries,
and they are considered the property of first their fathers and then their
husbands. As a sign of their entry into womanhood, they undergo a ritual
of scarification which literally marks their role in society. Interestingly, while
Walker indicates here the African women's suffering, the only form of
resistance she provides them is the Western education they surreptitiously get
from Nettie and Olivia. When whites appropriate the land, the very traditions of generosity and trust which the Olinka display lead to the destruction
of the land and the tribe. The only option for the group is the *mbele,* a hidden area from which occasional acts of resistance can be carried out. But such
a space is essentially an escape from rather than an engagement with the
oppressive world. Significantly in this context, the missionaries return to
America rather than stay to share the Africans' fate.

Afro-American women, in contrast, develop with models for resistance
as well as healing. The first of these is the "crazy" woman, mentioned in the
discussion of Bambara. The story of Sofie is explicitly the story of a woman
who will not accept the rules of an oppressive order. She refuses to allow Harpo
to beat her and in fact always wins their physical battles; some of the most

humorous moments in the book are his attempts to explain away his inability to control her: "He say, Oh, me and that mule. She fractious, you know. She went crazy in the field the other day. By time I got her to head for home I was all banged up. Then when I got home, I walked smack dab into the crib door. Hit my eye and scratch my chin. Then when that storm come up last night I shet the window down on my hand." Her more serious struggles are against white authority figures who presume to dictate her role. She talks back to the mayor's wife and then strikes the mayor when he attempts physically to put her "in her place." She is then beaten by the police and thrown in jail for assault. In prison, she constantly dreams of murder.

She is saved from further violence when Harpo, Celie, and Mr. ———— devise a Brer Rabbit scheme to ameliorate her situation. They send Harpo's new girlfriend, Squeak, who is an unacknowledged relative of the warden, to tell him that Sofie would rather rot in prison than work as a maid for the mayor's wife. He, of course, immediately assigns her that task. Because this woman has already seen what she considers the black woman's crazy behavior, she is intimidated and Sofia suffers much less than she would have otherwise. "Craziness," then, is a form of resistance that allows for the expression of the frustrated humanity and creativity of black women.

Celie herself functions at one point as a conjure woman. When she decides to travel to Memphis with Shug, she delivers herself of a curse on Mr. ————: "Until you do right by me, I say, everything you even dream about will fail. I give it to him straight, just like it come to me. And it seem to come to me from the trees." Walker uses here Zora Neale Hurston's notion that the voice speaking is in fact that of a god using a human instrument: "A dust devil flew up on the porch between us, fill my mouth with dirt. The dirt say, Anything you do to me, already done to you." The voice, whatever its source, speaks the truth of Celie's pent-up anger and sense of injustice. Speaking forth carries with it its own authority; the voice exposes the suffering that has been her life and gives her an interiority and humanity that others have denied her. Her conjuring, in other words, has creative moral force. Its effect is shown in Mr. ————'s decline, both physical and mental, during her absence; only when he takes steps to right the wrongs he has done her does his strength return. Significantly, his major wrong has been the withholding of correspondence between Celie and Nettie. When he accepts their right to expression, the curse is lifted.

The most important of the folk figures is the female blues singer Shug Avery. Like her music, she embodies both love and trouble. For Mr. ————, who has always loved her, she is the source of his dissatisfaction over everything, including Celie, that is not her. Moreover, she has had a negative impact on his reputation in the community; Celie's father uses their affair as an excuse not to allow him to marry Nettie. But that same love is his one saving virtue. When Shug becomes ill, he brings her to the house and nurses her back to health. Similarly, her encouragement allows Squeak (Mary Agnes) to find her own voice as a blues singer and to demand that she not be "called out of her name" by Harpo, who has previously treated her as insignificant.

Her most complex effect is on Celie. From the very beginning she makes a powerful impression: "Shug Avery was a woman. The most beautiful woman I ever saw. She more pretty than my mama. She bout ten thousand times more prettier then me. I see her there in furs. Her face rouge. Her hair like somethin tail. She grinning with her foot up on somebody motocar. Her eyes serious tho. Sad some." Shug exists as something other than the reality in which Celie lives, and yet she is connected with that reality through Mr. ———. Thus she is not pure fantasy, a being representing escape from the harsh world of the present. The seriousness and sadness in her face suggest that she too has had unpleasant experiences and has lived through them. In addition, she opens for Celie the realm of the unconscious, giving this cipher another dimension of being.

The emergence of this dimension (which makes possible the conjuration described above) receives expression in the connection between Shug and Celie's gradual awareness of her own body. Walker emphasizes a relationship between the development of selfhood and the acceptance of female biology. Repeatedly, Celie talks of making herself wood, of not responding to either abuse or sexual intercourse. She protects herself, much as Velma did in *The Salt Eaters,* by denying the reality of her own flesh and emotion. Her rehumanization begins with her involuntary response to Shug's body: "First time I got the full sight of Shug Avery long black body with it black plum nipples, look like her mouth, I thought I had turned into a man." Since Celie herself has never experienced sexual arousal, she assumes that stimulation is a male attribute. She feels urges that frighten her: "I feel like something pushing me forward. If I don't watch out I'll have hold of her hand, tasting her fingers in my mouth." Part of what elicits this response is Shug's beauty, which sets a standard that Celie, who believes in conventional notions of female attractiveness, cannot hope to meet. Only when she learns the beauty of her own femaleness can she begin to accept her body and the self of which it is a part: "Stick the looking glass tween my legs. Ugh. All that hair. Then my pussy lips be black. Then inside look like a wet rose. It a lot prettier than you thought, ain't it? she say from the door." The discovery, not of an abstract, spiritual beauty, but of a physical one inherent in womanhood begins the psychological change in Celie. She now becomes someone worthy of the love of Shug, and someone who did *not* deserve the treatment she received from her stepfather and Mr. ———.

For both Celie and Mr. ———, Shug's beauty is linked to her singing. She can give voice to the pains they each endure silently. For Celie, she implies the possibility of creativity in a context other than the endless cycle of reproduction:

> What that song? I ast. Sound low down dirty to me. Like what
> the preacher tell you its sin to hear. Not to mention sing.
>   She hum a little more. Something come to me, she say.
> Something I made up. Something you help scratch out my head.

Though Shug sings the "devil's music," Celie must balance this "sin" against her affection for the singer/sinner. A tension is created between the rules of the church and the attractiveness of the violation. Again Celie is implicated in a crime of verbal expression, just as she was at the beginning of her story.

But if Shug brings love and creativity, she also brings and experiences troubles. She holds herself responsible for the death of Mr. ———'s first wife, who took a violent lover when she could not counteract her husband's infatuation with the singer. Moreover, her story of her inability to stay with one man is a tale of loneliness; she loved Mr. ——— (whom she calls Albert), but she wanted her freedom more than love. Thus, her history is the classic blues dilemma she describes in her songs. She creates the same tension for Celie, whose very love for Shug makes her vulnerable to despair when her beloved finds another man; the opening of her life involves pains which she did not experience before she felt worthy of love. Thus, Shug as a folk figure opens possibilities rather than constructs completed orders of reality.

However, another of her contributions to creativity leads to a resolution of the text's conflicts that is more appropriate to the fairy tale than to Afro-American folklore. At her suggestion, Celie begins making pants, especially purple ones (a color associated with Shug's regal bearing), for herself and others. At first, this traditional art works in a folk manner; though she desires to kill Albert for suppressing the letters, she puts her energy into sewing instead: "A needle and not a razor in my hand, I think." But, when the immediate motive passes, pants making becomes a business and Celie a petty capitalist who turns her farm into a home factory. When it is revealed that Albert has always enjoyed sewing, any lingering hostility vanishes, and they sit on the porch stitching "folksy" pants and shirts.

This resolution is part of a larger pattern of closure in the narrative. Harpo turns his house into a blues club where Shug and Mary Agnes sing, while he works at his favorite activity, cooking. When the stepfather dies, a long-hidden will appears which shows that the land, house, and store he had possessed for years in fact were left to Celie and Nettie. And, finally, the long-lost sister escapes from Africa and turns up at the farm with Celie's children, Olivia and Adam, who has scarified his own face to identify himself with the suffering womanhood of his African bride. Thus, all the characters are reunited in a feminized space with female traits and free of the hostility, oppression, guilt and cruelty of the male and white worlds.

But this very liberation contradicts the nature of the folk sensibility on which it is based. History, with the suffering and joy it brings, cannot, in the folk worldview, be transcended; it must be lived through. Walker seeks to resolve the dialectic by making all males female (or at least androgynous), all destroyers creators, and all difference sameness. In this process, she must move outside the very conflicts that generated the sewing, the blues singing, and the voice of Celie herself. Such an effort makes sense for one who wishes to articulate a political position; resolution creates a sacred, utopian space which justifies the ideology on which it is based. But this creation is in fact another system that requires the same denial of history and difference as the order it has supplanted. To live "happily ever after," as the folk characters do in *The Color Purple,* is, ironically, to live outside the folk world.

Alice Walker's feminist and antiracist perspective has given her access to new literary material by allowing her to see the value of the folklore of black women and the history which has shaped that lore. In *The Third Life of Grange Copeland, In Love and Trouble,* and *Meridian,* she has emphasized suffering and the struggle to resist it through folk values. In much of *You Can't Keep a Good Woman Down,* she moves away from storytelling into polemic, even within narratives. Questions of race and sexual identity become more absolute, and much of the complexity of historical sensibility that feeds folk material is lost. In *The Color Purple,* she has in effect moved to allegorical form in order to transcend history and envision the triumph of those principles she espouses. But in doing so, she has neutralized the historical conditions of the very folk life she values.

MAE G. HENDERSON

The Color Purple:
Revisions and Redefinitions

*T*he *Color Purple* subverts the traditional Eurocentric male code which dominates the literary conventions of the espistolary novel. As a genre, the English epistolary novel, a form invented by men writing about women, embodies male control of the literary images of women. By appropriating a form invented and traditionally controlled by men, but thematicizing the lives and experiences of women, Alice Walker asserts her authority, or right to authorship. Signing herself as "A.W., author and medium," Walker suggests that her purpose has been not only to create and control literary images of women, and black women in particular, but to give voice and representation to these same women who have been silenced and confined in life and literature. *The Color Purple* is a novel which deals with what it means to be poor, black, and female in the rural South during the first half of the twentieth century. In an interview in *Newsweek* in June 1982, Walker explains that Celie, the protagonist of *The Color Purple,* is modeled after the author's own grandmother, who was raped at the age of twelve by her slave owner (and Walker's grandfather). Celie's fate, however, is brighter. "I liberated her from her own history," remarks Walker, "I wanted her to be happy." Walker hopes that "people can hear Celie's voice. There are so many people like Celie who make it, who came out of nothing. People who triumphed." Thus, for Walker, art is liberational and life-saving; it is an act for reconstruction and reclamation of self, of past, of women, and of community.

As an epistolary novel, *The Color Purple* employs a narrative technique singularly appropriate to the author's subject. The portrayal of women's friend-

From *Sage: A Scholarly Journal on Black Women* 2, no. 1 (Spring 1985). © 1985 by Mae G. Henderson.

ships in literature is formally linked to the development of the epistolary novel that can be traced back to the beginnings of the modern novel in eighteenth-century England. As Janet Todd argues in *Women's Friendship in Literature,* "the fictional friendship between women grew out of the idea of the confidant—the correspondent in the epistolary novel." Moreover, recent feminist scholarship has recovered and reclaimed letters, diaries, journals, and similar forms of expression associated with the culture of women who have been historically denied access to the popular and commercial print media. Black and third-world women of color, in particular, have begun to appropriate the epistolary form, as represented, for example, in Cherrie Moraga and Gloria Anzaldúa's *This Bridge Called My Back.* By choosing an epistolary style, Walker, like these authors, is able to draw on a form which places her work in a tradition associated with women, allows a feminine narrative voice, and establishes a bond and intimacy between women.

Although there are a number of letters to Celie from her sister Nettie, the story is told primarily from the point of view of Celie, who addresses her letters first to God, and later to Nettie. Such a form is uniquely suited to Walker's subject in that it allows an uneducated, black, southern woman to speak for herself. The form also allows Walker to link a formal and Western tradition to an oral and distinctly Afro-American folk expression. Celie's letters transpose a black and oral mode into a Western epistolary tradition (a form also adapted effectively by modern African writers such as Camara Laye and Ferdinand Oyono, whom Walker acknowledges as influences). Walker's use of the vernacular (sometimes called Black English) has invested an old and somewhat rigid form with new life.

In adopting the epistolary form, the vehicle for the eighteenth-century novel of sentiment, Walker draws on certain codes and conventions of the genre, but revises them in such a way as to turn the sentimental novel on its head. Like the Pure but Betrayed Maiden of the sentimental story, Walker's heroine is a victim of sexual abuse. At age fourteen, Celie is raped by her stepfather. Forcing himself on her, he warns Celie, "You better not never tell nobody but God." Consequently, Celie's early letters are written to God.

After bearing him two children who are taken away from her, Celie is married off by Alphonso, her stepfather, to an older widower. Saddled with farm work as well as the care of four "rotten" kids and domestic chores, she is overworked, beaten, and reduced to virtual bondage by her husband. Celie's status is suggested as her stepfather negotiates her marriage to Albert:

> She ugly. He say. But she ain't no stranger to hard work. And she
> clean. And God done fixed her. You can do everything just like

you want to and she ain't gonna make you feed it or clothe it.
. . . She can take that cow she raise down there back of the crib.

When Albert, whom Celie calls "Mister," returns for a second inspection, the transaction is completed:

He say, Let me see her again.
    Pa call me. . . . Like it wasn't nothing. Mr. —————— want another look at you.
    I go stand in the door. The sun shine in my eyes. He's still up on his horse. He look me up and down.
    Pa rattle his newspaper. Move up, he won't bite, he say.
    I go closer to the steps, but not too close cause I'm a little scared of his horse.
    Turn round Pa say.
    I turn round.

The arrival of Mister represents an ironic reversal of the fairy tale in which the steed-mounted knight in shining armor arrives to save the damsel in distress. Resonating through this passage, however, are not the chimes of medieval chivalry, but the echo of the slavers' auction block in the sale and bartering of a human commodity in a quasi-feudal Southern economy. Celie's status as slave, or chattel property—subservient to father and later to husband (and to God)—expected to perform domestic, field, and sexual labor, is confirmed when Albert is assured that the "cow [is] coming."

The inscription of slavery is critical to understanding Walker's intentions. If Mister has inherited from his father, Old Mister, the farm which belonged to his grandfather, the white slaveowner, he has likewise inherited from Old Mister the values of ownership, mastery, and domination bequeathed by the white slaveowner. These values, he attempts, in turn, to impose on his own son, Harpo. For Walker, it is the institution of slavery and its legacy which are largely responsible for setting into motion the oppressive mode characterizing relations between men and women, white and black, powerful and powerless.

The indirect impact of white violence on black women and children is suggested by Walker in her treatment of Celie's (natural) father, owner of a prosperous dry-goods store, who is lynched by local white businessmen threatened by his success. While this episode exposes the economic bases of racial oppression, it also suggests the far-reaching consequences of violence directed toward black men. It is the murder of Celie's father which results in her mother's mental derangement and subsequent marriage to Alphonso—

the stepfather who violates Celie. Even more subtle perhaps are the relations of violence initiated by a racial episode which sets the pattern for other forms of racial and sexual violence throughout the novel. The message, however, is an elaboration rather than a restatement of that in *The Third Life of Grange Copeland* in which Walker links the sexual oppression of black women by black men to the racial oppression of black men by white men. What Walker demonstrates in *The Color Purple* is the necessity for each person to struggle against unjust oppression, whether it is in the home, in the community, or in a racially hostile society. As she has written elsewhere, "freedom should force us to stop relating as owner to owned" ("In the Closet of the Soul: A Letter to an African-American Friend").

Marriage perpetuates Celie's plight. Like the central character in the novel of sentiment, Celie finds herself beleaguered and victimized by what Todd describes as the "scheme of patriarchy." Laying claim to the "right" of pater familias, Albert attempts to impose a pattern of dominance and submission on his wife and children. "He beat me like he beat the children," writes Celie, "It all I can do not to cry." Advising his son Harpo, Albert declares, "Wives is like children. You have to let 'em know who got the upper hand. Nothing can do that better than a good, sound beating."

The model for the patriarchal scheme in the novel has already been established by Albert's father, who has dissuaded his son from marrying the only woman he has ever loved, Shug Avery ("She black as tar, she nappy headed. She got legs like baseball bats"). Like his father before him, Albert attempts to prevent his own son from marrying Sofia, the woman of his choice and the mother of his child: "No need to think I'm gon let my boy marry you just cause you in the family way. He young and limited. Pretty gal like you could put anything over on him." Although Harpo, in defiance of his father, finally does bring home Sofia and his baby, he tries to beat her just as his father beats Celie.

Yet, the women in *The Color Purple* represent a radical departure from the "sentimental friends" who, Todd argues, "lead conventional lives." Walker's women transform their lives. In the sentimental novel, the women frequently expire or ultimately succumb in form—if not always in spirit—to the patriarchal condition. The women in Walker's novel, however, reform the essential bases of the relationships, codes, and values of their world, and at the same time, strengthen and extend the bonds of female friendship.

When Nettie escapes from her stepfather, she comes to live with Celie and Albert. Because she rebukes Albert's amorous attentions, however, she is forced to leave, and is not heard from for many years. Celie later discovers that Albert has been intercepting Nettie's letters from Africa where she has gone with a missionary couple, Samuel and Corrine, who have adopted Celie's two children. Albert's unsuccessful attempts to expropriate or conceal Nettie's letters suggest, again, Walker's intention to subvert male efforts to suppress black women in life as well as letters. Thus, if on a formal level, Walker subverts white and male literary codes and conventions on the level of plot and theme, she subverts the codes and conventions which dominate social and sexual relationships.

Over and over again, Celie accepts abuse and victimization. When Harpo asks her what to do to "make [Sofia] mind," Celie, having internalized the principle of male domination, answers, "Beat her." When Celie next sees Harpo, "his face [is] a mess of bruises." Sofia, then, becomes Celie's first model of resistance to sexual, and later, racial subjugation. Cheeky and rebellious, Sofia is described as an "amazon" of a woman. She scorns rigid gender definitions and prefers fixing the leaking roof to fixing the evening dinner. Moreover, as Harpo quickly learns, Sofia gives as well as she takes. "All my life I had to fight," Sofia explains to Celie, "I had to fight my daddy. I had to fight my brothers. I had to fight my cousins and my uncles. A girl child ain't safe in a family of men." Not only does Sofia resist Harpo's attempts to impose submission, she is also jailed for "sassing" the mayor's wife and knocking the mayor down when he slaps her for impudence.

Unlike Sofia, however, Celie submits to a system of beliefs and values which reinforce conventional notions of race, class, and sex—and relegate her to a subordinate status. Celie submits to male authority because she accepts a theology which requires female subjugation to father and husband. Having been taught to "honor father and mother no matter what," Celie "couldn't be mad at [her] daddy because he [her] daddy." She suffers Albert's abuse for the same reasons: "Well, sometime Mr. —— git on me pretty hard, I have to talk to Old Maker. But he my husband. I shrug my shoulders."

"Old Maker" is, for Celie, "big and old and tall and graybearded and white." In linking her notion of divinity to a white, male figure, Celie accepts a theology of self-denial. It is a theology which validates her inferior status and treatment as a black woman in a racist and sexist culture. Not only does she devalue herself, but she attaches little value to a world which reflects her image as "black. . . pore. . . [and] a woman. . . nothing at all."

If Albert separates Celie from Nettie, he introduces her to Shug Avery, his former mistress. Celie moves from a relationship with a stepfather who is sexually abusive to a relationship with her husband who exploits her labor and sex, to finally, a relationship with Shug Avery, who loves her, teaches her the reverence and mystery of her body, and the means of earning a livelihood through her own industry and creativity.

Afflicted with what one character describes as "the nasty woman's disease," Shug, a blues singer, arrives in a covered wagon one afternoon. Just as Celie has internalized Albert's principle of patriarchy, so Shug internalizes his demeaning attitude toward Celie. Upon first meeting Celie, Shug "looks [Celie] over from head to foot and cackles, "You sure *is* ugly. . . like she ain't believed it.""

Opposite Celie in every way, Shug has the reputation of a high-living, adventurous, independent blues singer, whose life-style gives her greater freedom than Celie's more conventional status. Yet when Celie nurses and coaxes Shug back to health, the two women become intimate friends instead of rivals. Unlike the men who have subjugated Celie, Shug seeks neither to control nor to possess her. Celie subsequently forms a relationship with Shug which evolves from a maternal, to a sororal, to an erotic attachment.

Shug initiates Celie into an awareness of her own sexuality and an appreciation of her body—for despite the fact that she has had two children, Celie remains a "virgin" in that she has never shared a loving relationship. Until Shug introduces her to the beauty of her own body, Celie remains devoid of any sense of self-esteem or self-value:

> [Shug] say, Here take this mirror and go look at yourself down there, I bet you never seen it, have you?
> Naw. . . .
> She say, What, too shame even to go off and look at yourself? And you look so cute too, she say, laughing. . . .
> You come with me while I look, I say.
> And us run off to my room like two little prankish girls.
> You guard the door, I say.
> She giggle. Okay, she say. Nobody coming. Coast clear.
> I lie back on the bed and haul up my dress. Yank down my bloomers. Stick the looking glass tween my legs. Ugh. All that hair. Then my pussy lips be black. Then inside look like a wet rose.

Celie's passivity and self-indifference are transformed into receptivity and responsiveness first to Shug, then to herself:

> It a lot prettier than you thought, ain't it? she say from the door.
> It mine, I say. Where the button?
> Right up near the top, she say. The part that stick out a little.
> I look at her and touch it with my finger. A little shiver go through me. Nothing much. But just enough to tell me this the right button to mash. Maybe.

> She say, While you looking, look at your titties too. I haul up
> my dress and look at my titties. Think bout my babies sucking
> them. Remember the little shiver I felt then too. Sometimes a big
> shiver.

If her body has been devalued by the men in her life, Celie not only
discovers her own sexuality in the relationship with Shug, but she also learns
how to love another. The recognition of herself as beautiful and loving is the
first step towards Celie's independence and self-acceptance. If Celie, however,
becomes more self-reliant, Shug becomes more nurturing and caring. In the
course of the friendship, both women are transformed.

Unlike Celie, who derives her sense of self from the dominant white and
male theology, Shug is a self-invented character whose sense of self is not male-
inscribed. Her theology allows a diving, self-authorized sense of self. Shug's
conception of God is both imminent and transcendent:

> God is inside you and inside everybody else. You come into the
> world with God. But only them that search for it inside find it.
> And sometimes it just manifest itself even if you not looking, or
> don't know what you looking for. . . . I believe God is everything.
> . . . Everything that is or ever was or ever will be.

Shug rejects the scriptural notion of God: "Ain't no way to read the bible and
not think God white. . . . When I found out I thought God was white, and
a man, I lost interest." Describing her god as "it," Shug explains that "god
ain't a he or a she." God, for Shug, is not only someone to please, but to
be pleased: "I think it pisses God off if you walk by the color purple in a
field somewhere and don't notice it."

Celie begins to revise her own notions of God and man and her place
within the scheme of patriarchy when she discovers, through the agency of
Shug, the cache of letters which Albert has concealed from her. Not only does
she discover that her sister and children are in Africa, perhaps separated from
her forever, but that her real father had been lynched and her mother driven
mad. These calamities and misfortunes shatter Celie's faith in the "big. . .
old. . . tall. . . graybearded" white man to whom she has been "praying and
writing." "He act just like all the other mens I know," writes Celie, "trifling,
forgetful, and lowdown." Resisting the authority of a patriarchal god as well
as that of her husband, Celie learns to assert herself both in writing and speaking. When she recognizes that "the god [she] has been writing is a man" who
does not listen to "poor colored women," she begins to address her letters
to sister Nettie.

Writing thus becomes, for Celie, a means of structuring her identity—her sense of self—in relationship to her sister, and by extension, a community of women. The subsequent letters between Celie and Nettie stand as a profound affirmation of the creative and self-creative power of the word. Because the letters, due to Albert's expropriation, are never answered, it is apparent that they function primarily for the benefit of the writers, rather than the recipients. The dedication of the book ("*To the Spirit:* Without whose assistance / Neither this book / Nor I / Would have been / Written") suggests that to create a book is to create a life. Celie (like her creator, Walker) writes herself and her story into being. Moreover, the transformation of the letters represents and parallels, to some extent, the growth and change in the lives of the writers. Not only do Nettie's letters become more formal and didactic in style as she is educated in the manners and mores of the Olinka tribe, but Celie's letters become longer and more sophisticated as she articulates a more reflective and complex sense of self. The correspondence between Celie and Nettie attests to the power of literacy and, at the same time, reinforces the motifs of community and female bonding that underlines the novel.

Celie's defiance of Albert is both a mark of increasing literacy, as well as a milestone in her journey toward maturity and independence:

> Mr. ———— start up from his seat. . . . He look over at me. I thought you was finally happy, he say. What wrong now?
>
> You a lowdown dog is what's wrong, I say. It's time to leave you and enter into the Creation. And your dead body just the welcome mat I need.

Just as the power of literacy affirms Celie's relationship with Nettie, and moves her closer to a sense of self-in-relationship, so the power of voice severs her dependency upon Albert, and moves her toward a more autonomous sense of self. If writing demonstrates the creative potential of the word, then conjuration gives powerful testimony to its destructive possibilities:

> I curse you, [Celie] say.
>
> What that mean? he say.
>
> I say, Until you do right by me, everything you touch will crumble.
>
> He laugh. Who you think you is? he say. You can't curse nobody. Look at you. You black, you pore, you ugly, you a woman. Goddam, he say, you nothing at all.
>
> Until you do right by me, I say, everything you even dream about

will fail. I give it to him straight, just like it come to me. And it seem to come to me from the trees.

Whoever heard of such a thing, say Mr. ———. I probably didn't whup your ass enough.

Every lick you hit me you will suffer twice, I say. Then I say, You better stop talking because all I'm telling you ain't coming just from me. Look like when I open my mouth the air rush in and shape words.

Shit, he say. I should have lock you up. Just let you out to work.

The jail you plan for me is the one in which you will rot, I say.

Shug come over to where us talking. She take one look at my face and say Cclic! Then she turn to Mr. ———. Stop Albert, she say. Don't say no more. You just going to make it harder on yourself.

I'll fix her wagon! say Mr. _____, and spring toward me.

A dust devil flew up on the porch between us, fill my mouth with dirt. The dirt say, Anything you do to me, already done to you.

Then I feel Shug shake me. Celie, she say. And I come to myself.

I'm pore, I'm black, I may be ugly and can't cook, a voice say to everything listening. But I'm here.

Amen, say Shug. Amen, amen.

Not only does the word have a transformative effect on Celie, but in the form of conjuration, it has the power to change, or at least deflect, the hostility and negativity emanating from an ill-wisher—or, as Hurston describes the power of a curse, to place "damnation and trouble. . . on the head of [her] enemy and not on [her] head" (*Mules and Men*). Moreover, as conjure woman, Celie not only has the power to free herself from unjust oppression, but also the potential to release Albert from the burden of his own oppressiveness.

Ultimately, it is Celie's sewing which saves Albert's life. With "a needle and not a razor in [her] hand," Celie channels her anger and violence into creativity. Later, in Memphis, Celie's skill with the needle and her talent for designing pants provide her with the means of earning a comfortable livelihood. Thus, if Walker emphasizes the importance of popular culture (singing) in the character of Shug, she stresses the centrality of material culture to women's creativity and survival in her depiction of Celie.

Sewing and quilting are occupations in the novel in which women—and sometimes men—participate. Sofia, Shug, and Celie all share in the art of quilting. Both Sofia and Shug contribute to making a quilt ("Sister's Choice") by donating patching material to Celie. It is both a utilitarian and decorative art, and, equally important, represents the collective and collaborative labor of women. Although associated with women and women's culture, quilting is an art particularly associated with the culture of rural, black, working-class women. It is a fitting emblem of the bonding between women.

Sewing is an enterprise, however, which is sometimes performed by men. The Olinka [African] men are known for their "beautiful quilts which are full of animals and birds and people." Moreover, at the end of the novel, Albert significantly begins to make tops to accompany Celie's pants. Thus textile culture not only forges a bond among black women, it also serves as a link between Africans and Afro-Americans as well as between women and men.

Just as Walker's use of the epistolary form allows her to transpose a formal tradition into a vehicle for expressing the folk voice, so her emphasis on material and popular modes of expression allow us to revise our conventional notions of "high" art and culture. The significance of these expressions of folk culture is particularly compelling for black women whose creativity has had a direct relationship to personal and political survival. Walker uses the quilt, then, as a metaphor for the black and female aesthetic as well as an emblem of bonding.

Both Celie and Shug have doubles in the novel. Celie and "Squeak," Harpo's mistress, duplicate each other in some measure: both are victims of rape and incest by black and white men respectively. Sofia and Shug also function as doubles: both resist the conventional submissive and obedient roles expected of women, thus subverting the system of patriarchy. Tiring of Harpo's attempts to control and dominate her, Sofia leaves and Harpo takes up with Squeak, who is as submissive to him as Celie is to Albert. When Harpo begins to lose interest, however, Celie, under Shug's tutelage, realizes that Squeak has surrendered her right to self-entitlement by giving up her name. Celie advises Squeak to make Harpo address her by her real name, Mary Agnes.

The women in the novel forge bonds in other ways as well. Celie accedes to the violation of her body in order to protect her sister Nettie from the sexual advances of their stepfather. Squeak (Mary Agnes), with her own body, secures Sofia's release from jail. When Squeak decides to pursue a career as a blues singer, and leaves with Shug, it is Sofia who promises to care for Squeak's daughter while she is in Memphis. Even Eleanor Jane, daughter of the white mayor's wife (for whom Sofia has been forced to work as a maid) prepares special foods as a curative for Sofia's youngest child, who is victim to a rare blood disease.

Each of these relationships, however, forms part of a vaster network of communal relationships in which female bonding is the dominant and connecting link. Challenging the hierarchal power relations exercised between men and women (and by implication, whites and blacks) are the relationships among the women based on cooperation and mutuality. Women share the children, the labor, and even, at times, the men. Ultimately it is the female bonding which restores the women to a sense of completeness and independence. The relationship between Celie and Shug, on the one hand, and between Celie and Nettie, on the other, exemplify the power and potential of this bonding.

Although blacks in the American South as well as the Olinka tribe in Africa are impacted by the presence of whites, and function, to some degree, as satellites in a white sphere of influence, it is the black (American/African) community which provides the central focus for the action of the novel. Nettie's letters educate Celie and the reader on the customs and rituals of West Africa. Reportorial rather than expressive, they illuminate the similarities between the condition of black women in the American South and black women in Africa.

If Celie is degraded and devalued as a black woman in the American South, Nettie discovers that, as an unmarried female, she is regarded with pity and contempt by the Olinka. She also learns about scarification and clitoridectomy, rituals of female mutilation in a patriarchal society. Tashi, the young Olinka woman whom Celie's son marries, submits to both these rites in order to preserve some vestige of tribal culture and identity in the face of white encroachment upon traditional village life. Tashi's choice suggests, of course, the conflict between the demands of race and the demands of sex confronting black women. With these rituals, black patriarchal culture replicates the historic occidental relationship between whites and blacks. Scarification and cliteridectomy both externalize the historic victimization of black women and symbolize gender debasement in patriarchal culture.

In Africa, however, Nettie discovers among the Olinka the value of female bonding in a polygynous society. "It is in work that women get to know and care about each other," she writes to Celie. Moreover, in the missionary household where she lives with Samuel, a black minister, and his wife, Corrine, Nettie shares the responsibility of rearing the children and administers to the spiritual and medical needs of the Olinka.

Yet, it is Celie and Shug who epitomize the complementarity as well as the autonomy of the women—which extend to include not only other women, but also the men. While developing an individual sense of self, Celie nevertheless respects Shug's rights. Although heartbroken that Shug has run off with Germaine, a young musician in her band, Celie recognizes that "[Shug] got a right to look over the world in whatever company she choose. Just cause

I love her don't take away none of her rights. . . . Who am I to tell her who to love? My job just to love her good and true myself." Albert's feelings for Shug, together with his desertion by Shug and Celie, constitute the catalyst for a similar recognition in his life: "I have love and I have been love. And I thank God he let me gain understanding enough to know love can't be halted just cause some peoples moan and groan. It don't surprise me you [Celie] love Shug Avery. . . . I have love Shug Avery all my life." Finding consolation in each other's company, Albert and Celie become friends for the first time, and spend their evenings sharing interests and reminiscing about Shug.

By the end of the novel, we see that Walker has developed a new model for relationships based on new gender roles for men and women. Not only do Albert and Harpo extend their interests to include activities such as sewing and cooking but, perhaps more importantly, they begin to relate more affectively to each other. When Albert is nearly dying, Harpo bathes and nurtures his father back to health. Walker suggests here that less rigid and oppressive roles are necessary in order for men and women to live together and fulfill their individual potential. Celie's notions of "manliness" and "womanliness" challenge rigid gender categories and allow for individual variations and preferences:

> Mr. ——— ast me the other day what it is I love so much bout Shug. He say he love her style. He say to tell the truth, Shug act more *manly* than most men. I mean she upright, honest. Speak her mind and the devil take the hindmost, he say. You know Shug will fight, he say. Just like Sofia. She bound to live her life and be herself no matter what.
>
> Mr. ——— think all this is stuff men do. But Harpo not like this, I tell him. You not like this. What Shug got is *womanly* it seem like to me. Specially since she and Sofia the ones got it [Emphasis added.]

Walker not only redefines male and female roles, she also suggests a new paradigm for relationships. During the course of the novel, Shug leaves Albert and returns married to Grady, "a skinny big toof man." She later runs off with the youthful Germaine. The intimacy between Celie and Shug, however, survives and incorporates each of these relationships.

In Memphis, the initial triad of Shug, Celie, and Albert gives way to a triad consisting of Celie, Shug, and Grady (or alternately, Squeak, Shug, and Grady). When Shug takes up with Germaine, a new triad develops—Celie, Shug, and Germaine. Other triads in the novel include Squeak, Harpo, and Sofia and Nettie, Corrine, and Samuel. The final triad in the novel, formed when Shug returns to Celie, is, in fact, a reconstitution of the first—Shug, Celie, and Albert—with *radically redefined roles*.

Walker's final paradigm, then, is neither the male/female nor the female/female dyad, but a variation on the eternal triangle in which women complement rather than compete with each other, and at the same time, share an equal status with the men. Thus, the novel moves from a male/female coupling in which the woman is subjugated, to a female/female coupling based on mutuality, to a female/male/female triad based on new and re-defined roles. In Walker's new model, conventional heterosexual relationships and nuclear families give way to a triad which radiates outwards into an extended family network linked by women. Walker's paradigm is confirmed by the work of contemporary feminist scholars such as Nancy Chodorow and Elizabeth Abel who hold that primary bonding exists between women. Moreover, like Chodorow, Walker's resolution to sexual inequality depends on fostering an increased sense of male self-in-relationship and a greater sense of female autonomy. If Harpo learns to "mother" his father, Celie learns to earn her own livelihood. Walker's women, through their unconventional lifestyles, gain greater access to the public sphere. (Celie replaces her real father as owner of a dry-goods store, while both Shug and Squeak, as blues singers, perform in public. Both Harpo and Albert, on the other hand, in their enjoyment of cooking and sewing, as well as their heightened sense of nurturance and connectedness, move further into the private or domestic arena.)

The novel ends on a theme of reunion between lovers, family, and friends, symbolizing on a personal level, the psychic reintegration of personality dif-ferences and on a social level, the reconciliation of gender differences. Having enrolled Germaine in Wilberforce, Shug returns to join Celie, now the suc-cessful owner of a house and business, and Albert, who is content to sit back and learn "to wonder." Finally, drawing again on the conventions of the senti-mental novel, Celie is reunited with her two children who have returned with her long-lost sister from Africa.

Embracing and consecrating all forms of existence on the planet, Celie's final letter—addressed, once more, to God—expresses her new concept of the deity: "Dear God. Dear stars, dear trees, dear sky, dear peoples. Dear Everything. Dear God." Her letter is not only a private prayer of thanks for the reunion of her family, but a liturgical lection affirming the rites, rituals, and experiences of the black community. Significantly, the occasion for the reunion and the setting for the closing letter is the fourth of July—the day on which "white people [are] busy celebrating [their] independence" and "black folks . . . celebrating each other." Walker's emphasis, once again, is on the psychic reintegration of the self and the reconciliation of community (as opposed to social integration).

Yet, finally, *The Color Purple* is a novel about the right to *write* (oneself) and the right to *right* (a wrong). Not surprisingly, the form Walker chooses is one which confers not only literary authority with its emphasis on the written word, but moral authority in its rewriting of the Scriptures. In a refiguration of the apostle Paul's Letter to the Philippians, Celie addresses her epistles not to the Church, but to God. If the apostle Paul wrote from prison to affirm his belief in death as a blessing for the faithful, Celie writes to affirm her faith that "This life soon be over. Heaven last always." Like Paul, she writes in the midst of persecution and in the hope of divine deliverance. In Philippi, Paul's church was formed as a result of the efforts of a small group of women. Lydia, a dealer in purple cloth, was his first convert, followed by his jailer. If Celie (like Paul) ultimately succeeds in the conversion of her jailer (Mister), she herself is converted by the dealer in purple (Shug) and a small group of women. In rewriting Paul's Letter to the Philippians, Walker, in effect, subverts his more popular Letter to the Ephesians in which Paul prescribes in detail the duties of wives and servants to husbands and masters.

Walker's accomplishments in her third novel are considerable. Not only does she liberate her women from the narrow confines of male-inscribed roles in the literary sphere and male-prescribed roles in the social sphere, but perhaps more important, Walker celebrates the centrality of black women in the reclamation of the past and transformation of the notion of community. Further, Walker creates a new literary space for the black and female idiom within a traditionally Western and Eurocentric form. In the process of merging two forms and two traditions, *The Color Purple* extends both.

SUSAN WILLIS

Walker's Women

Be nobody's darling
Be an outcast.
Take the contradictions
Of your life
And wrap around
You like a shawl,
To parry stones
To keep you warm.
—Revolutionary Petunias
and Other Poems

What the black Southern writer inherits as a natural right is
a sense of community.
—In Search of Our Mothers' Gardens

The strength of Alice Walker's writing derives from the author's inexorable recognition of her place in history; the sensitivity of her work, from her profound sense of community; its beauty, from her commitment to the future. Many readers probably associate Alice Walker with her most recent novel, *The Color Purple,* for which she won the Pulitzer Prize. But the best place to begin to define the whole of her writing is with the semi-autobiographical novel, *Meridian,* and in that novel I suggest we first consider a very minor character: "Wile Chile." For "Wile Chile" is not gratuitous, not an aberrant whim on the part of the author, but an epigrammatic representation of all the women Walker brings to life. I think this is how Alice Walker intended it, precisely because she begins telling about Meridian by describing her confrontation with "Wile Chile," a thirteen-year-old ghetto urchin, who from the

From *The New Orleans Review* 12, no. 1 (Spring 1985). © 1985 by Loyola University, New Orleans.

age of about five or six when she was first spotted, has fed and clothed herself out of garbage cans. More slippery than a "greased pig" and as wary as any stray, the Wild Child is virtually uncatchable. When it becomes obvious that the Wild Child is pregnant, Meridian takes it upon herself to bring her into the fold. Baiting her with glass beads and cigarettes, she eventually catches "Wile Chile," leads her back to the campus, bathes and feeds her, then sets about finding a home for her. However, Meridian's role as mother comes to an abrupt end when "Wile Chile" escapes and bolts into the street where she is struck by a speeding car.

If we consider the story of "Wile Chile" against the events which shape Meridian's development from childhood (the daughter of school teachers), through college, into the Civil Rights movement and finally to embark upon her own more radical commitment to revolutionary praxis, the two pages devoted to the Wild Child seem at most a colorful digression. Her only language comprised of obscenities and farts, "Wile Chile" is Meridian's social antithesis. Nevertheless, the story of "Wile Chile" is central to our understanding of *Meridian* and the woman whose name is the title of this book, for it includes certain basic features, present in different forms in all the anecdotal incidents which make up the novel and through which Meridian herself must struggle in the process of her self-affirmation.

When Meridian drags the stomach-heavy "Wile Chile" back to her room, she puts herself in the role of mother and enacts a mode of mothering which smacks of liberal bourgeois sentimentality. On the other hand, "Wile Chile's" own impending motherhood represents absolute abandonment to biological contingency. These are only two of the many versions of womanhood which the problem of mothering will provoke in the book. While Meridian and "Wile Chile" do not share a common social ground, they come together on one point, and that is the possibility of being made pregnant. For "Wile Chile" and Meridian both, conception articulates oppression, to which "Wile Chile" succumbs and against which Meridian struggles to discover whether it is possible for a black woman to emerge as a self and at the same time fulfill the burdens of motherhood.

The story of "Wile Chile" also raises the question of Meridian's relationship to the academic institution and the black community which surrounds the university. Her outrageous behavior causes Meridian (and the reader) to reflect upon the function of the university as a social institution whose primary role is to assimilate bright young black women, who might otherwise be dangerously marginal, to dominant white culture. "Wile Chile's" unpermissible language draws attention to the tremendous pressures also placed upon Meridian to become a "lady" patterned after white European cultural norms. This is not a cosmetic transformation, but one that separates the individual from her class and community and forever inscribes her within the bourgeois world. That the university serves bourgeois class interests is dramatized when Saxon students and members of the local black community attempt to hold "Wile Chile's" funeral on the campus. Barred from entering the university, the funeral procession is isolated and defined as "other" in the same way that the local neighborhood, which ought to be the university's community of concern, is instead its ghetto.

In *Meridian,* childbearing is consistently linked to images of murder and suicide. In this, the figure of the Wild Child is as much a paradigm for the book's main characters, Meridian and Lynne, as it is for another minor anecdotal figure: Fast Mary. As the students at Saxon tell it, Fast Mary secretly gave birth in a tower room, chopped her newborn babe to bits and washed it down the toilet. When her attempt to conceal the birth fails, her parents lock her up in a room without windows where Fast Mary subsequently hangs herself. In posing the contradictory social constraints which demand simultaneously that a woman be both a virgin and sexually active, the parable of Fast Mary prefigures the emotional tension Meridian herself will experience as a mother, expressing it in fantasies of murder and suicide. The tales of "Wile Chile" and Fast Mary also pose the problem of the individual's relationship to the group. Fast Mary's inability to call upon her sister students and her final definitive isolation at the hands of her parents raise questions Meridian will also confront: namely, is there a community of support? And is communication possible between such a community and the individual who is seen as a social iconoclast?

The problem of communication, and specifically the question of language, is at the heart of another of *Meridian*'s anecdotal characters: Louvinie, a slave woman from West Africa whose parents excelled in a particular form of storytelling, designed to ensnare anyone guilty of having committed a crime. Louvinie's duties as a slave are to cook and mind the master's children. The latter includes her own superb mastery of the art of storytelling, which for Louvinie, as for all oppressed peoples, functions to keep traditional culture alive and to provide a context for radical social practice. The radical potential of language is abundantly clear when the master's weakhearted young son dies of heart failure in the middle of one of Louvinie's gruesome tales.

At the level of overt content, the story of Louvinie focuses on the function of language while in its structure it reproduces the features associated in the book with motherhood. Louvinie, who does not have children of her own, nevertheless functions as a mother to the master's offspring. She, like

"Wile Chile," Fast Mary—even Meridian and Lynne—kills the child defined structurally as her own. In more narrow terms, Louvinie provides a model closer to the way Meridian will resolve her life. Her actual childlessness suggests in asexual terms Meridian's choice not to be fertile and bear children. Moreover, when Louvinie murders the child in her charge it is clearly a politically contestatory act, which is not the case for either "Wile Chile" or Fast Mary—but is true for Meridian when she chooses to abort her child.

Louvinie's punishment rejoins the problem of language when the master cuts out her tongue. Louvinie's response is to bury her tongue under a small magnolia tree, which, generations later, grows to be the largest magnolia in the county and stands at the center of Saxon College. As a natural metaphor, the tree is in opposition to the two social institutions: the plantation and the university; it suggests an alternative to their definition of black history and language. Just as the university excludes women like "Wile Chile," so too does it seek to silence black folk culture typified by Louvinie's stories. The magnolia casts the university in stark relief, exposes its version of history as a lie, its use of language as collaborative with the forces of domination.

The magnolia also provides a figural bridge linking the struggle of black women from slavery to the present. In the past, it offered a hiding place for escaped slaves and in the present its enormous trunk and branches provide a platform for classes. Named The Sojourner, the magnolia conjures up the presence of another leader of black women, who, like Louvinie, used language in the struggle for liberation. In this way, Walker builds a network of women, some mythic like Louvinie, some real like Sojourner Truth, as the context for Meridian's affirmation and radicalization.

The stories of "Wile Chile" and Fast Mary demonstrate that anecdotes are the basic narrative units in Walker's fiction. They reveal how Walker has managed to keep the storytelling tradition among black people alive in the era of the written narrative. The anecdotes are pedagogical. They allow the reader to experience the same structural features, recast with each telling, in a different historical and social setting. Each telling demands that the college students (and the reader) examine and define their relationship to the group in a more profound way than in the explicitly political gatherings where each is asked to state what she will do for the revolution. In this way, Walker defines story writing in the radical tradition that storytelling has had amongst black people.

It is not surprising that language is crucial to Meridian's process of becoming. From slavery to the present, black women have spoken out against their oppression, and when possible, written their version of history. However, their narratives have fared less well in the hands of publishers and the reading public than those written by black men. Only very recently, and with the growing interest in writers like Toni Morrison, Paule Marshall, and Walker herself, have black women enjoyed better access to recognized channels of communication outside those of home and church. As testament to the very long struggle for recognition waged by black women and the deep oppression out of which their struggle began, the literature is full of characters like Zora Neale Hurston's Janie Woods, whose husband sees and uses her like a "mule" and will not allow her to speak, to Walker's most recent female character, Celie, in *The Color Purple,* also denied a voice, who out of desperation for meaningful dialogue writes letters to God. For black women writers, the problem of finding a viable literary language—outside of the male canon defined predominantly by Richard Wright—has generated a variety of literary strategies. Toni Morrison's solution was to develop a highly metaphorical language, while for Alice Walker the solution has been the anecdotal narrative, which because of its relationship to storytelling and the family more closely approximates a woman's linguistic practice than does Morrison's very stylized discourse.

The fact is no black woman has ever been without language, even the tongueless Louvinie who uses the magical preparation and planting of her tongue to speak louder and longer than with words. The question of language is not meaningful except in relation to the community. Louvinie's example affirms that the community of struggle will always exist and that the actions of a single black woman join the network of all. In contrast, "Wile Chile" represents a negation of the individual's need for community. With language reduced to farts and swears, hers is a one-way communication whose every enunciation denies integration with the group and proclaims her absolute marginality. Contrary to the Wild Child's self-destructive marginality, Meridian must define a form of oneness with herself which will allow her to speak and work with the community while at the same time prevent becoming submerged by it. Meridian's quest for a language and a praxis is analogous to Walker's work as a writer, which demands both distance from and integration with the people.

When in the book's first chapter Meridian is asked if she could kill for the Revolution, she finds herself unable to make the required revolutionary affirmation, and defines instead what will be her more difficult form of revolutionary praxis: "I'll go back to the people" People means the South, the small towns, the communities for whom the Civil Rights movement passed by too quickly to transform embedded racist and sexist practices. In this, she is the antithesis of "Wile Chile," who never was a part of any community and hence can never return to it.

Meridian's decision is her way of defining the single most common feature in fiction by black women writers: that of return to the community. From Zora Neale Hurston's landmark text, *Their Eyes Were Watching God,* to Toni Morrison's widely read novels, the trajectory of departure and return is the common means for describing a woman's development and structuring the novel. In every instance, return raises the fundamental question of whether a community of support exists and what will be the individual's relationship to it.

For Hurston's Janie Woods, the journey to selfhood takes her through three husbands and just as many social strata. Yet return is as crucial to her development as her initial departure from her mother's traditional aspirations and town's inbred domination. Janie's three husbands define three modes of a woman's being with and for a man and they represent three stages which Janie must transcend for her affirmation of self. First, as the wife of a farmer, she is nothing more than a beast of burden; then, as wife to a small town mayor and storekeeper, she becomes a well-dressed commodity. Only later, as the wife of a migrant field worker, does she attain equal partnership with her man and the larger community of the migrant camp. This is the book's one utopian community, where women are not only allowed to speak but sing and dance as well. The camp gives the illusion of being separate from the world of white domination, which the black ghetto or small town cannot achieve. Then, too, the camp is so low on the economic scale that accumulation and property do not exist to define class relationships.

Janie's decision to leave the camp and return to the small town of her childhood represents a commitment akin to Meridian's determination to confront the struggle in the real world where black communities are strongly determined by their relationship to the white world. Janie's return begs the question of whether in the course of her own development the town might not have undergone some positive social change. The prognosis is at best mixed, although given the fact that Hurston is writing in the 1930s, the outlook is more favorable than might have been expected. Janie returns to find the same old gossipy pack of male-dominated women, but for one girlhood companion, Pheoby, who after hearing Janie's life story remarks, "Ah done growed ten feet higher jus' listenin' tuh you, Janie. Ah ain't satisfied wid mahself no mo'. Ah means tuh make Sam take me fishin' wid him after this. Nobody better not criticize yuh in mah hearin.'" In her refusal to be relegated to "women's work" and in her statement of solidarity with Janie, Pheoby demonstrates that she has taken a tremendous leap in consciousness. The two women's sisterhood suggests a nucleus out of which a women's community very different from that defined by male domination might grow.

The case is very different for Toni Morrison's *Sula,* written in the 1970s but about a woman growing up during Hurston's epoch. Here, return articulates the tragic plight of an extremely sensitive and perceptive black woman, in many ways ahead of her time, who goes to college, sees the world and a fair number of men, only to find herself dispossessed of place. While the community of her girlhood has undergone economic progress, neither the town's new golf course nor its convalescent hospital testify to deep social transformation. In contrast to Hurston's version, Sula returns home to find her girlhood friend deeply stigmatized by male sexual domination. Traumatized by his abandonment, she has become a sterile shell living out a life whose only excuse is her moral and economic enslavement to her children. There is no community of possibility for Sula, who dies, alone with her dreams and aspirations—a halcyon symbol of a future womanhood which can never be the basis for a community in this society.

Alice Walker's rendering of return involves elements present in both Hurston's and Morrison's versions, but set in an entirely different context: the Civil Rights movement, which historically was not a factor for Hurston and geographically does not significantly enter into Morrison's tales usually set in the Middle West. Only in Walker, a writer of the southern black experience, do we come to understand how important Civil Rights was. Not that it solved anything, but it definitely marks the moment after which nothing can ever be the same. Meridian's mission is to help discover the shape of the future.

Return is the developmental imperative in all of Walker's novels, where the journey over geographic space is a metaphor for personal growth and, in a larger sense, historical transformation. In her first novel, *The Third Life of Grange Copeland,* Walker's conception of geographic space embodies a dialectical understanding of history. When Grange Copeland abandons wife and child to seek his self and fortune in New York City, he leaves behind a rural community historically representative of the plantation system for the North and the industrial mode. The third moment of the dialectic is marked by Grange's return to the South, not as a penniless sharecropper, but with money in his pocket to buy his own land. The farm Grange brings into being suggests Walker's vision of a very different basis for black community, one which has experienced and transcended two forms of enslavement: first to the plantation, then to wage labor. In Walker's vision of the future, property ownership will not be for the purpose of accumulation as it is under capitalism, but will provide for the satisfaction of basic human material and spiritual needs.

The epic of Grange Copeland is doubly transformational in that the character who will bear his experience into the future (both of the distant past which Grange passes along in the form of folk tales, and of the more recent past which Grange has directly known) is not a male heir, as more traditional literature might have it, but his granddaughter, whose coming of age is marked by sit-ins, voter registration and the speeches of Martin Luther King, Jr. His own life marred by his struggle against bigotry, his own acts of violence, and the terrible racism and sexism of which he has been both a victim and an agent, Grange cannot be the embodiment of the future. Rather some great moment of rupture from the past is needed, and this Walker achieves in the transition from the male to the female principle. The novel ends on a note of affirmation—but not without uncertainty over the shape of the future. Ruth, Grange's granddaughter, is an adolescent and her future as well as the post–Civil Rights black community in the South cannot yet be told, but is, like the sixteen-year-old Ruth, on the threshold of its becoming.

In geographic strokes less broad, Walker's most recent novel, *The Color Purple,* also articulates personal and historical transition. In it, Celie is married as an adolescent to a man who makes her cook and keep house, tend the fields and look after his unruly children, and who pretty much conceives of her as a "mule." Celie's abuse is deepened by the fact that before marriage she had already been repeatedly raped by the man she calls "father" and made to bear his children only to have them taken from her soon after birth. If there is to be any transformation in this book, its starting point is the absolute rock bottom of a woman's economic and sexual enslavement in a male-dominated and racist society.

The possibility of Celie's transformation is brought about by her journey away from the rural backwater and to the big city: Memphis, where she comes to support herself—not by means of wage labor, and it is clear that Walker sees no hope for liberation in the transition to the industrial mode, but by means of learning a trade—which is both artistic and necessary. She designs and sews custom pants.

If Celie's transformation is to be thorough, it must not just be economic, but sexual as well. Celie's ability to question what would otherwise be her "lot in life" and to break with her passive acceptance of her husband's domination is made possible by her friendship and eventual lesbian relationship with a black blues singer: Shug Avery. Unlike the monstrous inequality between husband and wife, theirs is a reciprocal relationship—Celie giving of herself to heal the sick and exhausted Shug (even though Celie's husband has for years been enamoured of the singer), and Shug giving of herself, patiently and lovingly teaching Celie to know the joys of her own body and to follow the intuition of her mind. Neither the economics of pants-making nor the sexuality of lesbianism represents modes of enslavement as do the economics of industrial capitalism and the sexuality of male-dominated heterosexual relationships. At book's end Celie is neither seen as a pants-maker in the way one might see an auto worker as a particular species of human, nor as a lesbian lover the way one sees a wife and mother.

Out of Walker's three novels, *The Color Purple* defines return in the most auspicious terms and offers—not a prescription for—but a suggestion of what a non-sexist, non-racist community might be. No longer a voiceless chattel to her man, Celie is able to converse with her husband. Having undergone liberation in both economic and sexual terms, she is for the first time perceived—not as a domestic slave or the means toward male sexual gratification—but as a whole woman: witty, resourceful, caring, wise, sensitive and sensual. And her home—the site of an open and extended family where family and friends merge—suggests the basis for a wholly new community. The Fourth of July picnic which concludes the book and reunites Celie with her sister and children redefines the traditional family group in the context of a radically transformed household.

Of the novels, *Meridian* offers the clearest view of the process of radicalization. For Meridian, the autobiographical embodiment of Walker herself, coming of age in the 1960s does not offer a free ticket, but provides an atmosphere of confrontation and the questioning of contradiction with which the individual must grapple. Early in the book it becomes clear that one of the most profound ideologies to be confronted and transcended is the acceptance of mystical explanations for political realities. Meridian's childhood is steeped in Indian lore, the walls of her room papered with photographs of the great Indian leaders from Sitting Bull and Crazy Horse to the romanticized Hiawatha. Moreover, her father's farm includes an ancient Indian burial mound, its crest shaped like a serpent, where, in the coil of its tail, Meridian achieves a state of "ecstasy." Absorbed in a dizzying spin, she feels herself lifted out of her body while all around her—family and countryside—are caught up in the spinning whirlpool of her consciousness. It is not odd that Walker focuses on mystical experience. After all, this is a book about the 1960s whose counterculture opened the door to more than one form of mysticism. It is also not strange that Meridian's mystical experience derives from Native American culture given the long co-historical relationship between blacks and Indians (in the southeastern United States) whose radical union goes back to the time of cimarrons and Seminoles.

However, ecstasy is not the answer. While Meridian will learn from the mystical experience, it will not be sufficient to her life's work to rely upon the practice of retreat into the ecstatic trance. What, then, of the historic link between Indians and blacks? If, in the course of the book, Meridian learns to transcend ecstasy, is this a denial of her (and her people's) relationship to the Indian people?

Definitely not: the book's preface gives us another way of defining Meridian's relationship to Native Americans, which the great lesson taught by her radicalization will bring into reality. Taken from *Black Elk Speaks,* this is the book's preface:

> I did not know then how much was ended. When I look back now . . . I can still see the butchered women and children lying heaped and scattered all along the crooked gulch as plain as when I saw them with eyes still young. And I can see that something else died there in the bloody mud, and was buried in the blizzard. A people's dream died there. It was a beautiful dream . . . the nation's hoop is broken and scattered. There is no center any longer, and the sacred tree is dead.

Black Elk's words remember the massacre of Wounded Knee which for Indian people was the brutal cancellation of their way of life. The dream Black Elk refers to is the vision he, as a holy man, had of his people and their world: "The leaves on the trees, the grasses on the hills and in the valleys, the waters in the creeks and in the rivers and the lakes, the four-legged and the two-legged and the wings of the air—all danced together to the music of the stallion's song."

This is a vision of a community of man and nature, which Black Elk, as a holy man, must bring into being—not individually, but through the collective practice of the group. As he sees it, the nation is a "hoop" and "Everything an Indian does is in a circle, and that is because the Power of the World always works in circles, and everything tries to be round." These are images of a community's wholeness, which Meridian takes as her political paradigm—not the particulars of Indian culture: not the beads which Hippies grafted on their white middle-class identities, not the swoons of ecstasy—but the Indian view of community, in which the holy man or seer is not marginal, but integral to the group. So when Meridian says she will "go back to the people," and when she leads them in demonstration against racist practices, she enacts Black Elk's formula for praxis. As an intellectual and a political activist, she understands that the individual's inspiration for social change can only be realized through the group's collective activity.

By far the greatest test of Meridian's radicalization is to overcome the social and sexual categories ascribed to all women, and black women in particular. Because she does not choose the lesbian alternative as does Celie in

The Color Purple, Meridian's struggle is within and against heterosexual relationships. As Walker describes it, the two most fundamental categories of womanhood as defined under male-dominated heterosexuality are bitches and wives. The first category is composed of white women, while the second is made up of black women and is essentially the same as saying "mothers." The bitch in the book is Lynne, who in many ways is Meridian's antithetical parallel. A white woman, from the North, Jewish, a student and fellow Civil Rights worker, Lynne is the third factor in a triangular love relationship which includes Meridian and Truman, also a Civil Rights worker and the man both Lynne and Meridian love. The tension produced by love and jealousy is the ground upon which Walker examines social categories and defines the process through which Meridian eventually liberates herself from male sexual domination.

She begins her adult life a high school dropout and teenage mother married to a restaurant bus boy. Motherhood for Meridian is fraught with contradictory impulses. Caressing her child's body, she imagines that her fingers have scratched his flesh to the bone. At other times she thinks of drowning her baby; and when not fantasizing her child's murder, she dreams of suicide. Murder and suicide are the emotional articulation of social realities. This is the experience of futility—the mother's purposelessness as an individual, whose only function is to add yet another little body to the massive black underclass, and the child's bankrupt future, another faceless menial laborer.

In contrast to the futility is the one moment—equally profound for its singularity—when Meridian beholds her child with loving wonderment and sees him as a spontaneous, unasked-for gift, absolutely unique and whole. In response to the possibility for her child's selfhood and in recognition of her own desperate need to redefine her life's course, Meridian chooses to give her child away when, as if by miracle, her high IQ makes her a college candidate. In relinquishing her child, Meridian recognizes her relationship to the history of black motherhood, which, under slavery, defined the black woman's struggle to keep her children as a radical act, making the mother liable for a beating or worse; to the time of freedom, which, in giving black women the right to keep their children, provided the fetters of enslavement to poverty and sexism. Meridian's mother is very much a part of this tradition. Although morally outraged at her daughter's decision to "abandon" her child, the mother exemplifies the plight of black mothers, "buried alive, walled away from her own life, brick by brick" with the birth of each successive child.

In giving her child away, Meridian makes it clear that mothering as it has been defined by heterosexual relationships in racist society is the single most unsurmountable obstacle to a black woman's self-affirmation. Only by refusing ever to be a mother in the particular can she carve out a new social function, which includes a form of mothering, but in the larger sense of an individual's caring for her community. We get a sense of what this might involve when Meridian first appears in the novel leading a band of children in demonstration. But for the most part, Meridian's practice is less an indication of future possibilities and more a critique of the way heterosexual relationships have individualized a woman's relationship to *her* children, making them *her* property. This is the mother/child relationship which Meridian violently denies for herself when, becoming pregnant for a second time, she chooses to abort her lover's baby. Her decision is also a dramatic refutation of Truman's overtly male chauvinist invitation to "have [his] beautiful black babies" for the Revolution. For Meridian, the subsequent decision to have her tubes tied represents another step in the direction toward a new form of womanhood where heterosexuality will not be the means towards oppression but a mode within which sexual partners will one day set each other free. But for the time being, her espousal of a selfless, nun-like celibacy suggests that the day is a long way off.

For Lynne, however, heterosexuality, complicated by the pressures upon the biracial couple in a racist society, leads not to liberation and the affirmation of a new social mode, but rather the rock bottom debasement of self. Notwithstanding her marriage to Truman, Lynne will always be the white bitch, and notwithstanding their child's African name, Camara, the mulatto does not represent a hope for a non-racist future. This is because American society—before, during and after Civil Rights—remains racist and sexist. Camara's brutal murder graphically puts an end to any liberal thoughts about a new, hybridized society of the future. The death of this child—and all the book's children, either by abortion or murder—dramatizes Walker's radical intuition that the future as something positive and new cannot be produced out of genetic or personal terms, but demands, as Black Elk saw it, the selfless involvement of the individual with the community. When Truman criticizes Meridian for never having loved him, she responds, "I set you free." Meridian has chosen to relinquish personal and sexual relationships, which in this society cannot help but be the means and form of a woman's oppression, as a way of advancing her own struggle—and that of her loved ones—toward their liberation.

For the most part, Walker's writing is not figural, but there is in *Meridian* one very important metaphor, whose function is to synthesize the many levels of Meridian's struggle. This is the significance of Meridian's sickness, which goes by no medical name but is characterized by dizziness, temporary blindness, swooning faints, loss of hair, paralysis, and general bodily weakness.

The illness strikes Meridian immediately after she first sees the Wild Child. Because many of the symptoms coincide with her childhood experience of mystical ecstasy, the illness is a link between her early confrontation with cultural ideology and her later struggle as an adult against social and sexual oppression, typified by the plight of the Wild Child. The illness allows the reader to perceive at the level of experience the absolute energy-draining work of political praxis, as with each demonstration Meridian must struggle to regain her vanquished strength, patiently forcing her paralyzed limbs to work again. Meridian's trademark, a visored cap to cover her baldness, articulates the contradictory notions attached to a black woman's hair—her crowning glory and sign of sexuality, for which the headrag was both a proclamation and refutation. With each confrontation with white male authority—be it under the abortionist's knife or facing down an army tank—Meridian's swoon and faint proclaim, not surrender, but absolute commitment to the struggle. Coming back to consciousness, Meridian awakens to find the struggle—an ongoing process—renewed upon a higher, more exacting level.

At the novel's conclusion, Walker gives us to understand that Meridian has mastered—not the whole struggle—but herself in that struggle. Rid of the sickness, her wooly head restored, she discards her cap and packs her bag to set out once again upon the road to confrontation. While one individual's coming to grips with self can be a lesson for others, it cannot be their solution. The novel closes upon Truman, dizzily crawling into Meridian's sleeping bag, pulling her cap upon his head, and accepting for himself the long process of her struggle. The transition from Meridian to Truman lifts the book out of its sexual polarization and suggests that everyone, regardless of socially ascribed sex roles, must work to de-essentialize sex. Now it will be Truman who works for the community and in its care to bring the collective dream into being.

Although not by his choosing, Truman, at book's end, is no longer capable of being perceived either as a lover or a father. The course of Meridian's struggle to liberate herself from sexually prescribed categories has been the means for Truman's unwitting relinquishment of positions from which men have traditionally exerted domination. The transcendence of sexual domination undermines other forms of domination including racism, but this does not mean that race itself has been neutralized. Rather, blackness is affirmed. Meridian's new crop of wooly hair testifies directly to her renewal as a black woman. Nor has transcendence brought about her separation from the community, whose coherent presence is the novel's core. In contrast to the strength of the black presence, white people enter *Meridian* incidentally and are always perceived as individuals, bereft of any relationship with their own community. Almost freakish in their singularity and behavior, white people in general closely approximate their symbolic representation in the form of a mummified white woman, a side show attraction, whose husband carts her from town to town earning money off her exhibition.

Walker's affirmation of blackness uses racially specific traits—not to define a form of black racism—but to delineate the look of a class. Black is the color of the underclass. And all Walker's women are peasants, from Celie in *The Color Purple,* whose abusive treatment is the context of Ruth's childhood in *The Third Life of Grange Copeland* and Meridian's experience of her mother's and grandmother's history. Bound to the land and their husbands (or fathers), worn by toil in the fields and the demands of child-bearing, these women are the underclass of the underclass. This is why literacy and education are so crucial to the way Walker depicts the process of liberation. Her radical understanding of education lies at the heart of literacy campaigns from revolutionary Angola to Grenada and Nicaragua. Clearly, the ability to raise questions, to objectify contradictions, is only possible when Celie begins writing her letters. Similarly, for Meridian, education (notwithstanding its inspiration in liberalism) and the academic institution (notwithstanding its foundation in elitism) offer the means for confronting social and sexual contradictions which she, as a black teenage mother, would not have been able to articulate—either for herself or anyone else.

To understand the author's perception of class and the role of women in class politics, I recall that in a workshop on black women writers held at Yale University (spring 1982), Walker stressed the importance of rediscovering Agnes Smedley, particularly the latter's highly perceptive descriptions of Chinese women during the years of the Revolution. Both Smedley and Walker would agree that the radical transformation of society can only be achieved when the bottommost rung attains liberation; in fact, the wellspring of revolution is the rebellion of the peasant class. This is the great historical lesson of revolution in the twentieth century from China to Cuba and Central America. And it lies at the heart of all Smedley's "sketches" of women revolutionaries, who, when their class background and education more closely approximate Meridian's, must, like Walker's character, turn to the people and be one with their struggle. The individual who becomes separate from the peasantry is truly lost—like Walker's Lynne, who never outgrew her liberal background and the tendency to see black people as works of art; and Smedley's the "Living Dead," women reclaimed by the aristocracy and abandoned to opium dreams or so traumatized by the White Terror that they wander about dazed.

There is a great deal of similarity between the real life Agnes Smedley and the fictional Meridian—and her autobiographical inspiration, Alice Walker herself. Smedley, born in the South (Missouri), was also a peasant woman. Her childhood grounded in poverty, she, although white, knew a form of enslavement when, at the age of eleven, she was hired out as a domestic. Education and, later, left politics were her way up and out of poverty, just as writing was her way back to the people. Always an advocate of feminism, both in journalism and in fiction, Smedley, like Walker, depicts the contradictions of womanhood as they relate to abortion, birth control and mothering. Finally, while Smedley's community was the revolutionary Chinese, her relationship to that community as a foreigner and an intellectual bears striking similarity to Meridian's relationship to her community.

Perhaps the best way to characterize all three—Smedley, Meridian and Walker—is with the title of one of Walker's collections of poems: *Revolutionary Petunias*. It captures the spirit of revolutionary women both in beauty and struggle. Certainly, there was a great deal of flamboyance in Agnes Smedley as she donned a Red Army uniform and marched into Sian. Rather than a simplistic identification with the Communist forces, her act was intended to draw the attention of the world press (which it did) and to articulate a joyous celebration of struggle (which it does) in the linguistics of gesture and play acting often used by women in lieu of those modes of communication—like speech and writing—which have been traditionally defined by male discourse. This is a form of revolutionary praxis very like the moment when Meridian, at the head of a pack of kids, faces down the town militia and a World War II tank. Not to be confused with the flower children and the politics of counter-culture, "Revolutionary Petunias" are those women who with grace, strength and a fair amount of wit, have put their lives on the line.

W. LAWRENCE HOGUE

Discourse of the Other:
The Third Life of Grange Copeland

Alice Walker's *The Third Life of Grange Copeland* was published in 1970 during the midst of the seventies feminist movement in America. As a feminist text, *The Third Life* reproduces and reinforces many feminist values, codes, conventions, and myths. It produces a feminist narrative which invents what Frederic Jameson calls imaginary "formal resolutions" to "unsolvable social contradictions" in the social real.

Michel Foucault's concept of discursive formation provides the theoretical framework and vocabulary to explain how social discourse informs literary texts. For Foucault, a discourse is any group of statements or facts that exists under the positive condition of a complex group of relations. He calls this group of relations *discursive*. The regularity that binds the object's relations he calls *discursive formations*. A discursive formation does not connect concepts or words with one another. Instead, it offers concepts the objects of which they can speak. It determines the group of relations that discourse must establish before it can speak of a particular object. These relations characterize not the language used by discourse, but discourse itself as a practice. The conditions to which the group of relations are subjected Foucault calls the *rules of formation*.

Within discourse, there exist relations of mutual delimitation. The whole group of relations forms a principle of determination that permits and excludes a certain number of statements. This means that a discourse does not occupy all the possible space that is open to it by the mere nature of its system of formation. It is essentially incomplete. The incompleteness is manifested in gaps, silences, discontinuities, and limitations. Foucault's concept of discursive

From *MELUS* 12, no. 2 (Summer 1985). © 1985 by W. Lawrence Hogue.

formation gives us the theoretical tool to show the various ways in which
discourse or forms of representation delude. This paper will show how *The
Third Life of Grange Copeland* is informed by the seventies feminist discourse.
It will show how *The Third Life* produces a myth about the American and
Afro-American historical past and how that myth functions ideologically.

In its attempt to show the historical oppression of black women, to further
undermine established, one-dimensional, stereotypical American images of
the black woman, *The Third Life* produces a feminist representation of the
American and Afro-American historical past that gives meaning, coherence,
validity, and a mythical history to a contemporary feminist set of supposi-
tions about women's reality and existence. In an interview with John O'Brien,
Walker, in discussing the writing of *The Third Life,* states:

> I am committed to exploring the oppressions, the insanities, the
> loyalties, and the triumphs of black women. In *The Third Life
> of Grange Copeland,* ostensibly about a man and his son, it is
> the women and how they are treated that colors everything. . . .
> I knew when I started *The Third Life of Grange Copeland* that
> it would have to cover several generations, and nearly a century
> of growth and upheaval. It begins around 1900 and ends in the
> Sixties . . . all along I wanted to explore the relationship between
> parents and children: specifically between daughters and their
> fathers . . . and I wanted to learn, myself, how it happens that
> the hatred a child can have for a parent becomes inflexible. And
> I wanted to explore the relationship between men and women, and
> why women are always condemned for doing what men do as an
> expression of their masculinity. Why are women so easily "tramps"
> and "traitors" when men are heroes for engaging in the same
> activity? Why do women stand for this?

The idea that "the women and how they are treated . . . colors everything"
becomes the major determining factor in the text's reconstructed historical
past. It selects heterogeneous facts from the historical past. It determines the
group of relations the text must establish to make its enunciation about the
historical oppression of women.

Also, in describing the discursive facts which form within *The Third Life,*
we can discern how the text's discursive formation reproduces statements
and facts different in forms and dispersed in time and have them relate to
the same object or enunciation. In the text's discursive formation, these facts
are taken from their original context, intersected, and juxtaposed in what
Jameson calls the "ideologeme" of the text—the "amphibious formation,

whose essential structural characteristic may be described as its possibility to manifest itself either as a pseudo-idea—a conceptual or belief system, an abstract value, an opinion or prejudice—or as a protonarrative, a kind of ultimate class fantasy about the 'collective characters' which are the classes of opposition." In the "ideologeme" these facts take on new meanings. M. M. Bakhtin writes:

> These heterogeneous stylistic unities [facts], upon entering the novel, combine to form a structural artistic system, and are subordinated to the higher stylistic unity of the work as a whole, a unity that cannot be identified with any single one of the unities subordinated to it.

The Third Life, then, becomes a product of Walker's feminist intention, her unconscious and conscious transformation of facts (stylistic unities) from the American and Afro-American historical past that combine to form a "structural artistic unity."

The text's title, *The Third Life of Grange Copeland,* signifies that Grange Copeland, the protagonist within the text, has three lives and that it is "the third" life that has the most significance. Grange's first life is dominated by his response to an oppressive, dehumanizing social structure which deprives him of his personhood and causes him to abuse his wife Margaret and to deny parental love and care to his son, Brownfield. Grange's second life concerns his sojourn to New York where he undergoes transformation in preparation for his third life. (Brownfield's first life repeats a life cycle, a set of relations, that is quite similar to his father's.) Grange's "third" life concerns his return South, his attempt to exorcise past iniquities, to break the desolate social structure, to interrupt a set of relations, in which he and his son have fallen victim. It shows Grange's uncompromising attempt to create a new social structure, a new set of relations, where his granddaughter Ruth can have more options and opportunities in her life than he or his son.

The opening pages of *The Third Life* are filled with actions, symbols, and conventions. These pages show a father who, for some reason, cannot touch or communicate with his son: "Brownfield's father almost never spoke to him unless they had company." Several scenes later, Grange's wife, Margaret, is presented as a hard working, loyal, and submissive wife who works in the fields from sun up to sun down, who raises a son and manages a household: "His mother agreed with his [Brownfield's] father whenever possible." Margaret as the hardworking, loyal, and submissive black woman becomes a discursive fact which forms within the text. Margaret's scene is juxtaposed immediately by another scene that repeats Grange's refusal to acknowledge his son's presence: "His father never looked at him [Brownfield] or acknowledged him in any way."

Next, *The Third Life* juxtaposes the scene about the father's refusal to acknowledge his son's existence with the scene where Brownfield is watching "his father freeze in the presence of a white man." Here, we see a master-servant relation between the plantation owner, who is powerful, and Grange, who is subservient and powerless, being constituted in language. The white man as an ominous force who points out Grange's powerlessness, who turns Grange into "a stone or a robot," and who turns the other black men into "objects" becomes a second discursive fact which forms in the text. Grange as a powerless black male becomes a third discursive fact which forms in the text. Lastly, in this first chapter, Brownfield as the abused and neglected child becomes another discursive fact in the text.

The scene where Brownfield witnesses his father being humiliated by the white landowner is followed immediately by a scene where Grange is drinking and using abusive language with his son: "I ought to throw you down the goddam well." Here, we see the father-son relation being constituted in a language of violence and domination that reflects the master-servant relation between Grange and the white landowner.

With new and repeated discursive facts, *The Third Life* reveals the life cycle, or the set of relations, which not only embraces and embodies Grange Copeland's first life, but which also reveals the series of discursive facts and categories, their conditions for existence, their limits, and their correlations which form the immediate materials within the text:

> On Monday, suffering from a hangover and the after effects of a violent quarrel with his wife the night before, Grange was remorseful, sullen, reserved, deeply in pain under the hot early morning sun. Margaret was tense and hard, exceedingly nervous. Brownfield moved about the house like a mouse. On Tuesday, Grange was merely quiet. His wife and son began to relax. On Wednesday, as the day stretched out and the cotton rows stretched out even longer, Grange muttered and sighed. He sat outside in the night air longer before going to bed; he would speak of moving away, of going North. He might even try to figure out how much he owed the man who owned the fields. The man who drove the truck and who owned the shack they occupied. But these activities depressed him, and he said things on Wednesday night that made his wife cry. By Thursday, Grange's gloominess reached its peak and he grimaced respectfully, with veiled eyes, at the jokes told

by the man who drove the truck. On Thursday night he stalked the house from room to room and pulled himself up and swung from the rafters of the porch. . . . By Friday Grange was so stupefied with the work and the sun he wanted nothing but rest the next two days before it started all over again.

On Saturday afternoon Grange shaved, bathed, put on clean overalls and a shirt and took the wagon into town to buy groceries. While he was away his wife washed and straightened her hair. She dressed up and sat, all shining and pretty, in the open door, hoping anxiously for visitors who never came. . . . Late Saturday night Grange would come home lurching drunk, threatening to kill his wife and Brownfield, stumbling and shooting off his shotgun. He threatened Margaret and she ran and hid in the woods with Brownfield huddled at her feet. Then Grange would roll out the door and into the yard, crying, like a child in big wrenching sobs and rubbing his whole head in the dirt. He would lie there until Sunday morning, when the chickens pecked around him, and the dog sniffed at him and neither his wife nor Brownfield went near him. . . . Steady on his feet but still ashen by noon, Grange would make his way across the pasture and through the woods, headlong, like a blind man, to the Baptist church, where his voice above all the others was raised in song and prayer. Margaret would be there too, Brownfield asleep on the bench beside her. Back home again after church Grange and Margaret would begin a supper quarrel which launched them into another week just about like the one before.

Within this life cycle, we can identify all the discursive facts mentioned earlier. Grange, the black man, finds himself in a subservient and powerless position to the white man "who drove the truck and who owned the shack they occupied." Oppressed and abused by the white man, Grange abuses and mistreats his wife and son. Margaret is, again, loyal and submissive; and the white man as an oppressive force and Brownfield, the child who is neglected, are also repeated facts.

With this life cycle, *The Third Life* begins to show the conditions of the existence of these facts, their limits, and their correlations within the text. With Grange and the white landowner, a master-servant relation is constituted in a language of violence and domination. Frustrated by his powerless position, Grange turns to violence, drinking, and domination. He establishes with his wife and son relations that have the same violence and domination that characterize his relationship with the white landowner. Grange's actions and behaviors become the features of his function within the text's group of relations. The white man's sole function within the text is to signify an oppressive and dehumanizing force. Margaret, the wife, who is oppressed indirectly by the white man and the existing social structure and directly by Grange, the black man, has limited options within the text's group of relations. She can attend to her son when time allows, remain loyal and submissive to Grange, or commit suicide. With both parents caught up in relations that render them powerless and subservient, Brownfield is neglected. The reproduction of these social relations shows how they are transmitted in and through language.

In the production of Grange's first life, *The Third Life,* through its selection, transformation, and arrangement of facts and categories from the American and Afro-American historical past, produces a particular ideologeme which is different from those made by dominant American discursive formations: the American social system, whose power is exercised by the white male, crushes and emasculates the black man. It stifles his feelings and emotions and it destroys his dreams, hopes, and chances for a better life. The American social structure turns the black man into a beast—suppressing his human qualities and accenting his animal tendencies. The black man, in turn, reflects his violent relation with his white landowner in his relations with his wife and son. He takes his anger and frustration out, not on the social system or the people who exercise its power but on his children and on the black woman, who, as he does in the master-servant relation, remains loyal and submissive. Just as the white man becomes the symbol of his oppression, the black man becomes the symbol of the black woman's oppression. Within the set of relations established in the text, we see images of the black woman—as someone who is battered, abused, scarred psychologically, who is "profound, tragic, mysterious, sacred, and unfathomable"—which undermine and violate the dominant image of the black woman, to use the words of Mary Helen Washington, as "the one-dimensional Rock of Gibraltar—strong of back, long of arm, invincible."

These sets of relations within the text possess the problem which the text must resolve: How will the historical oppression of women be ameliorated? How will the evil force that causes that oppression be obliterated? How will the parental love and care for the black child be reestablished? The seeming insolubility of the text's problem causes the reader to turn the pages, for each repetition of discursive facts presupposes a closure, an ending. It is this pressure to finish, to find the solution to the text's problem that pushes on the narrative.

The Third Life's "ideologeme," which is the "conceptual complex," is where, according to Julia Kristeva, the "knowing rationality grasps the transformation" of the text's set of relations, its facts, and allows it to project itself variously in the form of a value system, or in the form of a protonarrative. The text's ideologeme is the focal point where heterogeneous facts or "stylistic unities" lose their original contexts and meanings and combine to form a "structural artistic system" as determined by the text's discursive formation.

To generate its ideologeme, *The Third Life* repeats in various modes and by various means its discursive facts. They are repeated in Josie's rather traumatic life story. Josie's father is bitter towards the world because it has rendered him powerless. Therefore, he, like Grange Copeland, reproduces his violent and domineering relation with the world in his family relations. But in this reproduction, he has the power. He displays his anger and frustration by inflicting violence and humiliation on the members of his family. At a party Josie gives to earn his love, she falls and

> it was then and only then that her father rose from his chair, from the garish cushion of war . . . and, standing over her, forbade anyone to pick her up. . . . He pressed his foot into her shoulder and dared them to touch her. . . . "Let er be," growled her father, "I hear she can do *tricks* on her back like that."

And just as Margaret never intercedes when Grange is abusing Brownfield, Josie's mother refuses to intercede when her husband violates Josie's person and humiliates her in public: "Josie's father rode her. . . . Her mother was a meek woman and though she rarely agreed with Josie's father she never argued with him."

The Third Life repeats its discursive facts in the cases of the "overworked deacons" that Grange encounters in New York. They beat "their women to death when they couldn't feed them." The discursive facts are repeated again with Grange's Uncle Buster who beats his wife. Each repetition of the text's discursive facts reinforces the signification of the oppressive ideologeme and reformulates the text's problem.

The second life of Grange Copeland, which is the first life of Brownfield Copeland, finds Grange undergoing transformation in New York. As Grange undergoes transformation, Brownfield falls victim to the same dehumanizing social structure that Grange encountered in his first life and Brownfield comes to exhibit the same violence as Grange.

In the text's strategy to generate its ideologeme, it repeats its discursive facts in Brownfield's life story. Brownfield lives a relatively happy and sedate life until he marries Mem, Josie's niece, and the two move into the Southern sharecropping system. Once in the system, Brownfield gradually finds himself becoming devastated. Despite the fact that he works from sun up to sun down, he becomes deeper in debt. Also, as in the case of Grange, Brownfield is denied his role and responsibility of being a husband to his wife and a father to his children—a role and responsibility that the dominant society has socialized him to believe is his. He sees himself becoming a failure:

> That was the year he first saw his own life was becoming a repetition of his father's. He could not save his children from slavery; they did not even belong to him.
>
> His indebtedness depressed him. Year after year the amount he owed continued to climb. He thought of suicide and never forgot it. . . . He prayed for help, for a caring President, for a listening Jesus. He prayed for a decent job in Mem's army. . . . He felt himself destined to become no more than overseer, on the white man's plantation, of his own children. That was the year he accused Mem of being unfaithful to him, of being used by white men, his oppressor.

Brownfield, like his father and the other black men in the text, finds himself in the powerless and subservient position in a master-servant relation. As with Grange and the other black men, he reproduces this master-servant relation in his relations with his wife and children. He adopts a false sense of pride where controlling his family becomes his only source of power—even if it means resorting to violence. When Mem defies his authority and purchases a home in town, he lies in wait for the first opportunity to destroy her assertive spirit and to bring her back into his fold:

> He was determined at such times to treat her like a nigger and a whore . . . and if she made no complaint, to find her guilty.
>
> He was expected to raise himself upon air, which was all that was left over after his work for others. Others were always within their rights to pay him practically nothing for his labor. He was never able to build on it, and was never to have any land of his own.
>
> His crushed pride, his battered ego, made him drag Mem away from school teaching. Her knowledge reflected badly on a husband who could scarcely read and write. It was his great ignorance that sent her into white homes as a domestic, his need to bring her down to his level. It was his rage at himself, and his life and his world that made him beat her from an imaginary attraction she aroused in other men. . . . His rage could and did blame everything, *everything* on her. And she accepted all his burdens

along with her own and dealt with them from her own greater knowledge.

Thus, just as Grange's inability to come to grips with his debased and powerless position in society is a principal factor in Margaret's suicide and Brownfield's misguided life, Brownfield's inability to come to grips with his destituted existence is a principal factor in his murder of Mem and his mistreatment of his three daughters.

As Brownfield acts out the drama of Grange's first life, Grange, in his second life, is undergoing transformation in New York where he encounters experiences that will give him a new and informed perspective on his past and will determine how he shapes his future. In Harlem and other parts of the world, Grange has the opportunity to view blacks from a larger social context. He learns about Africa and he teaches himself the history of the black man in America. The culmination of Grange's education is provoked by an encounter in New York's Central Park. When he helps a pregnant white woman from drowning in a pond of water, he is rebuffed and is called a "nigger" which prompts him to allow her to drown. Reproducing Wright's *Native Son* where Bigger Thomas feels free psychologically after accidentally killing white Mary Dalton, *The Third Life* states:

> Her contempt for him had been the last straw; never again would he care what happened to any of them. She was perhaps the only one of them he would ever sentence to death. He had killed a thousand, ten thousand, a whole country of them in his mind. She was the first, and would probably be the only real one.
>
> The death of the woman was simply murder, he thought, and soul condemning; but in a strange way, a bizarre way, it liberated him. . . . It was the taking of the white woman's life . . . that forced him to want to try to live again.

Allowing the woman to drown, Grange is liberated from his fear of whites, a fear that has caused him to mistreat the women and children in his life. With Grange's realization, *The Third Life* hints at a possible resolution to its problem, a possible answer to its question: How will the historical oppression of black women be ameliorated?

To live his "third life," Grange returns South where things are different: he has psychological freedom. The soul searching, life experiences outside the South, and educational exposures allow him to define himself outside the dominant myths, conventions, and stereotypes:

> But soon he realized he could not fight all the whites he met. Nor

was he interested in it any longer. Each man would have to free himself, he thought, and the best way he could. For the time being, he would withdraw completely from them, find a sanctuary, make a life that they need not acknowledge, and be always prepared, with his life, to defend it, to protect it, to keep it from whites, inviolate.

"The white folks hated me and I hated myself until I started hating them in return and loving myself. Then I tried just loving me and then you, and *ignoring* them as much as I could."

His one duty in the world was to prepare Ruth for some great and herculean task, some magnificent and deadly struggle, some harsh and foreboding reality.

Grange's "one duty" is to nurture, through Ruth, a new and whole black life into existence, which is done at the expense of killing his own son: "Survival was not everything. *He* had survived. But to survive *whole* was what he wanted for Ruth."

Grange's third life serves as a catalyst for the destruction of a social structure which posits definitions of manhood and responsibility which the black man does not have the opportunity to attain; it also resolves the text's problems. As the transformed discursive fact within the text's discursive formation, Grange causes a new social formation, a new ideologeme, to emerge. Now that Grange has replaced his fear and hatred of whites with his love for Ruth, he no longer needs to oppress women and abuse children. Grange's psychological liberation resolves the text's problem.

But, in this resolution, we see how *The Third Life* constitutes what Frederic Jameson calls a "symbolic act" whereby "real social contradictions, insurmountable in their own terms, find a purely formal resolution in the aesthetic realm." The oppressive, violent white male who causes the black male to be subservient and powerless is still unresolved in the social real. This explains why *The Third Life*—by resolving in the aesthetic realm the historical oppression of black women by killing Brownfield and transforming Grange— has to exclude or distance itself from this real political and social contradiction—the oppressive white force—because it cannot directly and immediately conceptualize it.

In addition to the repetition of its discursive facts, *The Third Life* uses other strategies to generate its ideologeme. It uses characters to espouse or to articulate certain cultural, ideological, and sociological forms whenever a given detail needs motivation or reinforcement. For example, when *The Third Life* presents Margaret as hard-working, loyal, and submissive, it invests Brownfield with certain sociological and cultural forms which generate this presentation and the text's ideologeme: "He thought his mother was like their dog in some ways. She didn't have a thing to say that did not in some way show her submission to his father."

These sociological forms, which are masquerading as Brownfield's thoughts, have the penetration, psychological insight, and understanding not of a youth, but of an adult. On the one hand, this feminist sociological form supports the text's ideologeme. On the other hand, it contradicts Brownfield's chronological years and intellectual maturity.

This strategy is repeated again when Brownfield comments on Josie suffering at the hands of black men:

> Josie, Brownfield was sure, had never been young, had never smelled of milk or of flowers, but only of a sweet decay that one might root out only if one took the trouble to expose inch after inch of her to the bright consuming fire of blind adoration and love.

This adult Brownfield has been characterized as being evil, as being void of feelings and emotions, as being the symbol of black women's oppression. Yet, in the above commentary, he suddenly has insightful and sympathetic comments about Josie's difficult plight in life. Though his comments function to reproduce a feminist perspective, they violate the character Brownfield conceived in realist terms of a coherent array of actions and remarks.

This strategy of using characters to espouse ideological forms is further exploited in Grange's transformation. To accent the transforming and redeeming qualities of Grange, *The Third Life* allows Ruth to believe that

> Grange drank because of his murderous son and because of Josie. Grange and his wife now rarely spoke to each other; the house was often miserable because of their coldness. But Grange's crimes, she [Ruth] believed, were never aimed at any one but himself, and his total triumph over his life's failure was the joy in him that drew her to him.

Like Brownfield's, Ruth's analysis possesses an intellectual insight that is from a perspective that is much more mature than her chronological years and intellectual development. But, Ruth's analysis reinforces the text's narrative move to transform Grange to resolve its problem.

As stated earlier, this strategy of using characters to articulate certain ideological forms causes internal dissonance within the text and contradictions in character development. These ideological forms, when spoken by characters, are inconsistent with the actions and remarks that have come to characterize the characters. Pierre Macherey, in *A Theory of Literary Production,* argues that this dissonance arises from the text's peculiar relation to its discursive formation which permits certain facts and excludes others. The text's determinate absences twist its various facts into conflict and contradictions.

Also, *The Third Life* uses certain established conventions—ideological fragments and sixties ideological jargon which can be appealed to as acceptable justifications—to generate its ideologeme. It reproduces the psychological rationale conceptualized by Fanon and textualized by Wright to motivate and justify a textual move—Grange's transformation. Killing one's master as the first prerequisite for the oppressed's psychological liberation was an acceptable ideological form in nationalist circles in the sixties. When Mem, with gun in hand, has the upper hand on Brownfield, she says:

> And just think of how many times I don got my head beat by you just so you could feel a little bit like a man, Brownfield Copeland. You going to take the blame for every wrong thing you do and stop blaming it on me and Captain Dabis and Daphne and Ornette and Ruth.

Brownfield responds to Mem's established cultural form with an "authoritative" sociological form:

> "Mem," he whined, assuming weakness from her altered face, "you know how hard it is to be a black man down here. . . . You knows I never wanted to be nothing but a man! Mem, baby, the white folks just don't let nobody feel like doing right.

In reproducing these "knowing" references, these established and authoritative forms, *The Third Life* is able to reinforce or motivate its ideologeme that when the black man is bruised and dehumanized by the dominant social structure, he, in turn, maims and beats his wife, who is loyal and submissive, and mistreats his children.

Lastly, *The Third Life* enters into further internal dissonance when it asks from Brownfield a particular statement which its discursive formation denies. To generate the text's resolution to its problem of blaming other rather than self, the text invests Grange with a moral speech condemning Brownfield for refusing to become a man:

> I figured he could blame a good part of his life on me, I didn't offer him no directions and, he thought, no love. But when he

becomes a man himself, with his own opportunity to righten the wrong I done him by being good to his own children, he had a chance to become a real man, a daddy in his own right. . . . But he messed up with his children, his wife and his home, and never yet blamed himself.

But, despite the text's insistence, can Brownfield become a man? Within the text's discursive formation, does Brownfield have the "opportunity to righten the wrong"? Can he become self-critical? Except for the short period, early in their marriage when Mem teaches Brownfield to read, where is Brownfield exposed to those social institutions—tradition, examples, education, parental guidance—that will teach him to grow and change? What conditions will cause him to change and grow? Are they present in *The Third Life?* In *The Archaeology of Knowledge*, Foucault argues that there are "conditions necessary for the appearance of an object of discourse . . . which means that one cannot speak of anything at any time."

The text's discursive formation never provides the necessary condition for Brownfield to talk of change or to be a man, as it does for Grange. On the one hand, *The Third Life* reproduces an established definition of manhood—taking care of self and family—that becomes the model for measuring the worth and value of the Afro-American male. On the other hand, the text places that definition of manhood in an Afro-American constellation where it has no chance to materialize. The text even admits that there are no chances: "He [Brownfield] was never able to do more than exist on air."

Yet, in Grange's moralizing speech, the text insists that Brownfield is responsible for his own demise. Grange changes because he removes himself from the existing oppressive situation. Unlike Grange, Brownfield never has the option of viewing his debased existence outside the rhetoric of the existing social structure. The only life he knows is the life of the brutal sharecropping system and the language of oppression with which his life represents "reality." Nor does Brownfield, like Grange, have anyone to touch him with love. This internal conflict, again, arises from the text's relation to its discursive formation. The text cannot talk about statements and concepts which its discursive formation denies.

The discursive strategies of including certain facts and excluding others, of arranging these facts hierarchically, of manipulating characters to articulate certain ideological forms—which generate the text's ideologeme—allow *The Third Life* to produce a particular representation of the American and Afro-American historical past from the turn of the century to the late 1960s. *The Third Life*'s produced representation of the historical past makes it possible for it to show the structure and operation of the Southern sharecropping system, certain values, ideas, and feelings which dominated and perpetuated the operation of that system. It also makes it possible for *The Third Life* to show how and why black men made certain decisions about their lives, exhibited certain behaviors, and committed certain violent acts.

In this representation of the historical past, black men—Grange, Brownfield, Josie's father and his friends, Uncle Buster, and the "overworked deacons"—are socialized to believe that being a man means taking control and being responsible for the members of their families. Yet, the nature of the dominant society's social structure denies them those controls and responsibilities. This disparity between expectation and actuality causes these black men to develop feelings of inadequacy. Bruised and beaten by the system, they beat their wives and deny guidance and love to their children. In short, they reproduce the relation they have with the system in the relations they have in their families.

This reproduced American and Afro-American historical past allows *The Third Life* to show the limited range in which black women had control over their lives and how this limitation makes them dependent upon and loyal to black men. Black women—Margaret, Uncle Buster's wife, the wives of Josie's father's friends, and the wives of the deacons, Josie, Lorene, and Josie's mother—lose respect for themselves and their husbands and fail, at times, to provide the necessary care and love for their children.

The Third Life shows how the actions of the men "color" everything about the women's lives. After being brutalized by Grange and the sharecropping system, Margaret changes from an earthy, caring, and strong woman to an obtuse street walker. Seeing her own life and her family destroyed by forces which she does not understand, Margaret resigns herself to death. Trudier Harris argues that "Margaret's murder and suicide are not defiance; they are a bow of defeat, a resignation to the forces outside. She is *destroyed* by forces that have dissolved her family." Margaret's inability to find a coping mechanism to give her life order and meaning makes suicide an inevitable choice.

Josie's life is also "colored" by the actions of the men in her life. But, despite the fact that she is constantly abused, misused, and abandoned, Josie is still able to care, to exhibit human qualities. After Brownfield kills her niece, she still visits him in prison. And even after Grange abandons her for Ruth, she still defends his honor to Brownfield. She is able still to "love in spite of all that had gone wrong in her life."

Perhaps, it is because the reader witnesses Mem's transformation from a shy, plump, quiet, and intellectual young woman to a skinny, ugly, mentally scarred, and physically maimed woman that he or she can begin to comprehend the devastating effects of the Southern sharecropping system and the black man on the black woman. After marrying Brownfield, Mem is dragged from one sharecropper's cabin to another. Her education threatens him; therefore, he embarrasses her in public. When Mem expresses a desire for a house and a better life for their children, Brownfield threatens her with physical violence. Because she spends most of her life struggling to survive amid verbal and physical abuse, Mem never has the time and option to develop those scholarly, creative, and spiritual interests she began as an adolescent. She is caught in a social web without an exit:

> She wanted to leave him, but there was no place to go. She had no one but Josie and Josie despised her. She wrote to her father, whom she had never seen, and he never bothered to answer the letter. From a plump woman she became skinny. . . . Even her wonderful breasts dried up and shrank; her hair fell out and the only good thing he could say for her was that she kept herself clean.

But, in spite of the abuses from Brownfield, Mem still possesses dignity and human warmth. She, like Margaret, continues to work hard to care for and love her family and she does not become bitter or anti-social. After observing how Mem handles her rather unpleasant predicament with Brownfield, Grange refers to her as a "saint."

It is these "other" images of the black woman—captured in Josie, Margaret, Mem, Lorene—in *The Third Life* that burst asunder or violate dominant, one-dimensional images of the black woman: the mammy, the tragic mulatto, the wench, and the matriarch.

Also, this representation of the American and Afro-American historical past makes it possible for *The Third Life* to show how, when children are neglected and denied parental love and guidance, they can come to hate their parents. After Grange and Margaret have abandoned Brownfield, Brownfield cannot forgive them for forgetting that they "were not alone." With no guidance from his mother and father, Brownfield is left to take care of himself, to learn and survive as best he can. Therefore, it comes as no surprise that when he marries and moves into the sharecropping system, his life begins to resemble his father's. His hopes, dreams, expectations, and person are destroyed. Having never been loved by his parents, he is incapable of loving his daughters. Thus, Brownfield passes on to his daughters the brutal kind of human relations that he learns from Grange and Margaret and their surroundings. This reconstructed American and Afro-American historical past shows how social systems and structures are reproduced through language. It shows how this brutal kind of relationship is passed from one generation to another.

In describing the facts which form within the text, we can discern how *The Third Life*'s discursive formation reproduces heterogeneous statements and facts—seventies feminist definition of history, sixties sociological jargon, images of black women from other texts, significations of the frustrated, angry, and violent black male from the Afro-American historical past, Fanon's resolution for the liberation of the oppressed class—different in forms and dispersed in time and have them relate to the same object or ideologeme. Brutal and violent facts of the American and Afro-American historical past are related to a seventies feminist definition of history only because the text's rules of formation produce the conditions. The fact of the white male as an insensitive, dehumanizing force is related to the fact of the black woman as being hard-working, loyal, and submissive only because the text's discursive formation needs both to make its enunciation. Sixties sociological jargons are related to the fact of the mistreated and misguided child because *The Third Life*'s rules of formation enable them to form as objects of a discourse. But for *The Third Life* to show certain insights into its produced American and Afro-American historical past and the black life it produces, it has to delimit certain facts and it has to be silent on others.

The Third Life is silent on the many historical moments where black men and black women, despite the oppressive nature of the sharecropping system, are able to love each other and to occupy the same mental space. These moments exist early in the marriage of Brownfield and Mem before they move into the sharecropping system or before they become adults. These moments also exist between the youthful Quincy and Helen and the old Grange and the young Ruth. But they do not exist during adult life. In comments made to David Bradley in *The New York Times Magazine,* Walker shows how her personal experiences inform her reconstruction of the historical past:

> I knew both my grandfathers, and they were just doting, indulgent, sweet old men. I just loved them both and they were crazy about me. However, as young men, middle-aged men, they were brutal. One grandfather knocked my grandmother out of a window. He beat one of his children so severely that the child had epilepsy. Just a horrible, horrible man. But when I knew him, he was a sensitive wonderful man.

In other discursive formations, which deal with the same historical period, black men and black women occupy the same space together. In Ernest Gaines's *The Autobiography of Miss Jane Pittman,* Jane Pittman and Joe Pittman are able to draw on the wisdom of the culture and their own inner strengths and determinations to protect themselves from the brutality of the dehumanizing system. Jane—unlike Margaret, Josie, and even Mem—understands the operations of the social system. Therefore, she is able to accept its limitations and live and love within its boundaries. But *The Third Life* cannot talk about black men and black women occupying the same space. To talk about the same space would undermine the text's ideologeme, its conceptual system, i.e., that the system's violent treatment of black men and their subsequent violent responses makes that togetherness impossible.

The Third Life is silent on the thousands of black women from the Afro-American historical past who refused to be loyal and submissive to black men, who refused to accept the daily abuse from black men. Janie Starks of Hurston's *Their Eyes Were Watching God,* a reconstruction of the same or a similar American and Afro-American historical past, is certainly more aggressive and more independent in spirit and body. Realizing that her first and second husbands practice values and hold ideas which are adverse to hers, Janie leaves both. But *The Third Life* has to be silent on rebellious black women, for they represent a category which its discursive formation denies. The presence of a rebellious black woman in the text would counter one of its principle enunciations: that despite the brutality inflicted on them by black men, black women remain loyal and submissive.

Also, in *The Third Life,* passive black women produce a sympathetic response from the reader. In denying the reader the chance to witness an aggressive woman's response to this male oppression, *The Third Life* manipulates the reader by having him or her identify with specific characters and situations. The presence of the category of passive black women solicits a sympathetic response from the reader because the reader always identifies with the helpless victim. It also generates the "saintly" image of the black woman. The absence of other options within the text's discursive formation for black men to relieve their frustration and aggressions makes their crimes more brutal and cruel. The reader always has contempt for the violent, aggressive character.

The Third Life is completely silent on other alternatives from the Afro-American historical past which black men used historically to neutralize the brutality of a racist and dehumanizing system. Thousands of black men maintained their humanity, their integrity, and their sanity by turning honestly and genuinely to the church and Christianity. Other black men openly and vehemently defied the system, even at the expense of their lives. There is Marcus Payne of Gaines's *Of Love and Dust,* also a reconstruction of the same American and Afro-American historical past, who refuses to accept the constrictions of the system. He strikes out against it and meets his death. There are Ned Douglass and Jimmy Aaron of Gaines's *Miss Jane Pittman* who meet their deaths because they refuse to accept the system's definition of who they are. The presence of discursive facts like Marcus, Ned, and Jimmy within *The Third Life*'s discursive formation would, again, counter the text's enunciation that the black man fears the white man and other menacing forces, and, as a result of this fear, becomes passive.

In making visible *The Third Life*'s discursive strategies and its silences, we can see how the seventies feminist discourse informs *The Third Life*'s discursive formation. The text takes certain heterogeneous facts—the domineering patriarch, the violent and oppressive male, the battered abused mother and child—which are essential to feminist ideology. Then, it establishes a group of relations between these facts which enable it to make a particular enunciation, to formulate a particular feminist ideologeme.

The Third Life—along with other feminist texts like Ntozake Shange's *For Colored Girls*, ... Gayl Jones's *Corregidora* and *Eva's Man*, Toni Morrison's *The Bluest Eye* and *Sula*, which reconstruct and emphasize the same American and Afro-American facts and categories as *The Third Life*, and other feminist series in political science, sociology, history, psychology, etc.—gives meaning, coherence, validity, and a history to the strivings and yearnings of a contemporary feminist set of assumptions about women's reality and existence. But, more importantly, we see how *The Third Life* and other feminist texts are "socially symbolic acts" which invent imaginary or formal solutions to the unresolvable social contradictions. These texts function as indices and cultural messages for Americans and Afro-Americans who embrace feminist ideologies because they explain certain lived experiences. With *The Third Life*, Alice Walker produces new myths about the American and Afro-American historical past—and especially about black women—to counter past and existing myths which have not portrayed women, and particularly black women, as complex human beings who have existed in oppressive and sexist historical constellations.

DIANNE F. SADOFF

Black Matrilineage:
The Case of Alice Walker
and Zora Neale Hurston

In their book on women writers and the nineteenth-century literary imagination, Sandra M. Gilbert and Susan Gubar revise Harold Bloom's psycholiterary
model of poetic precedence to make it applicable to the female writer. In
Bloom's Freudian model of poetic influence, the poet, like Oedipus, battles
his precursor father at the intertextual crossroads and metaphorically kills
him: he misreads and so swerves from, completes, or defines his discontinuity
with his literary forebear. Bloom defines an author's inevitable dependence
on tradition as necessarily anxious because writers deny obligation to precursors; they desire originality yet know it a fiction. The woman poet, however,
finds no place in this paradigm of authorial interaction. On the one hand,
she has few precursors who resemble herself, and on the other, she must come
to terms with her difference from male writers who (metaphorically) beget
the text upon the female muse. Gilbert and Gubar therefore posit that for
the woman writer the "anxiety of influence" becomes a "primary 'anxiety of
authorship.' " Her alienation from the male canonical tradition appears in
her text as marks, fissures, and traces of "inferiorization": rebellion mas-
querades as submission, poetic closure is ambivalent, structure and figurative
language undercut stated thematic material. The feminist study of literary
tradition seeks sympathetically to comprehend the strains of gender expectation and difference in texts, to reenvision female possibility, and to right (or
rewrite) the wrongs of literary history.

This theoretical perspective on feminism, texts, and literary tradition
focuses on the ambivalence and self-deprecation of the white woman writer in

From *Signs: Journal of Women in Culture and Society* 11, no. 1 (Autumn 1985). ©
1985 by the University of Chicago.

nineteenth-century England. Yet modern and contemporary women writers also have precursors. Both Bloom's masculinist and Gilbert and Gubar's Victorian-feminist paradigms of anxiety and influence need further revision once we alter the literary-historical prism through which we view texts. In Virginia Woolf's modern female version of literary influence, moreover, women writers "think back through [their] mothers." This maternal literary precedence means the contemporary woman writer seeks her precursors with enthusiasm and misreads their anxiety so as fully to enable her own enterprise. When we consider contemporary women writers of color, we must again revise Bloom's and Gilbert and Gubar's models of influence. Race and class oppression intensify the black woman writer's need to discover an untroubled matrilineal heritage. In celebrating her literary foremothers, however, the contemporary black woman writer covers over more profoundly than does the white writer her ambivalence about matrilineage, her own misreading of precursors, and her link to an oral as well as a written tradition. Study of Alice Walker's relationship as a writer to Zora Neale Hurston clarifies the relationship of gender and race in a revised theory of literary influence.

I

In numerous and diverse ways Walker proclaims Hurston her precursor and appears to find that precedence a source not of anxiety but of nurturance. For example, she dedicates the whole of *In Love and Trouble: Stories of Black Women* as well as the story in it, "The Revenge of Hannah Kemhuff," to the memory of Hurston. The story's narrator, a young woman who trains as a rootworker under the legendary Tante Rosie, recites a voodoo curse "straight from Zora Neale Hurston's book, *Mules and Men*" against the racist and classist Mrs. Holley; when she finishes her apprenticeship, the narrator, like Tante Rosie, will know this curse "by heart." Central to this passing on of knowledge from one woman to another is the quest for identification. For the rootworker, as for other black women, the double oppression of gender and race makes it doubly necessary to celebrate such continuity in the black experience. Reading about black heroines initiates a similar identification. Walker writes that if she were condemned to live on a desert island with only ten books, she would "unhesitatingly" choose as one *Their Eyes Were Watching God:* "I would want to enjoy myself while identifying with the black heroine, Janie Crawford, as she acted out many roles in a variety of settings. . . . *There is no book more important to me than this one*" ("Zora Neale Hurston—a Cautionary Tale and a Partisan View" [hereafter cited as "Zora"], in *In Search of Our Mothers' Gardens: Womanist Prose* [hereafter cited as

MG]). The multifaceted liveliness of the black heroine gives rise to Walker's sense of her own resemblance to Janie Crawford, and a similar sense of shared life and knowledge makes Walker identify with Hurston as well. The woman from Eatonton, Georgia, recognizes the woman from Eatonville, Florida, as a "model" for herself.

A tradition depends not only on identification with precursors but also on transmission by the belated or second-generation writer to later readers and writers. Walker writes that she would take *Mules and Men* to her desert island so as to "pass on to younger generations the life of American blacks as legend and myth" ("Zora"). In *Mules and Men,* Hurston herself has done just this: "Who you reckon want to read all them old-time tales about Brer Rabbit and Brer Bear," George Thomas asks the anthropologist. "Plenty of people," Zora replies; "we want to set them down before it's too late. . . . Before everybody forgets all of 'em." Alice Walker later takes *Mules and Men* to New York and Boston, to members of her family who "rapidly forget . . . their southern cultural inheritance." *Mules and Men,* Walker reports, "gave them back all the stories they had forgotten or of which they had grown ashamed (told us years ago by our parents and grandparents). . . . *This is not exaggerated.* . . . No matter how they tried to remain cool toward all Zora revealed, in the end they could not hold back the smiles, the laughter, the *joy* over who she was showing them to be: descendants of an inventive, joyous, courageous and outrageous people: loving drama, appreciating wit, and, most of all, relishing the pleasure of each other's loquacious and *bodacious* company." Walker thus undertakes a "fight for Zora and her work" because it "must not be lost to us"; this campaign Walker views as her "duty" ("Zora"). Transmission necessarily retrieves texts from the past and restores them to continuous use by later readers and storytellers, creating an intergenerational and contemporary cultural community.

Alice Walker's understanding of poetic history or literary influence, then, appears not at all melancholy or anxiety laden. Her essays about Hurston seem to share none of Woolf's modernist ambivalence about precursors: the "depressing" yet "triumphant" George Eliot, a woman "with no wish for intimacy"; the vehement yet angry and "self-centered" Charlotte Brontë; the discriminating yet "taciturn" and evasive—even dull—Jane Austen. Walker designates her precursor an author of black legend and black female liberation, a woman who facilitates what Adrienne Rich calls "re-vision" and who enables female possibility; her dedication—that is, her inscription and devotion—to Hurston acknowledges that, without predecessors, a writer cannot write, since texts enable other texts.

Walker's enthusiastic battle to restore both Hurston and her texts to the

Afro-American literary canon, however, masks an underlying anxiety about the black woman writer's singularity in white America that emerges, although disguised, in Walker's fiction. Needing a precursor to validate her own enterprise as a writer, Walker virtually invents Hurston before she defines herself as indebted to Hurston's example. In her forward to Robert Hemenway's biography of Hurston, Walker says of *Mules and Men,* "I became aware of my need of Zora Neale Hurston's work some time before I knew her work existed. In late 1970 I was writing a story that required accurate material on voodoo practices among rural southern blacks of the thirties; . . . it was then that I discovered *Mules and Men,* Zora's book on forklore, collecting, herself, and her small, all-black community of Eatonville, Florida. . . . Here was this perfect book!" ("Zora"). This deep need for a predecessor and her knowledge of black culture—in this instance voodoo—makes Walker idealize Hurston as model: *Mules and Men* is "perfect." As though to emphasize Hurston as ideal, Walker underscores that she does *"not exaggerate"* the folktales' effect on their audience, that *"no book is more important"* to her than *Eyes.* Hurston becomes not only predecessor but originator; her work, archetypal. Walker's essays on and editorship of Hurston designate the Renaissance writer precursor and obscure the Second Renaissance writer's fear of her cultural marginality, her own deep need for a foremother.

II

A woman who writes knows herself her precursors' metaphorical daughter. In Walker's journey to find Hurston's grave, however, she imagines herself to be Hurston's illegitimate niece. "The lie," as she calls it, is a figurative truth, for her precursor *is* her relation: "As far as I'm concerned, she *is* my aunt—and that of all black people" ("Looking for Zora," in *MG*). Yet Hurston is not only Walker's figurative aunt but her metaphorical mother as well. In her essay "In Search of Our Mothers' Gardens" Walker movingly pays tribute to the mute female poets of the enslaved South who are her precursors, her "mothers." Black women who were sexually exploited and politically oppressed by the system of slavery—"the *mule[s]* of the world"—dreamed dreams and saw visions. They could not have dreamed of being artists, but they might have been rootworkers, "saints," or singers. These "great-grandmothers," forbidden by law to read or write, kept alive the creative spirit among their people and passed on to their daughters that "living creativity," the *"notion of song."* Phillis Wheatley, Hurston, and Bessie Smith are among Walker's own "great-grandmothers," women who by their "songs" made it possible for her to "sing." Like Woolf, Walker believes a (black) female tradition includes silence as well as voice.

Walker concludes her essay, however, not with her figurative but with her literal mother. Although her mother spent her days in laborious tasks, she was an artist: she tended her garden daily, with the commitment necessary to art; she experienced the artist's radiance. Her materials were not paints but flower seeds, for like the unsung artists of any working or lower class, she "left her mark in the only materials she could afford, and in the only medium her position in society allowed her to use." Walker's mother also told stories, and Walker preserves these tales: her mother's stories about "strong horse tea" and voodoo curses become part of her own, just as her mother's "garden," her art, passes to her daughter and becomes her garden, her art. The literal and figurative genealogy of artists and storytellers enables and empowers the art of the contemporary black woman.

In this genealogical metaphor, the family resembles the poetic generations: ancestors on a family tree become by analogy literary precursors. In Bloom's original paradigm of such precedence, the Freudian "family romance" represents oedipal rivalry between the early or prior poet-father and the belated poet-son. Guy Rosolato describes the way in which the oedipal triangle at the heart of the family romance opens into the patriarchal and genealogical situation. If the rivalry between son and father over the mother's love is to conclude without parricide, the son must replace his loyalty to mother with devotion to patrilineage. In Rosolato's paradigmatic patrilineal narrative, God, Abraham, and Isaac battle over love and loyalty, and only by killing his own son, Isaac, can Abraham prove his obedience to his Father, God. When God inserts the ram into the oedipal equation, the mediating sacrifice allows the three generations of males to accept one another's sonhood or fatherhood and so create a patrilineage in which males inherit substance and identity one from another.

These masculine models of family structure and genealogy may be transformed into female-centered paradigms. In Nancy Chodorow's rethinking of oedipal models, the daughter as subject experiences her resemblance to her mother and never rejects the family as firmly as does the son; both girl and boy have their first and primary loving relationship with a woman. The tie between mother and daughter, then, unlike the tie between father and son, is in its beginning's based on love rather than rivalry. Although the later relationship between mother and daughter is often ambivalent, the early tie never is fully denied. The girl's sexual development may be troubled because she shifts the object of her affections from mother to father, but identification is less troubled for her than for the boy; she sees her mother in herself, and views her daughter as repeating—perhaps repairing—that matrilineal resemblance. This female genealogy makes woman the paradigmatic subject and defines her primary intersubjectivity as female.

As a model for literary priority, a female genealogy based on family structure alters Bloom's "anxiety of influence" to "matrilineal anxiety." The nineteenth-century white woman writer, for example, will find in the texts of her "motherly precursors" signs of inferiorization, self-hatred, and suppressed rebellion; she must seek her "lost literary matrilineage" and accept ambivalent matrilineal poetics so as herself to give birth to texts based on her precursors' strengths. The Second Renaissance black woman writer will not wholly fit this pattern, however, partly because of her history, partly her race.

For this paradigm unspokenly assumes the white nuclear family to be universal and without a history. Although radical American white women in the nineteenth century considered themselves metaphorically enslaved, their black sisters endured literal bonds. Moreover, slavery intervened in and altered the black family structure. The slave mother may have enjoyed more affective power in her family than did the white mother (whether northern or southern), yet the myth of "the black matriarch" current among twentieth-century liberals misreads maternal as though it were social authority. With terrible irony, this mystification originates in white resentment of the slave woman's seeming power through her sexual relationship with the master, when that relationship signifies instead her status as chattel. Forced to submit for survival, the black slave woman could yet resist her oppression because the dominant culture failed to define her as stereotypically "feminine." Although the master used rape in an attempt to crush the black woman's resistance and to humble the black man, her ironic freedom from the restraints of submissive white southern ladyhood allowed her to fight both alongside of and apart from the black man. Thus the black (slave) mother represents contemporary black woman's double history of enslavement and survival.

Notions that the contemporary black family is fatherless, unstable, and ruled by domineering women, like the myth of black "matriarchy," misinterpret matrifocality. Carol B. Stack examines extended clusters of urban black kin and finds that, although men are usually present, women "constitute the core of [the] network." Young women in the clusters, daughters and nieces, move often among households headed by their mothers, aunts, and women friends. Relationships between mothers and children, between women who are friends or kin, strengthen the network and provide its continuity; although the specific "household composition" may and does change, "members are selected or self-selected largely from a single network that has continuity over time." Rooted in slave culture and its adaptive strategies to the involuntary separation of mothers and fathers (exogamous marriage, extended inter- and intragenerational kin networks, naming of children for consanguineal kin, social acceptance of atypical female-headed families), black matrifocality serves as a response to poverty, urbanization, and oppression.

Her history and her race make the Second Renaissance writer appear less anxious about literary maternity or priority than is the modernist or contemporary white woman writer. She must create a tradition that restores to her people their "forgotten" culture, and so she seeks her motherly precursors without apparent ambivalence or anxiety, with a necessity to survive, even with idealization. Such precedence calls up matrifocal identification of daughter with foremother; it confirms and continues woman's rebellion, courage, and support. Walker's "In Search of Our Mothers' Gardens" transforms Woolf's model of the white female tradition by inserting in brackets the black equivalents for Woolf's exemplary writers and issues: instead of "Emily Brontë," "Zora Hurston"; instead of "wise women," "rootworkers." Yet the black and white female traditions are not, as Walker's substitutions imply, symmetrical or identical. The historical burden of black matrifocality and motherhood—slavery, sexual exploitation, forced loss of children, and economic marginality—also creates the special "duty," as Walker defines it, of black literary matriliny. Walker's own insistent affirmation of her foremother's perfection as example and uniqueness as precursor originates in the pressures of belatedness when superadded to the double bind of race and gender. Black and white women suffer similar oppression as women, but the black woman's double oppression intensifies her suffering and the beauty of her survival. Because she is black and female, Walker celebrates her matriliny with an idealism that counters her anger at her black slave mothers' "disinhertance," a disinheritance about which she knows her own mother can articulate anger only obliquely, about which for similar reasons the educationally deprived middle-aged black women she teaches in an Office for Economic Opportunity program know little. The evasions are strategies to escape the psychic deformity conscious anger entails. For Walker also, in the face of suffering and a history of oppression, idealized but necessary celebration masks anxiety about cultural disinheritance.

In "*One* Child of One's Own," the white female tradition calls up Walker's covert anger and her concomitant anxiety about the fragility of a black literary matrilineage. Articulating feminist theory and ideas about motherhood, Walker asks why white scholarship and art about women exclude the black woman. Judy Chicago, for example, in her feminist art piece "The Dinner Party" does not use for Harriet Tubman's plate the vaginal design found on most others. Walker states: "To think of black women as women is impossible if you cannot imagine them with vaginas. . . . And through that vagina, Children." White feminism obscures black women's sexuality and consequent motherhood. White women feel guilty and resentful about their relationship with black women, Walker theorizes, because they know their children get more from a racist society than do black mother's children—yet all mothers want the best for their children. Despite shared motherhood, race separates women; racism, not gender or motherhood, oppresses the black woman. Walker believes that her motherhood—surely literal but also metaphorical—will help overcome her oppression: "We are together, my child and I. Mother and child, yes, but *sisters* really, against whatever denies us all that we are" ("*One* Child of One's Own," in *MG*). Her conflation of the female generations, while describing the necessary political and cultural alliance of black women across generations, also confuses motherhood with sisterhood and idealizes the mother-daughter bond.

III

The tradition Walker sees passed on by foremothers is oral and Southern. In "Looking For Zora," then, Walker seeks in her precursor a writer of the black South and an exemplary black female "voice." The essay's structure and material imitates and so recalls *Mules and Men.* Hurston journeys back to Eatonville in her Chevrolet to seek the "city of five lakes, three croquet courts, three hundred brown skins, three hundred good swimmers, plenty guavas, two schools, and no jail-house"; Walker quotes this passage from *Mules and Men* as she writes about flying into an Eatonville still free, healthy, and black. In *Mules and Men,* Hurston rediscovers a people of "vivid imagination." She hears the tales of her childhood about the devil outsmarting God, blacks outsmarting Ole Massa, and animals allegorizing the black condition. These stories exist within an oral tradition that encourages both retelling and embroidering of the basic tale. Such repetition and variation knit the members of a community in their shared knowledge of their history, background, and culture, while rewarding individual inspiration and celebrating the verbal agility and metaphorical storytelling skill of black people. Storytelling happens socially: while men sit on the porch, while men and women flirt at a toe-party, while children play, while folks fish or play cards at a jook joint. Community members participate in telling "lies"—figurative and often hyperbolic truths about black life; the end of each story provides a verbal association that creates the next. Shug, for example, tells "The Quickest Trick" about three men who court one girl; Robert Williams follows with "How to Write a Letter" about a man and his daughter; Henry Byrd follows with another about a letter, "A Fast Horse." Hurston herself participates in this community self-creation. She urges her neighbors to tell as many stories as they can; one neighbor replies, "We kin tell you some lies most any old time. We never run outer lies and lovin'. "

The folklorist who returns south, however, is no longer herself Southern. Hurston chooses to collect folklore in Florida to be among black neighbors who know her: "I hurried back to Eatonville because I knew that the town was full of material and that I could get it without hurt, harm or danger," without "seeming acquiescence" or evasion. Yet her Northern education provides her a double perspective on Southern black life: "It was only when I was off in college, away from my native surroundings, that I could see myself like somebody else and stand off and look at my garment. Then I had to have the spy-glass of Anthropology to look through at that." Such double perspective aligns Hurston's narrative stance and voice. A white intellectual discipline and context provide another vantage point from which to examine her old cultural "garment," which, as Robert Hemenway demonstrates, is Eatonville idealized and removed from the Depression's economic hardship. To contain the difference between South and North, educated woman and townspeople, Hurston creates, as Hemenway says, a semifictional self-effacing narrator who presents her tales, a poseur. Although this "Zora" participates in porch sittings, parties, and high jinks at jook joints, her paradoxical distance from her ex-neighbors shows in her educated but "innocent" narrative voice; Hurston's record of her return South covertly exposes her distance from her home.

Walker, following her foremother back to the latter's home in the South, fails to find Hurston's unknown grave but marks a grave nonetheless in Hurston's memory. She encounters misinformation about and lack of interest in Hurston; she practices "evasion" to get her stories. The Eatonville that lived in her imagination, her self-irony implies, was, like Hurston's, an ideal. For she, like her foremother, has gone North, has become semi-assimilated to a white male literary world; she seeks her rural, Southern heritage with an idealism that tempers and compensates for her own lost past. Walker takes her trips back South to look for wholeness because, she believes, experience has fragmented and split apart herself and her people; she needs to confirm their faith and grace under the continuous pressures of racism, but she finds as well cultural disinheritance, symptomized by black co-operation in the neglect of Afro-American literature and of black women's writing. Black literary matriliny, like the structures of the black family, empowers daughters who write in the face of race and gender oppression, but it also sustains and conceals anxiety about the difficulties of writing as a woman of color. The difficulties appear, even if dispersed, in the fictional texts.

Like Hurston's semifictional narrator, Walker's fictional women find returning South bittersweet. Dee, of "Everyday Use," wants to make antique the Civil War quilts, butter churn, and rump-marked bench that are her Southern heritage; although Walker sympathizes with her Muslim heroine's "new day" for blacks, she sides with the narrator, Dee's mother, and with Dee's crippled sister Maggie, who will put her ancestors' things to daily use (*In Love and Trouble: Stories of Black Women*). The narrator of "To Hell with Dying" returns South to "resurrect" her old childhood friend Mr. Sweet, and, although her childhood "resurrections" worked, this one fails; yet Mr. Sweet lives on in the narrator's memory, in her story, and such figurative resurrection attempts to balance the violence and sexual exploitation other heroines in the stories of *In Love and Trouble* somehow survive. Sarah Davis, of "A Sudden Trip Home in the Spring," leaves New York to attend her father's funeral; she rediscovers her commitment to family and the South and decides to "come home." Quickly, however, she realizes that she must return North to study art so that she later may come home to sculpt a bust of her grandfather. In *Meridian,* Meridian ends up in Mississippi, gradually divesting herself of belongings so as to transcend herself. Lynne, Meridian's white friend and rival for Truman Held, wants to return South to rediscover the meaningful past of Civil Rights struggles; skeptical about both politics and the South, Truman declines to join her. In short, Walker's fiction reveals her own ambivalence about returning South as she rewrites Hurston's anxiety about separation from a rural past.

IV

The stories in *Mules and Men* articulate sexual politics with race and serve to normalize and regularize conflict between the sexes while permitting the community the appropriate stage on which to enact it. Man and woman, according to Mathilda, were once equal in strength. But the man wanted dominance, so he asked God to make him stronger; the woman got a set of keys from God, and the devil taught her how to use them to lock up the kitchen, the bedroom, and the cradle. For if the woman controls access to food, sex, and reproduction, she has more power than the man despite his strength. When the man "submit[s] hisself to de woman," Mathilda says, she opens the doors; "and dat's why de man makes and de woman takes." This tale of sexual difference portrays the necessity to mythologize such conflict so as to control it. The tale, indeed, follows an exchange between Gene and Gold in which each belittles the sexual prowess and gender privilege of the other:

[*Gene.*] "De trouble is you women ain't good for nothin' exceptin'

readin' Sears and Roebuck's bible and hollerin' 'bout, 'gimme dis
and gimme dat' as soon as we draw our pay. . . ."

[*Gold.*] "You mens don't draw no pay. You don't do nothin' but
stand around and draw lightnin'. . . ."

"You ain't seen me cryin'. . . ."

"Aw, shut up, Gene, you ain't no big hen's biddy if you do lay
gobbler eggs. You tryin' to talk like big wood when you ain't nothin'
but brush."

Such hyperbolic and richly metaphorical language inscribes power relationships between the sexes even while joking about them. Moreover, a quick
wit often defines a woman's power vis-à-vis men. "When Bertha starts her
jawin'," Jim says, "her tongue is hung in de middle and works both ways";
"her tongue is all de weapon a woman got," George Thomas chides. Big Sweet
nonetheless knows a woman's speech is authoritative; "Ah got de law in my
mouth," she claims (*Mules and Men*).

Hurston's finest novel, *Their Eyes Were Watching God,* examines gender
privilege and sexual politics from a feminist perspective. Janie Crawford's
Nanny, fearing routine sexual exploitation of her adolescent granddaughter,
marries her against her will to a domineering husband, Logan; Janie leaves
him to go off with Jody Starks, who promises she won't have to "follow a
plow" when she's married to him. But when the radiant attraction to "horizon"
and the feeling of possibility wear off between them, the raw power of sexual
domination once more appears in Janie's life. Jody founds an all-black town,
and, like Hurston's father, writes the laws for it; the account of the bringing
of light, the inscribing of laws, parodies biblical creation stories and suggests
Jody's exaggerated sense of "godliness." As mayor, Jody demands class
status—a "high chair"—for his wife, whom he assumes acquires her social
standing through his. "Ah aim . . . tuh be uh big voice," he says; "you oughta
be glad, 'cause dat makes uh big woman outa you." Janie disagrees, and the
novel relates the ensuing battle for power between husband and wife.

In *Their Eyes Were Watching God* and *Mules and Men,* male community
members gather to tell tales on Jody Starks's or Joe Clark's porch, the public
arena for sexual ogling, courting, and joking. But Jody denies his wife the
privilege of telling stories on his porch, just as he earlier denied her the right
to speak in public: "Mah wife don't know nothin' 'bout no speech-makin'.
. . . She's uh woman and her place is in de home." Jody wants Janie's "submission" and will fight to earn it. Jody makes Janie work in his store, forces
her to tie her abundant hair up in a headrag—sign of her oppression and self-
denial—and slaps her when the bread won't rise. Only slightly less forcefully,

the porch tales reveal the men's insistence on female submission and inferiority, while they enhance masculine pride and encourage male solidarity. One day the men heckle Mrs. Robbins for begging groceries when her husband provides for her:

> "If dat wuz *mah* wife," said Walter Thomas, "Ah'd kill her cemetery dead."
>
> "More special after Ah done bought her everything mah wages kin stand, lak Tony do," Coker said. "In de fust place Ah never would spend on *no* woman whut Tony spend on *her*. . . ."
>
> "[He] say he can't bear tuh leave her and he hate to kill her," [Jody responds], "so 'tain't nothin' tuh do but put up wid her."
>
> "Dat's 'cause Tony love her too good," said Coker. "Ah could break her if she wuz mine. Ah'd break her or kill her. Makin' uh fool outa me in front of everybody."

As Janie realizes when she hears this exchange, female obedience and chatteldom are a figurative death.

Their Eyes Were Watching God, however, tells about a woman who acquires the power to speak, who finds her voice and so learns to tell stories and create metaphors. Angered by the men's response to Mrs. Robbins, Janie for the first time "thrust[s] herself into the conversation": "It's so easy to make yo'self out God Almighty when you ain't got nothin' tuh strain against but women and chickens," she says, metaphorically describing the sexual pecking order. She's "gettin' too moufy," Jody fumes. Janie follows her verbal assault on male power with one on Jody's sexuality. When he humbles her in front of her store customers by calling her "old," she responds with a tongue lashing: "You big-bellies round here and put out a lot of brag, but 'tain't nothin' to it but yo' big voice. Humph! Talkin' 'bout *me* lookin' old! When you pull down yo' britches, you look lak de change uh life." Jody instinctively understands the challenge to male pride: Janie had "robbed him of his illusion of irresistible maleness that all men cherish." He goes to bed and never gets up. Janie accuses him of demanding she "bow down" and be "obedient" to him: he was "too busy listening tuh [his] own big voice." Narrative structure implies that Janie's learning to speak out, her willingness to use her tongue as weapon against masculine domination, kills Jody. Her words about his lack of sexual charisma send him into decline and disease; her verbal assault on his "big voice"—sign of his sexual prowess and political status—does him in. Janie's ability to play the signifying game, to allude indirectly to Jody's sexual inadequacy, instigates as well as insults; her imaginative skill with hyperbolic and metaphoric speech earns her power hitherto reserved for the men in the community, the right to tell tales. For the narrative opens with Janie's return to Hurston's fictional Eatonville and is framed by her telling the story of the novel to her friend Pheoby. Janie tells the community's "lies"—its fictional truths—and her own story as well.

V

Central to Bloom's theory of literary priority and influence is misreading. He believes weak talents "idealize," while strong ones "appropriate" space for themselves by misreading their precursors. Gilbert and Gubar view their nineteenth-century literary figures as producing incomplete texts well suited to misreading—texts that simultaneously conform to and subvert "patriarchal literary standards." These women writers, with few earlier models, are themselves unsure precursors to a modern female tradition; they often misrepresent themselves and so invite misinterpretation. As Gilbert and Gubar's revision demonstrates, Bloom's aggressive, even territorial, masculine model of misreading does not suit a woman's literary tradition. Female precursors, fearful of overt originality, facilitate misreading by their daughters; as precursor, the black woman writer, doubly culturally jeopardized by gender and race, will necessarily represent herself even more ambiguously in her texts than do white women writers. As literary daughter, meantime, the black woman writer will overtly idealize foremothers while disguising anxiety and covertly appropriating concealed rebellious thematic material. Her own texts may nevertheless revise and so expose this process of misreading, this idealized matriliny that covers over the troubling history of black women's motherhood.

Hurston, a first-generation writer in the black female tradition, does misrepresent herself, as a foremother must. Her texts bear the scars of disguise or concealment because she is black and female—doubly alienated from a white and patriarchal mainstream literature. Indeed, Arthur P. Davis judges Hurston's art "dishonest," her racial politics "incredible"; he accuses her of ignoring the effects of racism on the black community and of playing "darky" to white readers and patrons. Implicit in this reading is Davis's political rather than literary bias, his inability to regard concealed female rebellion as itself "political." Davis believes Hurston's fictional dialect mimics white conceptions of black speech, while on the contrary her folkloristic dialogue justly renders the rich metaphors, hyperboles, personifications, and allegorical urge of rural southern black language of the 1930s. Moreover, Hurston's much-criticized and problematic eccentricity, her posturings and evasions, got a woman of color published by the white literary establishment of her time, got her funds from universities and patrons, and so authorized and initiated her literary career.

In her autobiography, Hurston represents herself ambiguously by complying with, while covertly subverting, white male literary expectations. About *Dust Tracks on a Road,* Walker writes, "For me, the most unfortunate thing Zora ever wrote is her autobiography. After the first several chapters, it rings false. . . . But this unctuousness, so out of character for Zora, is also a result of dependency, a sign of her powerlessness" ("Zora"). Hurston's book both justifies and falsifies the self. The slighting of black influence and playing up of white friendships such as those with Fannie Hurst and Mrs. Mason, even the refusal to "kiss and tell" about her love affairs, may originate not only in uneasy self-justification but in the double necessity the black woman is under to write inoffensively about her life. When "looking for Zora," Walker reports, "you have to read the chapters Zora *left out* of her autobiography"; for Hurston truncated and revised her political and racial analysis in *Dust Tracks* in response to comments her editor at Lippincott made on the manuscript. She deleted, as Robert Hemenway demonstrates, discussions of colonial oppression in the Third World, American racism, and the failures of democracy. In the 1940s Hurston's political acuity and her racial bitterness must both have been considered by whites as inappropriate for verbalization by a black woman.

A woman born in an all-black Florida town who lost her mother at nine and left home at fourteen yet grew up to become a well-known writer must understandably have had difficulty reconciling her achievement with her race, class, and family background. In *Dust Tracks,* Hurston portrays herself as a survivor. Having left her family, she says she disregards all emotional ties to them. As a result, she appears to falsify her feelings about her mother's death: her exaggerated metaphors about the prowling "Old Master-Maker" cover over her unexpected loss; her insistence that she failed her mother by not heeding her last promise to Lucy appears to mask a child's normal anger at a dying parent for figuratively "failing" *her.* Hurston also evades knowledge of her oedipal jealousy of her stepmother, her anger so extreme that the sequence about this "skunk" who needed her "behind . . . kicked" gets narrated early and out of sequence (*Dust Tracks on a Road* [hereafter cited as *DT*]). No wonder this "survivor" idealized her long-suffering mother and vilified her womanizing father in the loosely autobiographical first novel, *Jonah's Gourd Vine;* no wonder she sought surrogate family in "godmother" Mason and "Papa" Franz Boas, her patroness and anthropology teacher, respectively. But the jealous and solitary girl must not surface in the successful woman writer's autobiography—the acceptable story of black girlhood and womanhood—and so she gets repressed.

Hurston also portrays her literary success as almost accidental in *Dust Tracks*. She happened to write a story her teacher sent out to *Story Magazine* which happened to get published, and publishers solicited an unwritten novel (she chose Lippincott, she says, because the letter did not frighten her); a friend typed her first manuscript for nothing, and—surprise—Lippincott took it. This account surely masks the drive necessary for a poor black woman to become educated, or, for that matter, to write at all. Hurston plays the passive role she deems proper for the woman of color dependent on others for her economic and literary security. Through her eccentric self-presentation in the 1920s and evasiveness in the 1940s, she was able to act out this sensed marginality to white male culture that her writing itself had to suppress. That repression, however, scars the written text. Robert Hemenway interprets sympathetically the "problem of voice" he perceives in *Dust Tracks*—a problem evident in my opinion even as early as *Mules and Men*—where the Northern-educated girl struggles to represent herself and her own speech in her "native village." This problematic voice inscribes Hurston's "contradictory understanding of her own success and her uneasy interpretation of it." Walker designates this double bind, in Virginia Woolf's terms, "contrary instincts" and ascribes it to lack of precursors on the one hand and the necessity to satisfy a white audience and publisher on the other.

Although in *Dust Tracks* Hurston masks her feelings about herself and her family, as well as her opinions about politics, race, and sex, her omitted material about gender appears in fictionalized form in *Their Eyes Were Watching God*. She wrote the novel in seven weeks after her second separation from Arthur Price and so "embalm[ed] all the tenderness of [her] passion for him" (*DT*). Indeed, many incidents between Janie and Jody, and Janie and Tea Cake are clearly transposed from her troubled relationship with Price. Janie's desire, for example, to tell stories and to achieve verbal power in the face of Jody's denial are figures for Hurston's drive to write novels and essays in the face of Price's insecure demand that she give up her career for their relationship. Like many women before and after her, Hurston used work to manipulate her relationship; when things got tough, she left home to do folklore research, to take her Guggenheim fellowship. But her insistence on writing won out, as does Janie's demand that she be free to tell stories. The committed writer's ambivalence about relationships betrays itself in her choice of language to describe her novel's genesis; it "embalms" her passion—kills and preserves it.

Hurston's ambivalent feelings about Price also appear concealed in the character of Tea Cake. In *Their Eyes Were Watching God,* a woman liberates her sexuality by taking as her third husband a man dedicated not to domination but to equality. The surface of the narrative supports this commonplace reading. Unlike Logan and Jody, Tea Cake asks Janie to participate in men's activities—shooting, playing checkers, and storytelling. He appreciates her achievements and individuality; he awakens her sexuality; he works side by side with her in the Everglades. Yet Hurston makes the reader distrust Tea Cake almost as soon as he and Janie settle down. When Janie discovers he has taken her two hundred dollars, she fears she's been jilted. When he returns, she forgives him. Tea Cake gambles to restore the money; "Ah no need no assistance tuh help me feed mah woman," he declares. This incident and Janie's uncertainties unsettle the reader's initial attraction to Tea Cake, even if Janie is temporarily reassured.

Hurston also arouses our suspicions about Tea Cake's dedication to sexual equality. As jealously becomes an issue in his and Janie's marriage, Tea Cake begins physically to abuse his wife and so to resemble Jody Starks, the manipulator of male power and privilege: "Before the week was over he had whipped Janie. Not because her behavior justified his jealousy, but it relieved that awful fear inside him. No brutal beating at all. He just slapped her around a bit to show he was boss." Afterward, he pets Janie, and she helplessly hangs on him. Hurston profoundly distrusts heterosexual relationships because she thinks them based on male dominance and willing female submission; yet such inequality appears necessary to the institution of marriage. In her autobiography, for example, Hurston blames her mother for not submitting fully to her father and so robbing him of "that conquesting feeling" (*DT*). In *Eyes*, Tea Cake rationalizes his jealous beating of Janie as serving to show that she is *his* woman and cannot possibly be attracted to a lighter-skinned man. The reader hardly believes the stated motivation and finds the novel's resolution of the incident unconvincing. The plot has broken down, has lost the link between sequence and consequence, between action and motive.

An event without narrative precedent follows: the flood. The characters interpret this catastrophe as an act of God; the novel places it in a pattern of biblical parody and black folktale. Yet neither the flood nor the rabid dog kills Tea Cake: Janie does. Janie kills the rabid man in self-defense; she guiltily accuses the mad dog of killing Tea Cake through her (as Hurston blames herself for failing her mother in *Dust Tracks*); language removes Janie as subject from the narrative description of the shooting. The novel declares Janie's innocence—a white jury acquits her of murder!—yet we remember she figuratively killed her second husband. Although plot and language manipulate events so that the heroine kills off her man metaphorically or unintentionally, Janie is clearly a dangerous woman. At the end of the novel, Janie banishes her male oppressors; although theme appears to affirm Tea Cake's eternal presence to Janie after his death, narrative structure ensures his absence. Pheoby had warned Janie about marrying Tea Cake—"You'se yo' own woman"—and by the end of the novel she is. Hurston has motivated her narrative, perhaps unconsciously, to act out her rage against male domination and to free Janie, a figure for herself, from all men.

The novel covers over this subversive material and so encourages us to misread it. Both literary critics and daughters have thus misread Hurston, their precursor, as a celebrator of liberated heterosexual love. Neither Hurston's subterranean thematic concern to punish dominating males in *Eyes* nor to idealize mothers while vilifying mother substitutes in *Dust Tracks* and *Jonah's Gourd Vine* appears in Walker's rhetoric about her literary foremother because the double bind of race and gender skews literary influence toward creative affirmation. Moreover, Hurston herself here misreads and covertly appropriates material from her contemporary, Nella Larsen, for whom the South, the return "home," and female sexuality were problematic. If Larsen's heroine embraces such goals, Hurston's Janie covertly refutes their force when she returns to her own house, alone, and surrenders her dependence on heterosexual love. While Alice Walker names Larsen—as well as Jean Toomer, whose *Cane* treats similar material—a precursor, her deep dedication to Hurston originates in that foremother's subversive material, which Walker herself covertly appropriates under the guise of idealized matriliny.

For while celebrating literary matrilineage in her essays, Walker subverts that celebration on the margins of her own fictional texts. In *Meridian,* for example, Walker restates yet revises the subterranean theme in Hurston's *Eyes* that women most truly become themselves without men. At seventeen, Meridian has married, divorced, and given up custody of her son; she views sex as a "sanctuary" from male aggression and, having never been aroused, at first refuses her future lover, Truman Held. "And for her part in what happened," the narrator states, "Meridian paid dearly." Consequently Truman dates white exchange students and eventually marries Lynne Rabinowitz; consequently, when she and Truman have sex once, Meridian has no orgasm, gets pregnant, aborts the fetus, and ties her tubes. Like Janie, Meridian surrenders her sexuality, not, however, for female voice and power but for politics. The novel begins at its story's chronological end when Truman encounters a parodic and corrupted emblem of capitalist endeavor: the circus wagoner who displays his wife's corpse for cash. He allows black children to view only on Thursdays, and to integrate the spectators, Meridian must ironically confront an army tank and stand before its guns. Despite Truman's shock, he and the reader see that the Civil Rights movement served not to eradicate Southern racism but to perpetuate parodies of itself, to keep poor black people in their place, and to teach black revolutionaries that racism will end only when the capitalist system alters. The ensuing retrospective narrative reveals the past, the unexpected consequences and complexities of political action: nervous breakdown, acquaintance rape, scapegoating of white (Jewish) women, divorce, and death. The terrible fictional price Walker exacts from her characters and in particular her heroine—Meridian "pays"—originates in Walker's own guilty ambivalence about political action; for despite her supposed apotheosis at the novel's end, Meridian has little visible effect on racist America. Politics becomes "performance," a personal yet powerless volunteer suffering.

The narrator implies and narrative structure confirms that Meridian persists in political performances—takes chances with her life—because she sacrifices her motherhood. As daughter, Meridian feels guilt for having shattered her own mother's frail independence and creativity, her "emerging self." Now anti-intellectual, prejudiced, and blindly religious, Meridian's mother nonetheless once fought her father's sexism, her own poverty, and the racist system to become a schoolteacher. The cost: *her* mother's life and willing self-sacrifice. As a daughter who becomes a mother and so participates in matrilineage, Meridian's mother represents the history of black motherhood: a legacy of suffering, endurance, and self-sacrifice. Meridian despises this "narrowing of perspective" yet also idealizes its self-righteous uprightness. Caught by such personal and historical guilt, Meridian views her own motherhood as "slavery," her wish to relinquish her child both his "salvation" and proof of her "monstrous" inadequacy; she desires to "murder" her son, but represses such unnatural thoughts and so turns them against herself; she abortively attempts metaphorical and compensatory motherhood in "adopting" an untameable, pregnant, and self-destructive "wild-child." A unique woman without "precedent" or precursor, Meridian considers herself unworthy of the black matriliny she idealizes and fails to see that her foremothers, unlike herself, were "compelled by necessity" to endure their suffering. She therefore refutes her own motherhood, despite knowing that her grandmothers—and by implication Meridian herself—defined freedom as keeping their children. Narrative structure exposes Meridian's consequent guilt: she gets ill, takes to bed, whispers "Mama, I *love* you" to her teacher, and rises to undertake her performances only when this mother surrogate responds, "I forgive you." Walker's fiction covertly exposes her own nonfictional misreading and idealization of matriliny.

In *The Color Purple,* Walker extends the conflation of motherhood and sisterhood she undertook in "*One* Child." In doing so, she appropriates the subterranean gender politics of Hurston's *Eyes.* As Celie reports in her letters to God, paternal incest has figuratively killed her mother and literally gotten her "big." Her father sells her children and barters her to a man who needs household help. Owned, beaten, and degraded by her husband's "climbing on top" of her, Celie survives only by learning her sister-in-law's lesson: fight back against the gender system based on male dominance and female submission that breeds violence against women and wives. Celie sees Sofia beat Harpo and Shug Avery talk back to Mr. —— and so learns to resist with fist and—as did Janie—with words. In addition she discovers Sofia's "amazon" sisters "stuck together." When Celie decides to leave her husband, she combines these sisterly lessons: she tells Harpo his attempt to make Sofia "mind" indirectly caused the white mayor to throw the uppity, talking-back woman in jail; she threatens Mr. —— that she, her children, and her sister Nettie "gon whup [his] ass"; she encourages Squeak, Harpo's lover, to laugh at male pride, go North to sing in public, and take back her proper name, Mary Agnes; and she goes off to Memphis with her female lover, Shug Avery.

This idealized sisterhood of women-loving women, however, masks a subterranean narrative violence against men and mothers that restates Hurston's. In *Purple,* Walker rereads and revises Hurston's concealed anxiety about motherhood and distrust of heterosexuality by idealizing sisterhood and economic progress. As Sofia, for example, fights back against Harpo, he begins to overeat and look "big" while Sofia constructs swings and shingles. At the end of the narrative, Mr. —— sews pants with Celie, and Harpo stays home with the kids while Sofia works in the sisters' dry goods store. Women gain strength by feminizing their men and creating a community of women and men who affirm female values of loving equality. In the same way, Nettie and Celie independently imagine a God neither man nor woman who loves "everything"; this God metaphorically calls Nettie home from Africa so the reunited sisters may inherit their rightful estate and become merchants. Walker's romanticized female economics revises the politics expressed in *Meridian* and misreads Hurston's analysis in which class aspiration and male dominance—Jody's "high chair," Nanny's organ in the parlor—cooperate to oppress the black woman. Moreover, in *Purple* mothers suffer death early or see their functions displaced onto sisters. Nettie raises Celie's children in Africa, where in a political subplot African daughters, like their American counterparts, must combat male violence against women (clitoridectomy, lack of educational and work opportunity) and so depend on idealized but ineffectual female support networks among mothers and daughters.

Other contemporary black women writers likewise question anxiety-free matrilineage. Toni Morrison's novel *Sula* values the black woman free enough to take her sexual pleasure without the middle-class security of "nesting," yet the novel rages against mothers as women who sacrifice contentment, limbs, and lives for their children. Sula watches her mother, Hannah Peace, burn to death because Hannah loves but does not like her daughter; Hannah as a child wanted her mother, Eva Peace, to play with her although the novel defines such play as a middle-class luxury: for a poor black woman, mother love means ensuring a child's survival. In *Sula,* black matrilineage breeds resentment and death, not affirmation; these free and mothering women pay with their lives, even though the author calls attention to her own motherhood in the book's dedication to her sons. Another example is *Corregidora* by Gayl Jones, in which black motherhood is portrayed as a scourge. Ursa's mothering ancestors were raped by their masters. The terrible knowledge of her history and that of all black women culminates in the novel's refusal to allow Corregidora motherhood; she has a hysterectomy. In *Eva's Man,* Jones explores the concomitant dangers of the black woman's sexuality: she is the queen bee who poisons men with love.

The black woman's history of suffering, however, necessitates her survival. Seeking survival and so matrilineal affirmation, the black woman writer paradoxically marks her texts with a heroine's suffering and the effects of oppression. Hurston explores the power while covertly disguising the danger of finding her black female voice; as literary precursor, she inscribes this danger on the margins of her fiction, her folktales, her autobiography. Yet the double bind of race and gender that scars her text also enables misreading. White feminist critics may misread narrative signs of concealment because of their double commitment to interpretation and feminist theory; black feminist critics, because of their commitment to reading, feminism, and affirmation of black community. Yet misreading, I would argue, makes reading and criticism possible. For a text inevitably bears scars and contains gaps, as blindness tempers all critical insight. My own readings here bear the trace of my race, no doubt, as well as my gender. Yet read we must, for this multiple and unavoidable misreading empowers poetic influence, facilitates understanding between women of color and white women, and creates literary tradition. As her literary daughters—and critics—misread Hurston, they also reread her and encourage other readers to do likewise. As we seek our matrilineage, we too will idealize, covertly appropriate, and conceal as we expose and revise our anxiety, our misreading, our history. Our mothers' gardens, like Hurston's, grow weeds as well as flowers, and rightly so.

DEBORAH E. McDOWELL

"The Changing Same": Generational Connections and Black Women Novelists

As Iola finished, there was a ring of triumph in her voice, as if she were reviewing a path she had trodden with bleeding feet, and seen it change to lines of living light. Her soul seemed to be flashing through the rare loveliness of her face and etherealizing its beauty.

Everyone was spell-bound. Dr. Latimer was entranced, and, turning to Hon. Dugdale, said, in a low voice and with deep-drawn breath, "She is angelic! . . . She is strangely beautiful! . . . The tones of her voice are like benedictions of peace; her words a call to higher service and nobler life."

As soon as dinner over, Shug push back her chair and light a cigarette. Now is come the time to tell yall, she say.

Tell us what? Harpo ast.

Us leaving, she say.

Yeah? say Harpo, looking round for the coffee. And then looking over at Grady.

Us leaving, Shug say again. Mr. —— look struck, like he always look when Shug say she going anywhere. He reach down and rub his stomach, look off side her head like nothing been said.
. . .

Celie is coming with us, say Shug. . . .

Over my dead body, Mr. —— say.

You satisfied that what you want, Shug say, cool as clabber.

Mr. —— start up from his seat, look at Shug, plop back down again. He look over at me. I thought you was finally happy, he say. What wrong now?

From *New Literary History* 18, no. 2 (Winter 1987). © 1987 by *New Literary History*.

You a lowdown dog is what's wrong, I say. It's time to leave you
and enter into the Creation. And your dead body just the welcome
mat I need.

The character being *spoken about* in the first passage is Iola Leroy, the
heroine of Frances E. W. Harper's 1892 novel of the same name. A group
of men are giving their approval of an impromptu speech that Iola has just
delivered on the ennobling effects of suffering and the necessity for Christian
service. They lay stress, simultaneously, on her physical beauty and saintliness.

In the second passage, from Alice Walker's 1982 novel *The Color Purple,* Celie, the novel's central character, *is speaking,* along with her spirit guide
and lover, the itinerant blues singer Shug Avery. Celie's, unlike Iola's, is an
audience of hostile, disapproving men; nevertheless, with force and
resoluteness, Celie announces her plans to move on in search of personal fulfillment and spiritual growth.

I cite these two passages as examples of two strikingly different images
of black female character in black women's fiction—one "exceptional" and
outer-directed, the other "ordinary" and inner-directed; two different approaches to characterization, one external, the other internal; and finally, two
different narrative voices, one strained, stilted, genteel and inhibited, the other,
spontaneous, immediate, fresh, and authoritative.

Although the passages are different, the novels from which they are
excerpted share important basic patterns. Both novels recount the problems
of familial separation and reunion, of lost and found identities. More
significantly, however, these novels represent the two most salient paradigms
in the black female literary tradition in the novel. Although manipulated differently, depending on the author, these paradigms derive from a common
center in black women's novels. Both revisionist in impulse, they are revealed,
most graphically, in the depiction of black female characters. Borrowing from
Susan Lanser's *The Narrative Act,* I call these paradigms, simply, public and
private narrative fiction. I see them posed respectively and most dramatically
in Frances E. W. Harper's *Iola Leroy* and Alice Walker's *The Color Purple.*

Of necessity, I use these terms not literally but metaphorically, for as
Lanser notes correctly, "obviously all fictional narration is 'public' in the sense
that it was written to be published and read by an audience. What I am
distinguishing here are fictional narrative acts designed for an apparently public
readership [or one 'outside' the text] and those narratives designed for reception only by other characters and textual figures."

In the following discussion, I would like to adapt and modify Lanser's
distinction between public and private point of view to posit a provisional

distinction between public and private narrative fiction. I wish to distinguish here between those novels by black women that seem to imply a public readership, or one outside the black cultural community, and those that imply a private readership, or one within that cultural matrix.

Given the complexity and ambiguity inherent in questions of audience, one can only speculate about the audience for whom a specific text seems intended. To be certain, authors cannot determine conclusively who their actual readers are. Nevertheless, all writers begin by fictionalizing or imagining an audience. As Peter Rabinowitz and other audience-oriented critics have argued, authors "cannot make artistic decisions without prior assumptions (conscious or unconscious) [stated or implied] about their audience's beliefs, knowledge, and familiarity with conventions," literary and/or social. Each text, then, selects, encodes, and images its targeted audience—what Wolfgang Iser calls its "implied reader"—through the style, language, and strategies it employs. (That does not preclude, of course, its being read by those outside the targeted reading group.)

I have chosen character as a springboard for examining these paradigms even though the current wave of literary/theoretical sophistication calls into question "naive commonsense categories of 'character,' 'protagonist,' or 'hero' " (Frederic Jameson, *The Political Unconscious: Narrative as a Socially Symbolic Act*) and rejects the "prevalent conception of character in the novel" which assumes that "the most successful and 'living' characters are richly delineated autonomous wholes" (Jonathan Culler, *Structuralist Poetics*). For, despite such positions, imaging the black woman as a "whole" character or "self" has been a consistent preoccupation of black female novelists throughout their literary history. That they frequently use the *Bildungsroman*—a genre that focuses primarily on the gradual growth and development of a "self" from childhood to adulthood—attests strongly to this preoccupation. It seems appropriate, therefore, to allow the critical concerns of black women's novels to emerge organically from those texts, rather than to allow current critical fashion to dictate what those concerns should be.

In considering character in black women's fiction as a reflection of the central paradigms in their tradition, other critical questions arise. Although the scope of this essay does not permit me to explore them in full and equal detail, the following interlocking questions are implied in my consideration of characterization. In that one of the most challenging aspects of characterization for any writer is the authentic representation of speech, what is the relationship between race/gender and literary voice? In turn, what is the relationship between author and audience, for that relationship largely determines and explains, not only narrative voice, but also a range of artistic strategies and choices. What do the configurations and variations of character in black women's fiction reveal about patterns of literary influence among black women writers, about their literary history? In other words, a study of how black women writers depict black female characters raises both aesthetic and sociological questions, illuminating vividly the intricate connections between the two.

I

Largely because degraded images of black women have persisted throughout history, both in and out of literature, black women novelists have assumed throughout their tradition a revisionist mission aimed at substituting reality for stereotype. Frances E. W. Harper and her female contemporaries Pauline Hopkins and Emma Dunham Kelley epitomized this revisionist mission, yoking it to a larger and related mission: to elevate the image of the entire black race. In so doing, they naively believed, they could eliminate caste injustices. They would manifest in literature the movement of racial uplift led by a widespread network of black club women of the nineteenth century whose motto was "Lifting As We Climb."

The impulse is at once the greatest strength and the greatest weakness of these early texts, for it results without exception in the creation of static, disembodied, larger-than-life characters. These early black heroines are invariably exemplary, characterized by their self-sacrifice and by their tireless labor for the collective good. But probably their most cherished and enduring mark is their chastity, a quality that black club women also struggled to defend in the uplift cause. To counter the widespread assumption that black women were sexually immoral, these club women "wanted to be remembered as upholders of puritan morality," hence, much of their work involved "encourag[ing] . . . masses of black women to accept the sexual morality of the Victorian bourgeoisie" (Wilson J. Moses, *The Golden Age of Black Nationalism, 1850-1925*). Ironically, despite the early writers' efforts to revise homogenized literary images, they succeeded merely, and inevitably, in offering alternative homogenization; they traded myth for countermyth, an exchange consistent with their public mission.

The countermyth dominates *Iola Leroy*. It is most striking in Iola's conscious choice to glorify the virtues of motherhood and domesticity, the mainstays of the mid-nineteenth-century cult of true womanhood. Although this ideology of domesticity was the veritable antithesis of the black woman's reality, Harper, like the majority of black writers of her era—both men and women—ironically accommodated her "new" model image of black womanhood to its contours. As Barbara Christian observes, "Since positive female qualities were all attributed to the white lady," black writers of the nineteenth century "based their counterimage on her ideal qualities, more than on [those] of any real black women." The image of the Lady combined and conflated physical appearance with character traits. Immortalized particularly in the southern antebellum novel, the image required "physical beauty [i.e., fair skin] . . . fragility, refinement and helplessness." "The closest black women could come to such an ideal, at least physically," Christian continues, "would . . . . have to be the mulatta, quadroon, or octoroon." Iola fulfills this physical requirement. "My! but she's putty," says the slave through whose eyes we first see her. "Beautiful long hair comes way down her back; putty blue eyes, an' jis' ez white ez anybody's in dis place." This ideal dominates novels by black women in the nineteenth century, due, as Alice Walker argues reasonably, to a predominately white readership "who could identify human feeling, humanness, only if it came in a white or near-white body." She concludes, " 'Fairness' was and is the standard of Euro-American femininity."

By giving Iola a role to play in the larger struggle for racial uplift, Harper modified the image of the Southern lady, but it is important to note that Iola's role in the struggle is enacted within the boundaries of the traditional expectations of women as mothers and nurturers, expectations that form the cornerstone of the cult of true womanhood. According to Iola, "a great amount of sin and misery springs from the weakness and inefficiency of women." In "The Education of Mothers," one of the two public speeches she gives in the novel (public speaking being largely reserved for men in the text), she appeals for "a union of women with the warmest hearts and clearest brains to help in the moral education of the race."

Not only does the content of such speeches contribute to Iola's exemplary image, the style and language do also. Ordinary or black folk speech has been historically devalued by the standard (white) English-speaking community, a devaluation that, as John Wideman maintains, "implies a linguistic hierarchy, the dominance of one version of reality over others." That devaluation and all that it implies was especially pervasive in Harper's era. Arlene Elder points out that "Blacks were ridiculed in white plantation and Reconstruction humor for the rough rhythms, slurred words, malapropisms, and quaint images in their language. In order to escape this degrading image, [early] Black novelists sped to the other extreme of creating cultured mulattoes" who used the elegant, elaborate, and artificial language found in much of the popular fiction of their day. At every point that Iola speaks in the novel, it is in the form of a carefully reasoned oration, in defense either of her virtue or of some moral or social ideal. Even in conversations at home with family and friends, Iola expounds, as in the following example: "To be . . . the leader of a race to higher planes of thought and action, to teach men clearer views of life and duty, and to inspire their souls with loftier aims, is a far greater privilege than it is to open the gates of material prosperity and fill every home with sensuous enjoyment."

In significant contrast to Iola's formal oratory is the more authentic folk speech of the novel's secondary characters, captured particularly well in the opening chapter entitled "Mystery of Market Speech and Prayer Meeting." The chapter describes the slaves' masterful invention of a coded language to convey secretly information to each other about battles won and lost during the Civil War. Their rich and imaginative language is self-consciously mediated in this chapter and throughout the novel by the stilted and pedantic voices of the narrator and the novel's major character. Nowhere is this pattern more strikingly illustrated in the novel than in the passage that describes the re-union between Iola's uncle, Robert, and his mother, from whom he was separated as a child. "Well, I'se got one chile, an' I means to keep on prayin' tell I fine my daughter," says Robert's mother. "I'm *so* happy! I feel's like a new woman!" In contrast Robert responds: "My dear mother . . . now that I have found you, I mean to hold you fast just as long as you live. . . . I want you to see joy according to all the days wherein you have seen sorrow."

In *Iola Leroy,* the propaganda motive, the hallmark of public discourse, largely explains these extreme differences of speech styles between the principal characters—all educated mulattoes—and the minor characters, all illiterate and visibly black servants and workers. The implications of such differentia-tions are clear: the speech of these secondary characters (which Iola finds "quaint," "interesting," and "amusing") must be mediated and legitimated in white terms by the more accepted language of the major characters.

In the course of *Iola Leroy,* as Iola fulfills her role as exemplary black woman she comes to resemble a human being less and less and a saint more and more. We learn very little about her thoughts, her inner life. Nothing about her is individualized, nor does this seem to be Harper's chief concern, for she is creating an exemplary type who is always part of some larger framework. That larger framework is moral and social in *Iola Leroy,* and every aspect of the text, especially character, must be carefully selected to serve its purpose. All of the novel's characters are trapped in an ideological schema that predetermines their identities. Every detail of Iola's life, down to the most personal experiences of family life, is stripped of its intimate implications and invested with social and mythical implications. It is significant that of all the Old Testament types, she identifies with Moses and Nehemiah, for "they were willing to put aside their own advantages for their race and country."

Iola's role as social and moral exemplar is paralleled by the novel's role as exemplum. Like its title character, *Iola Leroy* is on trial before the world. It aims for a favorable verdict by choosing its models carefully. Harper's most visible model is Harriet Beecher Stowe's *Uncle Tom's Cabin,* the most popular novel of the mid-nineteenth century in America. Space does not permit me to detail the striking similarities of plot, theme, style, and characterization between the two novels. Although Harper makes slight modifications, echoes of the most salient episodes of *Uncle Tom's Cabin* are present throughout *Iola Leroy.*

Harper's choice of *Uncle Tom's Cabin* as model is a logical and appropriate one, given the polemical and public role that she expected her novel to play, a role that Stowe's novel had played to unrivaled success with an audience comprised mainly of Northern white Christians. Harper addresses and appeals to this audience directly in the afternote of the novel: "From threads of fact and fiction I have woven a story whose mission will not be in vain if it awaken in the hearts of our countrymen a stronger sense of justice and a more Christlike humanity in behalf of those whom the fortunes of war threw, homeless, ignorant and poor, upon the threshold of a new era." Those Northern whites might be more inclined to lend their assistance to this homeless and displaced lot if the images of black life that Harper and her black contemporaries valued and affirmed accorded with that audience's horizon of social and literary expectations. In this respect, *Iola Leroy* is in company with a number of novels by black writers of its era, all dedicated to a public mission, all foundering on the shoals of two contradictory attempts: "to conform to the accepted social [and] literary . . . standards of their day and their almost antithetical need to portray their own people with honesty and imagination" (Elder).

II

The need to portray their people with honesty and imagination has been paramount for contemporary black women novelists. For many—Alice Walker, Toni Morrison, Gayl Jones, among others—that need has compelled them to transform the black female literary ideal inherited from their nineteenth-century predecessors. Although these recent writers have preserved the revisionist mission that inspired that ideal, they have liberated their own characters from the burden of being exemplary standard-bearers in an enterprise to uplift the race. The result is not only greater complexity and possibility for their heroines, but also greater complexity and artistic possibility for themselves as writers. Alice Walker is a good example of this paradigm shift.

In "Beyond the Peacock," an essay in her recent collection *In Search of*

Our Mothers' Gardens, Walker writes, "each writer writes the missing parts to the other writer's story. And the whole story is what I'm after." To Walker, a major if not *the* major missing part is the story of what she calls the "black black" heroine, described in the essay "If the Present Looks Like the Past." Unlike Iola Leroy and the other nineteenth-century black women characters that Walker surveys in the essay, the black black heroine cannot pass for white and is not protected by class privilege. While Walker isn't the only black female novelist to attempt an alternative to the Iola Leroy type, she has made a particularly skillful revision in the Celie letters of *The Color Purple.* These letters can be read as Walker's effort to write the missing parts of *Iola Leroy* and other black women's texts in its tradition. In other words, Celie is a revision of a revision of black female character, rendered, for the most part with the honesty and imagination lacking in *Iola Leroy.*

Whereas Iola Leroy as character is largely indistinguishable from the Southern Lady and is devoted to the mission of middle-class racial "uplift," Celie is a poor, visibly black, barely literate drudge devoted simply to avoiding and surviving the brutalities inflicted on her by every man with whom she comes into contact. Unlike Iola, no ornate and elevated speeches come trippingly to Celie's tongue. She speaks in black folk English, and, unlike Harper, Alice Walker provides none of the self-conscious assurances to the reader—apostrophes, contractions, corrections from more "well-spoken" characters—that she knows the standard.

But perhaps Celie's most striking difference from Iola is her sexual experience. Unlike Iola, Celie has been unable to fend off attacks on her virtue by predatory men as her very first letter makes starkly clear: "You gonna do what your mammy wouldn't. First he put his thing up gainst my hip and sort of wiggle it around. Then he grab hold my titties. Then he push his thing inside my pussy." Although Celie's introduction to sexuality is rape, as her narrative unfolds, she, unlike Iola, discovers how vital healthy sexual experiences are to the development of her self-esteem and her creative powers. Significantly, the only form of sexuality that aids that process is expressed with a woman, one of the few lesbian relationships explored in black women's literature.

Iola and Celie reflect their authors' divergent approaches to characterization as well. Whereas Harper approaches Iola's character largely from the outside through her physical characteristics and through what others say about her, Walker reveals Celie's character completely from the inside. Everything we learn about Celie is filtered through her own consciousness and rendered in her own voice.

In *Iola Leroy* the creation of a distinct self is sacrificed to the collective mission, and the result is a static symbol rather than a dynamic character. In *The Color Purple,* the collective mission, as imaged by Harper, is sacrificed to the self, and the result is the creation of a character in process, one more complex and thoroughly realized than Iola Leroy. Iola's energy is invariably directed outside of herself, and the narrative's action is, correspondingly, social and public in emphasis. Celie's energy, on the other hand, is primarily directed inward, and the narrative action of *The Color Purple* is correspondingly psychological, personal, and intimate in emphasis.

Unlike *Iola Leroy, The Color Purple* fits primarily into the private paradigm, suggested by its choice of the epistolary mode—by definition personal and private—and the finite focus of the Celie letters. One of their most striking features is the conspicuous absence of any reference to the "outside" world. Except for an occasional reference to Macon, Memphis, and one to World War I, the world is shut out. Instead, like epistolary novels generically, *The Color Purple* emphasizes the psychological development of character.

Celie begins her story at age fourteen in the form of letters to God, the only one who can hear her, she thinks. Feeling isolated and ashamed, she tells Him of her life of brutality and exploitation at the hands of men. Writing is all-important to Celie; her last resounding word to her sister Nettie before they separate is "Write."

While Celie's letters are an attempt to communicate with someone outside herself, they also reveal a process of self-examination and self-discovery in much the same way the letter functioned for the protagonists in Richardson's *Clarissa* and *Pamela.* In other words, Celie's growth is chartable through her letters to God, which are essentially letters of self-exploration, enabling her to become connected to her thoughts and feelings. That connection eventually liberates her from a belief in a God outside herself, whom she has always imagined as "Big and old and tall and graybearded and white," and acquaints her with the God inside herself.

The spiritual dimension of Celie's discovery of the God-in-self has striking implications for her experience as a writer—for a writer she is, first and foremost. A self-reflexive novel, *The Color Purple* explicitly allegorizes much about the process and problematics of writing for the black woman. For example, the process by which Celie comes to shift her addressee from God to Nettie suggests much about the relationship between writer and audience and its effect on narrative authority and autonomy, to forceful voice. *The Color Purple* makes clear that the black woman writer has written primarily without an audience capable of accepting and appreciating that the full, raw, unmediated range of the black woman's story could be appropriate subject matter for art.

The Celie letters addressed to God indicate that she is a writer without an audience, without a hearing, a predicament she recognizes only after discovering that her husband has intercepted and hidden in a trunk letters her sisiter Nettie has written to her from Africa over a thirty-year period. As Celie recovers from the shock, she announces to Shug that she has ceased to write to God, now realizing that "the God I been praying and writing to is a man. And act just like all the other mens I know. Trifling, forgitful, and lowdown." When Shug cautions Celie to be quiet, lest God hear her, Celie responds defiantly, "Let 'im hear me, I say. If he ever listened to poor colored women the world would be a different place."

Celie's decision to cease writing to God and to begin writing to her sister Nettie marks a critical point in both her psychological development and in her development as a writer. Significantly, before Celie discovers that God is not listening, her letters to him record passive resignation, silence, and blind faith in his benevolence. She can suffer abuses in this life, she confides to Sofia, because "[it] soon be over. . . . Heaven last all ways." In these letters, she identifies with Squeak who speaks in a "little teenouncy voice." She "stutters," "mutters"; her "throat closes," and "nothing come[s] out but a little burp." Celie admits that she "can't fix [her] mouth to say how [she] feel[s]." Appropriately, these letters record a distinct split between what she thinks and what she feels and says. For example, when Nettie leaves for Africa, she expresses sadness at leaving Celie to be buried by the burden of caring for Mr. ——— and his children. Celie writes, "It's worse than that, I think. If I was buried, I wouldn't have to work. But I just say, Never mine, never mine, long as I can spell G-o-d I got somebody along." Similarly, when Celie thinks she sees her daughter Olivia at the drygoods store in town, she strikes up a conversation with the woman who has custody of the child. The woman makes a joke about the child's name, and Celie writes: "I git it and laugh. It feel like to split my face." The image of the split functions here, as in so many novels by women, as a sign of the character's tenuous sense of self, of identity, if you will. The image objectifies the split between Celie's outer and inner selves that will ultimately be made whole as the novel develops.

It is further significant that none of the letters addressed to God is signed. In their anonymity, their namelessness, the letters further underscore Celie's lack of individuality. When she begins to write to Nettie, however, her inner and outer selves become connected. Her thoughts are fused with her feelings, her actions, her words, and the letters assume a quality of force and authority, at times of prophecy, as seen in Celie's conversation with Mr. ——— before she leaves for Memphis:

Until you do right by me, everything you touch will crumble.

He laugh. Who you think you is? he say. You can't curse nobody. Look at you. You black, you pore, you ugly, you a woman. Goddam, he say, you nothing at all.

Until you do right by me, I say, everything you even dream about will fail.

Celie concludes: "I'm pore, I'm black, I may be ugly and can't cook. . . . But I'm here." Thus these letters addressed to Nettie are alternately signed "Your sister, Celie" and "Amen," expressions of ratification, of approval, of assertion, of validation. The suggestion is clear: Celie is now ratifying, asserting, and validating her own words, her own worth, and the authority of her own experience. Celie's validation of her linguistic experience is especially important, for it is so critical to the establishment of her own literary voice.

Celie's story underscores sharply, as Iola's does not, the argument of many students of language that "ordinary" discourse can be continuous with "poetic," or "literary" discourse, and that any assumed distinctions between the two are unsupported by linguistic research. For considerations of Afro-American literature that argument is especially critical, for if both forms of discourse can be continuous with each other, the need for an external and legitimating filter is eliminated. Jerene and Darlene, Celie's helpers in her Folkspants, Unlimited enterprise, in wanting to teach her to "talk correctly," imply the popular belief that ordinary black speech must be "corrected" in order to have literate status, but Celie comes to understand that "only a fool would want you to talk in a way that feel peculiar to your mind."

The narrative links Celie's refusal to talk in a manner peculiar to her mind with a change of audience. That refusal—the mark of psychic wholeness as well as of narrative authority and autonomy—is licensed and buttressed by the sympathetic audience she imagines. Significantly, Celie directs her letters away from God, a "public" and alien audience outside herself and toward her sister Nettie, a private, familial, familiar, and receptive audience. The qualitative differences between the letters to God and those to Nettie imply a causal connection between a receptive audience (imaged as one with "kinship" ties to the writer) and the emergence of a forceful, authoritative, and self-validating narrative voice.

III

The question which immediately arises, however, is: Given this connection, what explains the comparative lack of force and authority in Nettie's letters? How do they serve the narrative? Early reviewers of *The Color Purple* rightly saw Nettie's letters as lackluster and unengaging compared to Celie's. While they advance the narrative line, they disrupt the immediacy and momentum of Celie's letters. That notwithstanding, Nettie's letters do function to unify the narrative by repeating its central images and concerns. Most significantly, they continue and expand its commentary on the act of writing and the role that context and circumstances play in the creative process.

But the Nettie letters have perhaps the most striking and intriguing implications for Alice Walker as a writer, for her discovery of her own voice. For Walker, as for as many women writers, the process of that discovery begins with thinking back through and reclaiming her female ancestors. While much has been made (with Walker's encouragement) of Walker's obvious debt to Zora Neale Hurston, there has been virtually no acknowledgment that she owes an equal though different debt to black women writers before Hurston. In "Saving the Life That Is Your Own: The Importance of Models in the Artist's Life," Walker admits that her need to know the oral stories *told* by her female ancestors, stories which Hurston transcribed in her folklore and writing, was equal to her need to know the stories *written* by nineteenth-century black women. Even if they had to be transformed or rejected altogether, the experiences that these earlier writers recorded were crucial to Walker's development as a writer.

Walker notes in an interview with Gloria Steinem that "writing *The Color Purple* was writing in my first language," in its "natural, flowing way." In the novel, that language is Celie's, not Nettie's, indicating that Walker identifies her own writing voice with Celie's. However, that identification does not require that she reject Nettie's. Both the oral and the literate are parts of her literary ancestry, and she conjoins them in the Celie and Nettie letters, respectively, reinforcing one of the novel's central themes: female bonding. Together their letters form a study of converging contrasts that are homologous with the relationship between Frances Harper and Alice Walker.

As their letters reveal, the correspondences between the sisters' experiences are striking, even strained and over-determined. Much of what Nettie writes to Celie describing the situation in Africa—the breakdown of male/female relationships, the power of male domination, and the bonding between women—is replicated in Celie's experiences in the rural south. Nettie writes to Celie of the paved roads in Africa; Celie, to her, of those in Georgia. Nettie describes her round and windowless African hut; Celie, Shug's difficulty including windows in her plans for a round house in Memphis.

While the sisters' experiences converge at these critical points, they diverge at others, perhaps most importantly in the voice, content, and style of their epistles. While Celie's letters are written in black folk English and record her personal traits and near defeat, Nettie's, written in more formal language, record the trials and decimation of a people and their culture. Nettie's personal relationships with Samuel, Corrine, and their children seem dwarfed and insignificant compared to the destruction of the Olinka culture. In other words, while the majority of Celie's letters can be said to represent the private paradigm of the Afro-American female tradition in the novel, the majority of Nettie's letters can be said to represent the public paradigm. I say "majority" because Nettie's letters to Celie are, significantly, in two distinct linguistic registers. Her first letters to Celie focus on personal matters and are largely indistinguishable from Celie's letters:

> Dear Celie, the first letter say,
>   You've got to fight and get away from Albert. He ain't no good.
>   When I left you all's house, walking, he followed me on his horse. When we was well out of sight of the house he caught up with me and started trying to talk. You know how he do.

The next letter reads: "I keep thinking it's too soon to look for a letter from you. And I know how busy you is with all Mr. ———'s children." Shortly after these letters, Nettie writes to Celie of the events leading to her decision to go to Africa as a missionary, explaining her agreement to help build a school in exchange for furthering her education. That letter reads: "When Corrine and Samuel asked me if I would come with them and help them build a school . . . I said yes. But only if they would teach me everything they knew to make me useful as a missionary. . . . They agreed to this condition, and my real education began at that time." From this point on, Nettie's letters shift from the personal to the social, the political, the historical. They assume the quality of lecture and oration, losing the intimacy more appropriate in correspondence to a sister. Nettie's has become an educated imagination, shaped by the context within which she moves as well as her function as a missionary in a colonizing enterprise.

Although Celie and Nettie are separated by a continent, by their lifestyles—one ordinary, the other exceptional—and by the style of their epistles—oral and literate—these separate realities become integrated in the novel and held in sustained equilibrium. Each sister is allowed to exist as an independent entity; each, through her letters, allowed to speak in her own voice without apology, mediation, or derision.

While one might expect it, there is no apology, mediation, or derision on Walker's part for her predecessor Frances Harper, the impulses of whose work she incorporates in the voice and experiences of Nettie. Reminiscent of Iola, Nettie guards her virginity. Her self-conscious and ambiguous description of her developing passion for Samuel brings to mind Iola's reticence about sexuality. In one letter Nettie recounts to Celie her "forward behavior" with Samuel. As she and Samuel embrace, Nettie writes, "concern and passion soon ran away with us," and "I was transported by ecstasy in Samuel's arms."

But the more important resemblance between Nettie and Iola is their sacrifice of personal needs and wishes for a larger social purpose. Nettie is swept up in a social movement and energized by its unofficial motto: "OUR COMMUNITY COVERS THE WORLD." She is, in her words, working for the "uplift of black people everywhere." The concept of racial uplift, of corporate mission, so central to *Iola Leroy,* is explicit in Nettie's letters and acts as counterpoint to Celie's more private and personal concerns. Further, together these letters objectify the pattern of intertextual relations among black women writers, a pattern which departs from what Harold Bloom describes in *The Anxiety of Influence* and *A Map of Misreading.* Bloom's linear theory of the oedipal war between literary fathers and sons does not obtain among black women writers, many of whom reverently acknowledge their debts to their literary foremothers. Unlike Bloom, I see literary influence, to borrow from Julia Kristeva, in the intertextual sense, each text in dialogue with all previous texts, transforming and retaining narrative patterns and strategies in endless possibility.

This pattern of literary influence from Harper to Walker is also distinct from that among black men. Henry Louis Gates's description of intertextuality in his discussion of Richard Wright, Ralph Ellison, and Ishmael Reed, for example, characterizes the formal relations between them as largely adversarial and parodic. While there is certainly much to parody in Harper's *Iola Leroy*—most notably, the stilted language that accompanied the uplift concept—Walker refrains from doing so, and perhaps therein lies a fundamental distinction between Afro-American male and female literary relations. We might argue that Walker has transformed and updated the concept of "uplift" associated almost exclusively with Harper and her generation, for a kind of uplift functions metaphorically in *The Color Purple.* The novel elevates the folk forms of rural and Southern blacks to the status of art. In a similar fashion, it elevates the tradition of letters and diaries, commonly considered a "female" tradition (and therefore inferior), from the category of "non-art" to art.

IV

But while Walker retains uplift as metaphor in *The Color Purple,* she rejects the burden it imposes on the writer, a burden that black writers have shouldered to excess throughout their literary history in fulfillment of a corporate mission. Certainly a major consequence of that mission for the writers of Harper's generation was a homogenized literary era that inhibited the writers' discovery of their unique voices.

The Color Purple is rich with images of voice, of singing, that complement and comment upon the novel's controlling metaphor of writing as seen in Celie's description of an exchange between Shug and Mary Agnes, aka Squeak:

> Shug say to Squeak, I mean, Mary Agnes, You ought to sing in public.
> Mary Agnes say, *Naw*. She think cause she don't sing big and broad like Shug nobody want to hear her. But Shug say she wrong.
> What about all them funny voices you hear singing in church? Shug say. What about all them sounds that sound good but they not the sounds you thought folks could make? What bout that?

Mary Agnes does go on to become a blues singer in her own right, singing in her own unimitative voice. Moreover, the narrative clearly implies that she can sing in public only when she discovers her own name (Mary Agnes, not Squeak) and her own "private," unique voice.

The Color Purple implies the regrettable fact that black writers have not been permitted the freedom to discover and then to speak in their unique voices largely because they have been compelled to use their art for mainly propagandistic (public) purposes. Ntozake Shange makes that point in her collection of poems *nappy edges*: "We, as a people, or as a literary cult, or a literary culture / have not demanded singularity from our writers. we could all sound the same, come from the same region. be the same gender. born the same year." She adds, "we assume a musical solo is a personal statement / we think the poet is speakin for the world, there's something wrong there, a writer's first commitment is to the piece itself," then comes the political commitment.

The work of Frances Harper implies no such choice. Her age demanded the reverse. The morality of black women was being rampantly impugned, black people were being lynched in numbers and were suffering rank injustices. Unarguably, the writer lifted the pen to uplift the race.

Walker sacrifices the impulse to uplift the race, although hers is no less than Harper's a project whose aim is cultural transformation. She envisions a new world—at times utopian in dimension—in which power relations between men and women, between the colonizers and the colonized are reconfigured to eliminate domination and promote cooperation. Further, in the structural arrangement of the letters—Celie's first, then Nettie's, then alternation of the two—she shows that self-development and corporate mission are not mutually exclusive but can be consonant with each other.

The Color Purple reflects Walker's awareness that the literary manifestations of racial uplift (or any social movement for that matter) are explained, in part, by the relationship between writer and audience. Unlike Harper, Walker could choose to ignore the fact that her audience was predominantly white, a choice strongly influenced, as was Harper's, by the social realities and literary circumstances of her place and time. We might pinpoint specifically the emergence of black nationalism in the 1960s and 1970s and the rise of the women's movement that followed closely on its heels. During this period, the writers and critics who formed the cultural arm of the larger political movement became convinced, as Houston Baker notes, that "their real audience, like the nation to come, was black." Accordingly, they directed "their energies to the creation of a new nation and their voices to an audience radically different from any [they] had ever conceived of," a black audience which would include, as never before, ordinary blacks from ghetto communities. They fashioned a critical methodology termed the "black aesthetic," a "system of isolating and evaluating the artistic works of black people which reflect the special character and imperatives of black experience."

Like the black aestheticians, those women in the vanguard of the women's movement's second wave called for women's release from unreal and oppressive loyalties. Feminist criticism became one literary manifestation of that political stance. Similar in spirit and methodology to the largely male-dominated black aesthetic movement, feminist critics likewise repudiated and subverted what they considered alien, male-created literary standards, and began to describe and analyze a female aesthetic which reflected women's unique culture.

It is necessary to note that, ironically, in their earliest formulations, the objectives and practices of both the black aesthetic and feminist criticism often came dangerously close to insisting on a different and no less rigid set of creative standards. Despite their own prescriptive leanings, however, these two modes of critical inquiry must be credited with opening up unprecedented possibilities for black and women writers. In isolating and affirming the particulars of black and female experience, they inspired and authorized writers from those cultures to sing in their different voices and to imagine an audience that could hear the song.

The narrative strongly implies that that audience is comprised mainly of Walker's "sisters," other black women. Its structure and plot—two black sisters writing to each other—lend support. It is not that Walker can or even desires to exclude writers outside this group; it is simply that she addresses her letters to them.

I am all too aware that the theoretical argument that Alice Walker addresses her letters first to black women raises at least two glaring empirical paradoxes: the novel has been enormously successful with a very diverse readership, a large part of which is white and often criticized by those to whom it seems addressed. However, the premise is recommended and supported by a major thread in the novel's plot: the act of reading letters that are written and intended for other eyes.

Just as the novel's letters lend themselves to Walker's reflexive depiction of the act of writing, they simultaneously lend themselves to her reflexive depiction of the act of reading. They offer a compelling model of the relationship Walker implies between herself and her readers, her own correspondents, her audience of "kissin' friends" who enter by the "intimate gate," to borrow from Zora Neale Hurston. In choosing them as her auditors and their experiences as her story, she has made the private public, and in the process created a new literary space for the black and the female idiom against and within a traditionally Eurocentric and androcentric literary history.

JOHN F. CALLAHAN

The Hoop of Language:
Politics and the Restoration
of Voice in Meridian

"I have experienced a revolution," Alice Walker writes in 1973, "unfinished, without question, but one whose new order is everywhere on view in the South." Walker's experience of revolutionary change intensifies her preoccupation "with the spiritual survival, the survival *whole* of [her] people" (*Interviews with Black Writers,* edited by John I. O'Brien). In *Meridian* Walker pursues the African-American subconscious through the inner voice of a young black woman. She confronts the desperation of the late 1960s and early 1970s when, despite the successes of the Civil Rights movement, Black Elk's words seemed a fitting epigraph for the chaos of America. "The nation's hoop is broken and scattered," he said, grieving over the violent end of his people's dream. On a preliminary page of *Meridian* Walker uses Black Elk's words to announce the political and spiritual desolation that must be overcome in the lives of individuals and society. Symptomatically, for her generation, the hoop of language—that continuum of voice going back to slavery and embodied in fiction by *The Autobiography of Miss Jane Pittman*—was broken and scattered. During the 1960s, as James Alan McPherson notes in *Elbow Room,* words "seemed to have become detached from emotion and no longer flowed to the rhythm of passion." That is the condition Walker and her character seek to overcome in *Meridian* as, together, they work to restore language, self, and nation.

For Walker and Meridian, silence and solitude become an essential prologue to speech and social action. Like Invisible Man, though for different reasons and in a different context, Meridian suspends the pursuit of eloquence.

From *In the African-American Grain.* © 1988 by the Board of Trustees of the University of Illinois. University of Illinois Press, 1988.

153

Like Zora Neale Hurston, Walker is a friend to her character. But she does not tell the story in a frame directly associated with the oral tradition. For one thing, she knows that Meridian, though brave and eloquent, is too preoccupied with her survival and the struggle of the people she works among, to focus on telling her story. For another thing, Meridian goes in search of a loving political voice after she finds that revolutionary rhetoric is often a mask for hate and emptiness and that the debased political language of the late 1960s upholds the condition of violence, egotism, and injustice she and her radical contemporaries seek to overthrow. To heal her soul and restore the spirit of words, Meridian listens and responds to the voices of the dead, particularly those black and Native American ancestors who haunt Walker's Georgia as they did Jean Toomer's. Consequently, the story unfolds gradually through visions and in remembered snatches of song and speech stitched together by Meridian's simultaneously meditative and political voice. And for her part, Alice Walker's pursuit of intimacy with her readers begins in her relationship with Meridian.

Meridian Hill is "an exemplary, flawed revolutionary" for her time, Walker has remarked. In the tradition of runaway slaves who became conductors on the underground railroad, she believes that "escape for the body and freedom for the soul [go] together." Therefore, according to Walker, she is a "revolutionary worth following." As a novelist, Walker *follows* Meridian by taking her form from the labyrinth of Meridian's mind. "I wanted to do something like a crazy quilt, or like *Cane*," she says, "something that works on the mind in different patterns." Or "like a collage," she adds, "like the work of one of my favorite artists, Romare Bearden" (quoted in *Black Women Writers at Work*). Like the gifted, often unknown black women who design and sew crazy quilts and like Toomer and, especially, Bearden, Walker's technique is (as Ellison writes of Bearden) "eloquent of the sharp breaks, leaps in consciousness, distortion, paradoxes, reversals, telescoping of time and surreal blending of styles, values, hopes and dreams which characterize much of Negro American history." Walker's discontinuous, apparently incongruous voices fuse personal, racial, and national history with myth so that, as Calvin Tomkins observes of Bearden's *Odysseus Collages,* "the images that he chooses and the manner in which he places them create vibrations, waves that carry us into regions not *visited but remembered,* dimly or vividly, from previous experience with the myth." In *Meridian's* case the myth is the myth of deliverance. True rescue, as Meridian Hill's story demonstrates, lies within those reaches of self beyond the babel of fashionably militant tongues.

To Meridian voice is a blessing and call-and-response an act performed in kinship with what is sacred to self, others, and the world. While those around her demand *correct* responses, she struggles to know the *right* response to dilemmas of personal and political experience. The ascent aspired to in Walker's title and Meridian's name requires a long painful descent into what Zora Neale Hurston calls the "infinity of conscious pain" (*Their Eyes Were Watching God* [hereafter cited as *Eyes*]). Although the effort alienates her from her contemporaries and brings her to the brink of madness and death, Meridian practices a politics that is "an expression of love" and not "politicized hate." Like her forebears in history and fiction, Meridian learns to tell false voices from true ones. She begins at home with her own voice, perhaps as one of those who has exhausted what Invisible Man calls "not much, but some—of the human greed and smallness, yes, and the fear and superstition" that keeps many Americans "running all over themselves" and the world. Like her rhetorically militant contemporaries, Meridian knows the tricks of speech, the *retrick* of a glib, false call-and-response. But to her, possession of a true personal voice is bound up with the creation of an authentic public and political voice. Like Janie Crawford, Meridian distinguishes true from false texts in her intimate life, and like Invisible Man and Miss Jane Pittman, she pursues connections between her inmost individual identity and her responsibility as a citizen.

II

Like Ellison in *Invisible Man,* Walker makes the chronology of her novel's opening mostly a matter of consciousness. She follows Meridian's mind back and forth through time in response to what is happening in the immediate present. But the historical narrative moment anticipates the nation's Bicentennial and leads Meridian to reconsider the old and new meaning of America's fate as a revolutionary society. Namely, Truman Held, Meridian's former Civil Rights coworker and briefly, *abortively,* her lover, interrupts work on his Bicentennial statue of Crispus Attucks and drives all night from New York to Georgia to see Meridian. Their encounter prompts her to reexperience the significance of language for personality and politics. In their conversation Meridian tries to persuade Truman to open the interior of his mind and memory:

> "I know you grieve by running away. By pretending you were
> never there."
> "When things are finished it is best to leave."
> "And pretend they were never started."
> "Yes."

> "But that's not possible."
> (*Meridian*)

Ironically, Truman's affirmation closes out dialogue, whereas Meridian's denial calls for consciousness in which the past informs the present moment.

Truman's silence is evasive, but in her reverie Meridian reenacts the principle of open consciousness learned the hard way nearly ten years before. Truman's cliches, characteristic of many emotional lives in his generation, remind Meridian of similar political evasions from the chaotic years of the late 1960s. In her mind she hears the two direct, apparently simple, self-evident questions posed by some black radical comrades in a former time of "extreme violence, against black dissidents, of the federal government and police," when the officially sanctioned policies of the state seemed to partake of politicized hate. To join the self-proclaimed revolutionaries Meridian must answer *yes* to both questions. She affirms easily and at once her "willingness to die for the Revolution." But she cannot answer the second question: "Will you kill for the Revolution?" Not because she necessarily opposes revolutionary violence, but because instinctively and viscerally, without the intimacy of language and experience that allowed Janie Crawford's "tongue" to be in her "friend's mouf" (*Eyes*), "Meridian's tongue could not manage"(*Meridian*).

Unlike the others, she cannot answer simply as an individual and a contemporary because for her social and political change is bound up with love and with the witnessing, participatory form that belongs to a true community. All the same, like her fellow radicals, Meridian views America as a society in extreme crisis, racially and otherwise, and she is disturbed by her interior dissent from their call. She looks for flaws in herself, not in the vague, unrooted, arrogant phrase, *the* revolution. Consequently, civil war breaks out within her, personified by "a small voice that screamed: 'Something's missing in me. Something's *missing.*'" Meridian is not a coward, far from it, but for her speech is action, the word her sacred bond with herself and her people, her history and theirs. She wishes she could join her contemporaries' call to arms. But because she takes them and their talk of revolution seriously, Meridian meditates on the question at hand in a silent call-and-response of the soul.

While Meridian struggles for the *right* response, the others wait impatiently for the *correct* response. In the break between their call and her response, Meridian discovers why her voice resists her comrades' expectations. Her inability to declare that she will kill for the revolution grows out of experiences in *her* past and the images and voices inside her from *the* African-American past. In her silence she is "not holding on to something from the past, but *held* by something in the past." Unlike many of her contemporaries,

Meridian does not surrender to that easily manipulated instantaneity in which "television became the repository of memory." Instead, her memory mediates between her interrogation in the present situation and those "old black men in the South who, caught by surprise in the eye of a camera, never shifted their position but looked directly back." For these men, whose breed Jean Toomer found in Georgia and Ernest Gaines in Louisiana, courage was a condition of being, a silent autonomy in response to the temptation to present a synthetic face to the world. Never easy, their stoicism hints at an inner ease and confidence, and their eloquent silence encourages Meridian to trust her refusal to speak in a pandering voice. In her mind she also sees and hears "young girls singing in a country choir, their hair shining with brushings and grease, their voices the voices of angels"; girls like these inspired Miss Jane Pittman with their bravery. Like Toomer, Meridian believes "she could actually *hear*" the singers' souls. These images and voices embody Meridian's conscious, reciprocal relationship with the past. She cannot imagine killing except in collaboration with those other black Americans whose lives are the comfort of her soul. For her sake and theirs, she speculates about the cultural consequences of violent politics in an inner voice of moral imagination: "If they committed murder—and to her even revolutionary murder was murder—what would the music be like?"

As she feels the hostile silence of her interlocutors, Meridian descends to another painful level of being. Here, too, she struggles against the loss of love she associates with failing to respond to the wishes of others. In her reverie she again sits in church "drunk as usual with the wonderful music, the voices themselves almost making the words of the songs meaningless." She basks in her father's sweet voice while resisting his wooing of death. But her mother, like the "revolutionary cadre" of the 1960s, demands Meridian's unconditional surrender to authority. In this case authority is not political or spiritual, but religious. Seeing her daughter's tears, Mrs. Hill presses her to "acknowledge Him as our Master." Then as now, Meridian "sat mute, watching her friends walking past her bench, accepting Christ, acknowledging God as their Master." As a consequence, she loses her mother's love but loves her mother in return because of her feeling that it is "death not to love one's mother." To survive, she lives with her mother's scorn as she will bear the rejection of her radical contemporaries rather than barter her soul for a conditional love.

Called back to the present "from a decidedly unrevolutionary past," Meridian struggles to overcome the paradoxical conflict between politics and personality. Her contemporaries, she realizes, "made her ashamed of the past, and yet all of them had shared it," whereas she keeps faith with the sustaining personal warmth of the past as a touchstone of contemporary politics. But she does not reject her comrades; "she felt she loved them," even though "love was not what they wanted, it was not what they needed." As she does with her mother (and also the young men who pursue her sexually), Meridian tries not to offend or alienate, even if she cannot please. Using the familiar pattern of call-and-response, she seeks common ground in the chaos and violence of American life. Slowly, she becomes the lead voice, and the others join her call believing she is about to announce her willingness to "kill for the Revolution":

> "I know I want what is best for black people."
> "That's what we all want!"
> "I know there must be a revolution. . . . "
> "Damn straight!"
> "I know violence *is* as American as cherry pie!"
> "Rap on!"
> "I know nonviolence has failed."

Meridian understands the struggle and the lingo. She has marched and been abused, beaten, and jailed, and she has gone back out on the line. She knows how to speak *to* her contemporaries and *for* them—so much so that they answer her rhythmic, repetitive *I knows* with one voice.

Her words invoke the simplicities of the current situation, but her pause implies its complexities as well as her refusal to enter the country of false eloquence. But Meridian's audience rejects the intimate, contemplative note her brief silence brings to the dialogue. They seek capitulation from her, not conversation with her. But their failure to let her respond individually to the collective call—"Then you will kill for the Revolution, not just die for it?" —chases her back to the private region of her mind. "I don't know" she says, and her truthful answers to this and subsequent questions make her an outcast. She is the victim of psychological political aggression reminiscent of Janie Starks's wifely experience in *Their Eyes Were Watching God*: "Mah own mind had tuh be squeezed and crowded out tuh make room for yours in me." Yet Meridian is not entirely a casualty. When a former friend among the revolutionaries asks her condescendingly, "What will you do? Where will you go?" Meridian keeps faith with those images and voices that persist in the depths of her mind as companions to her identity:

> "I'll go back to the people, live among them like Civil Rights workers used to do."
> "You're not serious?"
> "Yes," she said. "I am serious."

Unlike the others, because of her past (and her self-restoring sense of *the* past), Meridian cannot even pretend to disconnect political work from personal experience, particularly her surrender of her child and the related loss of her mother as psychological kin. Now in a simple courageous voice Meridian tells this hostile audience her choice: a life and politics committed to love and creation instead of hate and violence. She still does not know definitely whether or not she should or could kill for the revolution or for any other cause. But she does know that her answer must be her people's answer, and she cannot discover either in New York. (In her glossary Walker gives *southern* as a rare meaning for meridian, and Meridian is the name of the Mississippi town in which the murdered black Civil Rights worker, James Cheney, grew up and was buried in 1964.) Like Jean Toomer who went to Georgia seeking a loving artistic voice, Meridian goes south in quest of a loving political voice, rooted in her life and the people's—what Robert Hayden, in his poem for Frederick Douglass, calls "this beautiful and terrible . . . needful thing" of freedom. But Meridian alters Hayden's idea of "lives grown out of [Douglass's] life" (*Angle of Ascent*). Her new life will grow from the people, provided she is able "to see them, to be with them, to understand them *and herself*," while, true to her vision, they become next of kin "who now fed her and tolerated her and also, in a fashion, *cared* about her" (*Meridian,* my italics).

As Walker tells of Meridian's gradual personal revolution, her voice achieves a muted simplicity and eloquence. Her relationship with Meridian, like the people's, is sometimes tentative and always respectful of difference and otherness. Like a friend, she follows Meridian, sometimes up close in participation, and at other times from a distance in acts of witness, while Meridian digs out her story in response to her life's slow revolutionary trajectory after the sudden fits and starts of the 1960s. For although revolutions sometimes culminate in explosions, lasting change is prepared for gradually by grubby actions like those Meridian performs in one little Southern town after another. And true revolutions are never finished; like Meridian's life and story, they illustrate an elliptical pattern of continual change.

In her form Walker experiments with the idea of revolution. Her narrative follows a meridian along which Meridian's "mind-voice directs the flow of thought and action" (Barbara Christian, *Black Women Novelists*). By choice Meridian lacks a platform and an audience, but as she absorbs the other characters' voices, they, too, become threads in the crazy quilt of the novel. Because so many of her characters, especially those of Meridian's generation, live in fragments, Walker's narrative collage is often deliberately attenuated, as if she were guiding readers through individual and national labyrinths.

Nevertheless, *Meridian* is a meditation on wholeness and as such Walker's confession of faith. Its embrace of silence as a nest for speech protests against and overthrows false voices as the first act toward restoration of the word and the creation of genuine dialogue. By shunning the traditional office of storyteller, Walker, like Meridian, invites the "rest of them" (and us) to participate in a generation's unfinished personal and political work.

III

Jarringly, almost violently, Walker fires a succession of names at her readers in the no-man's land between Meridian's life in the present and her reconstruction of the past:

MEDGAR EVERS/JOHN F. KENNEDY/MALCOM X/
MARTIN LUTHER KING/ROBERT KENNEDY/CHE
GUEVARA/PATRICE LUMUMBA/GEORGE JACKSON/
CYNTHIA WESLEY/ADDIE MAE COLLINS/DENISE
MCNAIR/CAROLE ROBERTSON/VIOLA LIUZZO.

Like sounds from an automatic rifle, the slashes signify the political assassinations that open, close, and recapitulate the 1960s. The last five names belong to "those [four] black girls / blown up / in that Alabama church" (Michael S. Harper, "American History") in 1963 and a Northern white woman shot to death while driving Civil Rights workers back to Selma after the march to Montgomery in 1965. All were private persons whose names Walker restores to consciousness. Others, too, are victims of violence, and in *Meridian* Walker explores the relationship between voicelessness and the extremes of violence often visited on women and children. And among the young women in the novel an urge to violence sometimes shuts out the healing, sustaining presences from the past and leads to self-destructive acts performed in response to false inner voices.

The story of Wile Chile illustrates the obstacles in the way of Meridian's search for a usable voice. Apparently nameless, articulate only with curses, and visibly pregnant, Wile Chile embodies "how alone woman is, because of her body" (Walker, quoted in *Interviews with Black Writers*). After Wile Chile is run over and killed by a speeder, the young women at Saxon College realize instinctively and inarticulately that their fate is bound up with hers. But in their rage at the president's refusal to let them use the college chapel for the funeral, they turn on Sojourner, their protectress—"the largest magnolia tree in the country," an abiding, animate, magical maternal presence. Except for Meridian, the young women no longer remember or care that their ancestors in slavery "claimed the tree could talk, make music, was sacred to birds," and that "in its branches, a hiding slave could not be seen." They forget that the tree shields their lovemaking from detection and, as a ritual ground, offers them solace and strength to offset their vulnerability as women.

Powerless, the young women strike against a living presence signifying womanly power as far back as slavery. For as Meridian learns and shares, the Sojourner tree owes its magnificence to the severed tongue of the slave woman, Louvinie—a master storyteller "whose [family's] sole responsibility was the weaving of intricate tales with which to entrap people who hoped to get away with murder." In America, Louvinie's audience consists of the young Saxon children who "adored her." The last story she is able to tell reverses the familiar terms of slavery. In it, as written down later by one of the older Saxon girls, a very black African man captures "little white children," buries them alive up to their necks, and allows pet snakes to make them playthings. This and perhaps other of Louvinie's "new American stories" express her anger at captivity and also draw a moral and political lesson for the next generation of slaveholders. But the older Saxons fail to tell Louvinie that the youngest member of her audience, "an only son, suffered from an abnormally small and flimsy heart." In the midst of her tale, the boy has a fatal heart attack, and as punishment, "Louvinie's tongue was clipped out at the root." Mutely, she pleads for her tongue lest the singer in her soul be lost forever. Then she ministers to her severed tongue until, during the magically black sun of an eclipse, she buries it beneath "a scrawny magnolia tree" that eventually outgrows all the others even before her death. Among the Saxon students in the 1960s only Meridian understands that Sojourner is the living agent of Louvinie's voice and story—the dead slave's gift of life and eloquence to the black women who come after her. Spiritually, Meridian recognizes, Louvinie refuses to accept powerlessness or voicelessness, even though she is a slave who cannot speak. Louvinie's Sojourner tree also commemorates Sojourner Truth, an escaped slave who defied those white women who tried to deny her right to speak and whose eloquent call-and-response ("And a'n't I a woman?") electrified the 1853 Akron women's rights convention; like Louvinie, her mystical, earthy, sibylline voice exemplifies the struggle for wholeness. In her young womanhood, Meridian, too, like Hurston's Janie Crawford under the pear tree, experiences a oneness that is both cosmic and individual; imaginative and deeply sensuous.

But the young black women fail to respond to Meridian's lone dissenting voice. Though she "begged them to dismantle the president's house instead, in a fury of confusion and frustration they worked all night, and chopped and sawed down, level to the ground, that mighty, ancient, sheltering music tree." True to the story of Louvinie's tongue, the severed tree does not die. From the lives and stories of Louvinie and Sojourner Truth and the immense, intimate presence of the great blooming maternal tree comes a legacy of responsibility in response to oppression and injustice. Bred of the "fury of confusion and frustration," the students' act nevertheless signifies potentiality waiting to be rethought, revoiced, and refocused before personal or social revolution can occur. For when they cut down the Sojourner, these young women turn their anger against themselves and the black maternal tradition. Otherwise, they would have assaulted the literally forbidding authority of the president's house (his patriarchal tree).

For her part, Meridian's ability to speak truly follows from her willingness to identify her mother's false words and still love the person who brought her into the world. As she meditates on her childhood after the Sojourner is cut down, she hears her mother's old unsettling question. "Conscious always of a feeling of guilt, even as a child," Meridian confides in her mother; but in response "her mother would only ask: 'Have you stolen anything?' " In the past these words seemed mechanical, cruel, and immobilizing, but subsequently, when she reconsiders her mother's life, Meridian concludes that "it was for stealing her mother's serenity, for shattering her mother's emerging self that [she] felt guilty from the very first, though she was unable to understand how this could possibly be her fault." Her creativity "refused expression" because of her conviction that marriage and motherhood meant that "her *personal* life was over," Meridian's mother fights "a war against those to whom she could not express her anger or shout, 'It's not fair.' " But like the young women who chop down the Sojourner tree, Mrs. Hill displaces her anger. She uses a false voice and hands on values that have stifled her life. She speaks for her society and, in an act of perverse social allegiance, tells her daughter "things she herself did not believe."

For a while Meridian acts out her mother's distorted, determinist view of a black woman's fate. "Be sweet" is her mother's only sexual counsel, and because Meridian does not know the words are intended as "a euphemism for 'Keep your panties up and your dress down,' " she ends up pregnant and married to a man she neither loves nor desires. Following her son's birth, she dreams "of ways to murder him." A year later when Meridian gives up her child to accept a scholarship to college, her mother tells her only "some kind of monster" would not want her child, "and no daughter of mine is a monster, surely." Characteristically, Mrs. Hill intimidates Meridian with an apologia for her life: " 'I have six children,' she continued self-righteously, 'though I never wanted to have any, and I have raised every one myself.' " To which Meridian's friend Delores responds flippantly: "You probably could have done the same thing in slavery." But as soon as Meridian is away from home, these words trouble her, for she knows that in slavery her mother "would not, automatically, have been allowed to keep [her children], because they would not have belonged to her but to the white person who 'owned' them all." Meridian's honesty replaces her mother's mutually wounding, compliant rationalizations, but she pays a terrible price. At times of strain, as she works to become a serious productive student, she hears a subterranean voice.

"Why don't you die? Why not kill yourself?" the voice asks in another of those questions that lead Meridian to reconsider the terms of her existence. Meridian recognizes this as truly and terribly "her own voice": "It was talking to her, and it was full of hate." Part of her calls for annihilation as a punishment for her failure to "live up to the standard of motherhood that had gone before." She overcomes the urge to suicide in the same way she overcame her previous impulse to kill her son. Then, after her husband left her and their child, the murder of four people, three of them children, at the local Civil Rights headquarters prompted Meridian to volunteer. Now, in her second year at Saxon, she joins the Atlanta Movement and chooses dangerous, non-violent political action over Saxon's finishing school distractions and the turmoil of her mind. Rather than lose her life in a battle with her voice, she pursues a life of her own through participation in the Civil Rights struggle. In extremis, Meridian once again chooses the evolving wider world over the call to violence issued by the false voice in her heart. She recognizes that an absolutely final act of self-preoccupation like suicide is a paltry response to the universe around her and the world of feeling within.

In silent opposition to her voice of self-hate, she remembers moments of ecstatic oneness experienced beneath the Sojourner tree and, before that, at the Sacred Serpent, an Indian burial ground held in a trust of reverent ownership by her father but seized by the government and turned into a tourist attraction that, "now that it belonged to the public, was of course not open to Colored." As she knows the Sojourner partly through remnants of Louvinie's voice and story, she learned to reverence the Sacred Serpent through stories told about her passionate great-grandmother, Feather Mae. Then, in Meridian's time, she and her father also experience ecstasy at the Sacred Serpent. But they have different responses to the experience. For him "the body seemed to drop away, and only the spirit lived, set free in the world. But she was not convinced. It seemed to her that it was a way the living sought to *expand the consciousness of being alive*, there where the ground about them was filled with the dead"(my italics). Ecstasy confirms Meridian's belief in the possibility of fusing body and soul, life and death, in a way that intensifies experience. For her self-respect is bound up with respect for the ancestral presences that inhabit the earth and her consciousness. Moreover, the possibility of personal and sexual wholeness is confirmed by the presence of both the sheltering African-American maternal tree and the equally sheltering Native American paternal serpent. "Minuteness and hugeness"; "sorrow and ecstasy": these words are touchstones to memories of being and feeling that signify Meridian's communion with both African-American and Native American layers of the past in her consciousness. Her continuing awakening fortifies her against extrinsic correspondences to the ragged, violent, maddening fragments of her consciousness. For now in her "waking moments" everywhere in Atlanta she witnesses a patchwork nightmare of violence against black children and old women; "their humility of a lifetime doing them no good." Even more terrifying, she sees interior lives ravaged into blankness: "She saw young black men of great spiritual beauty changed overnight into men who valued nothing."

Meridian also suffers. In her inner civil war she is "too driven to notice" that her hair is falling out or that "her vision sometimes blurred." But the parts of her being do not secede from the whole; somehow, she will live or die an indivisible woman. Meanwhile, as her body responds to the call of her mind's guilt, she feels another factor of stress, a new tension that is more unpredictable, volatile, and incalculable than the others she has experienced in personal and political life. " Besides," she thinks and Walker writes, as if the emotion were an afterthought in the maelstrom of Meridian's consciousness, "she was in love with Truman."

Walker's understatement conveys her generation's casual understanding of passion and, therefore, calls attention to the danger Meridian faces as a woman. Two years earlier Meridian worked with Truman on voter registration in her hometown. There, attacked by white officers of the law, she breaks her disciplined silence only with a cry in her mind, "and the scream was Truman's name." She is *held* by him then, but not in the grip of sexual passion; rather, her interior voice utters a birth pang for both of them. "What she meant by it was that they were at a time and a place in history that forced the trivial to fall away—and they were absolutely together." But although Meridian believed the trivial to have fallen away, the *personal* lives of those in the movement were often marked by stereotypes of the previous decade, the 1950s. Black and white students challenge segregation in the separate but *un*equal public arena of American society, yet their relations as men and women follow old patterns of male dominance and female subservience and sometimes victimization. Namely, when Meridian acts on the basis of an intensely passionate attachment to Truman, she discovers that he is essentially a *true man* still held by unreconstructed urges to power within the old dispensation.

Now, years later, Meridian works through painful memories. For her soul's sake, she does not forget her former, too easy acceptance of Truman on his terms as "the conquering prince." Formerly, she imagined him having personal qualities commensurate with the courage he showed in the Civil Rights movement. But, in truth, Truman, with his French phrases and princely Ethiopian robe, acts as though his political commitment entitles him to be selfish, shallow, and self-indulgent in his private life as a man. For one thing, Truman construes his voice to be dominant and authoritative and misreads Meridian's subtle, simple statements as evidence of inexperience. On one occasion their divergent language prefigures the bitter, tragic consequences of the relationship.

> "Let's not go to the party," he pleaded. "Let's go back to the apartment. Everybody else is here, we'll be alone. I want you."
>
> "I love you," she said.
>
> "And we're going to the party, right?" Truman sat up and ran his fingers through his hair.
>
> "But do you understand?" Meridian asked. "I'm not a prude. Afraid, yes, but not a prude. One day soon we'll be together."
>
> "You're so young," said Truman, getting out and adjusting his robe. "I wish I could make you feel how beautiful it would be with me."
>
> "I feel it, I feel it!" cried Meridian taking his hand and walking up the street.

Truman interprets Meridian's unembarrassed declaration of love as merely a refusal. When she sends out more promising signals, Truman does not hear them, and he does not draw her out as a friend would by asking gently for her story. Instead, he stereotypes her and ignores her point about fear and love, her implied warning about the contingency of passion. At once inside and outside the moment, Meridian responds both to Truman and to her previous painful, empty, and *consequential* sexual experience. Her last words and her gesture of taking his hand promise intimacy in love and discourse, but at the party Truman pursues one of the seductive, white exchange students from the North. At the end of the evening when he takes Meridian home and she invites him in, he declines: " 'Maybe tomorrow night,' he said, stifling a yawn," in smug, callous disregard for *her* sexual need.

Later on, Truman and Meridian consummate their passion but still do not have a true conversation. "Come here, woman, I missed you," he declares on that occasion, but his command is fatuous and unnecessary, "since she was already lying, like a beached fish, across his lap." From Meridian's point of view, they do not make love; rather, "they fucked (she consciously thought of it as that)." Nevertheless, their sexual encounter, though casual for him, is consequential and traumatic for her. Afterward, "she remembered that he had not worn a condom—the only means of contraception she knew." She mentions none of this to Truman, and when she returns from the bathroom, he is gone, again without words or gesture. In their private lives neither Truman nor Meridian confronts the other as directly or effectively as they do in the public context of the Civil Rights movement—Truman because his macho solipsism makes him oblivious to Meridian; Meridian because her upbringing leads her to accept responsibility for sexual consequences as a woman's lot. She does not tell him she is pregnant; in the meantime he returns to the white exchange students. She decides to have an abortion and in an act of grief and rage at the doctor's coarse, criminal proposition has her tubes tied in self-punishment. Like the students who cut down the Sojourner, Meridian turns her anger against her own life-giving potential.

Months later, after the exchange students have left, Truman tries to resume things. Characteristically, his language betrays his assumption that his attention confers identity on Meridian. "Stone fox," he calls her, and "African woman." At first, she responds with an astonished, taut but uncombative civility. But he will not leave her alone. Grotesquely, he cites their sexual encounter as evidence of his prowess and his power to liberate her. "I can make you come," he blurts out. "I almost did it that time, didn't I?" As he continues, Meridian, perhaps remembering the undertaker's assistant from her girlhood, who seemed to fuck with a pornography of voice, "turned away, shame for him, for what he was revealing, making her sick."

As a last resort Meridian asks Truman to respect her privacy and be silent:

> "It's over. Let it stay."
> But he looked at her with eyes of new discovery.
> "You're *beautiful*," he whispered worshipfully. Then he said,
> urgently, "*Have* my beautiful black babies."

His voice puts language in the service of monstrous illusions. Invaded to the quick, Meridian abandons speech as an agent of communication. Truman is no longer someone she can listen or talk to; conversation is out of the question because he does not grant her even a minimal freedom from his narcissistic fantasies. At last, in direct action expressing her experience and identity as a human being and a black woman, she hits him with her book bag again and again in a refrain of wordless protest. This encounter is at once futile, fatal, and, finally, enabling: futile, because of Truman's shallowness, false pride, and hypocrisy, his failure to grasp or accept the responsibility that goes with being human; fatal, because as a man he exercises a certain power over other lives, especially women; and enabling because Meridian's instinctively violent response is therapeutic and restoring. Seeing and hearing that her words fail to penetrate Truman, she turns her anger outward silently and effectively. Taking her own advice, she retaliates against Truman's distorted masculine assertion of power. She will no longer allow the tree of her life and voice to be diminished by the words or actions of Truman or anyone else.

IV

Meridian's extrinsic act of womanly self-assertion leads to interior rejuvenation and reconciliation. Without warning, as she is about to graduate, she experiences "blue spells" of body and soul. Characteristically, she does not talk about her condition but in the privacy of her mind "felt as if a warm, strong light bore her up and that she was a beloved part of the universe." Formerly, Meridian's feelings of benevolent oneness came in response to powerful, unfathomable natural presences like the Sacred Serpent or the Sojourner; now she is transported by a serene energy in her own being. Ecstasy's promise is illumination and intimacy, its cost frailty and illness. To heal her soul, Meridian risks her body. Because her mother is not there, she does the work of reconciliation with Miss Winter, a teacher from her hometown whose insistence on teaching jazz and spirituals and blues earns her the enmity of the college administration and marks her as one of those courageous black women from Meridian's childhood who were always "imitating Harriet Tubman—escaping to become something unheard of."

As Miss Winter tends her, Meridian remembers an earlier occasion when the older woman intervened on her behalf. At a high school oratorical competition, "Meridian was reciting a speech that extolled the virtues of the Constitution and praised the superiority of The American Way of Life." In the middle of the speech she stops, seemingly because of a memory lapse but in reality, as she tries to explain to her mother, because "for the first time she really listened to what she was saying, knew she didn't believe it, and was so distracted by the revelation that she could not make the rest of her speech." Her mother does not listen; instead, she tells her daughter to trust in God. Coming upon Meridian, Miss Winter tells her, in effect, to trust her voice's impulse to halt a speech false to her sense of the truth. "It's the same one they made me learn when I was here," she tells Meridian, "and it's no more true now than it was then." To Meridian, then and now, Miss Winter, though single and childless, belongs to the tradition of nourishing, nurturing black women; she, too, has an identity in relation to African-American maternal history. Namely, her healing presence inspires Meridian's vision of her mother's place in the African-American maternal lineage. "Mrs. Hill," Meridian now acknowledges, "had persisted in bringing them all (the children, the husband, the family, the race) to a point far beyond where she, in her mother's place, would have stopped." For the first time Meridian sees her mother as a *giant* in an impersonal historical way rather than in the child's accustomed sense of her parent as a magnified, remote, but intensely personal presence. Almost despite her conscious intention, Mrs. Hill carries on the tradition she has not fully understood or accepted but has absorbed from her great-great-grandmother who three times stole back her sold-away children; from her great-grandmother who painted such lovely, arresting decorations on barns she was able to buy her family's freedom; and from her mother who at night trudged off to do others' washing so she could send her daughter to school.

Meridian does not tell this story of her maternal history to Miss Winter. But when she dreams that her mother is about to drop her into the sea—perhaps the equivalent of Mrs. Hill forcing Meridian to sink or swim alone in womanly matters of survival—Miss Winter comes forward and lovingly performs the motherly office:

> "Mama, I love you. Let me go," she whispered, licking the salt from her mother's black arms.
> Instinctively, as if Meridian were her own child, Miss Winter answered, close to her ear on the pillow, "I forgive you."

Unlike Janie in *Their Eyes Were Watching God,* who becomes autonomous only after she realizes that she hates her grandmother, Meridian breaks free only when she feels and declares her love for her mother. That bond, which she chooses freely in her time and place, allows her to call on her dream image of her mother to let her go. And Miss Winter responds in a voice able to mediate between Meridian and Mrs. Hill. She completes the ritual of exorcism that Mrs. Hill could not do with her daughter. Danger is bound up with intimacy, the dream implies, and having voiced love for her mother, Meridian prepares to enter the world on her terms. At stake is her place in the continuum of black women's struggle.

But as so often happens, Meridian's new kinship with her mother's generation costs her the allegiance of a contemporary. For at the moment of Meridian's reemergence, her friend and roommate, Anne-Marion, denies her. "I cannot afford to love you," she tells Meridian in an act of cruel calculation, and in her unearned surety passes absolute historical judgment. "Like the idea of suffering, itself, you are obsolete." But despite her spoken renunciation, Anne-Marion cannot *write* off Meridian. On the contrary, after

Meridian goes back South in disgrace with the cadre of polemical revolutionaries, Anne-Marion "discovered herself writing letters to her, making inquiries month after month to find out which town she lived in and to which address she should send her letters." She writes "out of guilt and denial and rage," but she writes. She begins to accept responsibility for the painful, shared story unfolding somewhere inside her and the others as well as Meridian. Somehow she knows that her act of denial actually affirms and sustains them both. Like that great music tree, the Sojourner, Meridian is strong enough to absorb the blows. Nevertheless, Meridian responds to Anne-Marion with silence, but it is the rich silence of potential responsiveness and collaboration. For she knows that in her generation the spoken word is still tethered to ideology, the written word too self-reflexively therapeutic to restore a reciprocal personal and political communication. Through her silence and her solitary life of action Meridian prepares a nest for the scarcely alive voices of her generation, a secret refuge where they can listen to the spirit of the word.

V

Meanwhile the promise of personality and politics turns into triviality and pathology in the lives of the characters and the nation. Truman marries Lynne Rabinowitz, "the last of the exchange students," but their vicarious, prurient motives doom the relationship and signal a general condition of emptiness. For Lynne, "the black people of the South were Art," and Truman gravitates toward the white exchange students because, in addition to fulfilling a long-tabooed sexuality, "they read *The New York Times*." Even before their young daughter, Camara, is sexually assaulted and murdered, Truman and Lynne separately look to Meridian for solace and strength. With her as a moral guide, they slowly come to see themselves and others in the world as individuals who happen to be black or white, male or female, not incidentally or deterministically but consequentially and dynamically. This acknowledgment of human personality leads to reconsideration of what it means to be black or white, male or female, in contemporary America. Truman, for instance, revolves painfully toward a new identity as a man. But he needs Meridian to remind him that confessions are *useful*, rather than self-congratulatory, when they lead to reformation of values. Thus, when Truman calls Meridian "the woman I should have married and didn't," her scrupulously responsive voice corrects him. " 'Should have *loved*, and didn't,' she murmured," and the truthful force of her words shrivels him in his formerly most prized and proudest place, namely, "he felt a shrinking, a retreating of his balls: He wanted her still, but would not have wanted (or been able) to make love to her." In order to be free and a friend to Meridian or any other woman Truman must purge his predatory, proprietary sexuality, and his *temporary* incapacity seems bound up with his need to create a whole personality.

His first act of liberation involves hearing Meridian's "voice of instruction." With her help he reconstructs his past repugnance at the discovery that she has had a son and given him up. He examines his values and motives impersonally, for his sake and not any longer from a hope that turning over a new leaf will win him Meridian. In Truman's and Lynne's lives politics has been an expression of desire, not love, and their desire comes more from exigent, desperate need than from any spontaneous overflow of self. Theirs is a sexuality reinforcing incompleteness rather than tending toward wholeness. For them and others politics debases sexuality, and sexuality distorts political impulse. Private and public experience are reversed with disastrous, destructive consequences. In Lynne's case, although "she often warned herself" that "I will pay for this" because "it is probably a sin to think of a people as Art," she fails to heed her inner moral voice. "And yet," Walker and Meridian testify, "she would stand perfectly still and the sight of a fat black woman singing to herself in a tattered yellow dress, her voice rich and full of yearning, was always—God forgive her, black folks forgive her—the same weepy miracle that Art always was for her." Walker's interjection repeats the old imperative and adds a new one. Black folks need to forgive Lynne; God cannot do it, and she cannot do it by herself.

Lynne, to overcome her glibness of spirit, needs to understand the human agency of black people. Gradually, she learns to speak in a voice compatible with her experience. As a Northern white woman abstractly worshipful of black American *images,* she marries one black man, is raped by another, his friend, and in pathetic misdirected retaliation sleeps around, taunting black women with her long-tabooed sexuality. Later, in her slow passage to companionability and intimacy with Meridian, Lynne works through secondhand idioms to a language genuinely hers. At times she speaks in tones "affecting a Southern belle accent"; at others a hostile imitation of black American speech: "So get up on me, nigger." Helped by Meridian's generous patience, Lynne reviews her life more in silence than in speech until at last she and Meridian understand each other and talk, "intimately, like sisters."

Before this breakthrough, Lynne frees herself from many illusions and stereotypes about black men and white women and, implicitly, black women, too. From her naive and sinister view of black folks as Art, she comes to regard them as varied, variable human beings whose responses to experience differ from both her dreams and her nightmares. For example, she is amazed to be the object of Tommy Odds's resentment when he loses an arm to a racist sniper's bullet. She misinterprets his calculation and hate when he shows up determined to possess her *by any means necessary*. Because of her sentimental ideology about black people, she is unprepared for the pathological form of his desolation. Grotesquely, as he is quick to sense, she pities him his blackness—"the one thing that gives me some consolation in this stupid world, and she thinks she has to make up for it out of the bountifulness of her pussy." Odds is cruel, his spirit hard and sharp as a razor, and he penetrates her because in her simultaneously self-denying, self-aggrandizing pity, she fails to take advantage of "a moment when she knew she could force him from her." Until much later, Lynne substitutes false pity for apprehension of another person's actuality. Odds acts out his sickness, not hers, and his is not about being black. But Lynne has not confronted her Jewish family and background; instead, she runs away into the arms of her *ideas* about black people. Her problem is vicariousness. She seizes simple, fixed, final versions of reality because of her predicament, not the African-American condition.

The day after her rape the simple manly voice of Altuna Jones rescues Lynne from her embrace of bestial stereotypes. Returning uninvited, Odds instructs Altuna and two other adolescent black boys on how to explore the "conquered territory" of Lynne's body: " 'Tits,' he said, flicking them with his fingers, 'ass.' " As the boys turn away, terrified, from Odds's cold pornographic voice, Lynne peoples her mind with vicious images of gang rape. Although the boys' faces look "horrified," Lynne denies their sympathetic human response and for a moment convinces herself that they "were no longer her friends" and that "the sight of her naked would turn them into savages." But like so many Southern black people, whose images Meridian sees clearly and sustainingly, the three boys remain true to their (and Lynne's) human dignity. Like a defrocked priest, Odds continues his obscene rite. "Go on," he commands, "have some of it." With eloquent courage Altuna Jones responds to Odds's prurient call with words that repudiate Odds's assumptions and deny his psychological power. He knows from experience that Odds's pronoun assaults the very basis of human personality. " 'It? *It?*' he said. 'What it you talking about? That ain't no *it*, that's Lynne.' " Altuna improvises out of his inviolable being, and affirms Lynne's, his, and, therefore, everyone's individual right to life and liberty. Lynne is Lynne, he asserts. She is a person, a human being who is also a woman, who is also white.

Altuna's simple genuine words set a salutary example for what is beginning to happen in *Meridian*. For a long time Meridian alone of the former Civil Rights activists understands the intense conscious effort required for personal or political change. In the mostly poor black village of Chicokema, her interior life so closely resembles the people's condition that soon "she

looked as if she belonged." Unlike others in her generation, Meridian, frail
and sickly, her physical and psychological survival at stake, goes to the oldest
African-American well: struggle. She recalls that in slavery her ancestors had
to bear up under Sisyphean toil—and still kept soul as well as body together.
Moreover, their energy overflowed into the spirituals, the tales, the sermons,
the blues, and the amazing quilts whose intricate form inspires Meridian's
design of self as well as Walker's narrative form.

Lynne, on the other hand, alienated from her experience and her tradition, resists change and projects her condition on the world. "Why did you
come back down here?" she asks harshly in a voice echoing those who called
on Meridian to kill for the revolution. "These people will always be the same,"
she continues. "You can't change them." Characteristically, Meridian revises
the question and shoulders the burden. "But I can change," she answers, and
reinforces her seriousness with a modest self-call: "I hope I will." In time,
Lynne, too, answers the call to personal revolution. In Meridian's presence,
she abandons her earlier view of African-Americans as works of Art. " 'Black
folks aren't so special,' she said. 'I hate to admit it. But they're not.' " From
here she renounces another idea given force by the history of race and sex
in the South. She sees that the peculiar power that in her worst moments she
has cynically, bitterly dared to exploit—her status as the desired tabooed white
woman—signifies pathology.

In interracial relationships the African-American often becomes the
cynosure, the bearer of burdens, and finally the metaphor for freedom in the
nation. Usually the apparent issue between black and white Americans is
whether their friendship allows them to talk about race, but too often race
refers only to being black in America. This compulsion evades the question
of what it means and feels like to be white in this country. In a reversal consistent with Walker's crazy quilt form, Lynne and Meridian test their newly
developing intimacy by considering white women. Appropriately, the two
women reach this topic through Truman, the temporary middle term who
is both a presence and an absence in their relationship.

> "No Truman isn't much, but he's *instructional*," said Lynne.
> "Besides," she continued, "nobody's perfect."
> "Except white women," said Meridian, and winked.
> "Yes," said Lynne, "but their time will come."

No more words are spoken between Lynne and Meridian and none need be
in the pages of the novel. But words on any subject *could* now be spoken
by them. When their lives touch again, they can resume talking with a certain
earned, assured freedom and intimacy. For this exchange with its ironic-

intimate tones of call-and-response settles past accounts and enables Lynne and Meridian to confront together the reversals of politics and sexuality so prominent in the lives of the women and men of their generation. To joke companionably about race and gender after everything they have gone through as women foretells a capacity to talk about anything, in a common voice expressive of what is happening to them singly and together in the unfolding of what Walker believes is one "immense story coming from a multitude of different perspectives" (*In Search of Our Mothers' Gardens*).

VI

Earlier in her life (and later in the novel), Meridian comes back to the South to restore herself and relearn the work of politics. But soon, in April 1968, she experiences a devastating low point that makes her journey to the people a categorical imperative. At first, like the speaker in Anna Akhmatova's "Requiem," she is a mere "witness to the common lot, survivor of that time, that place." She stands with the uninvited, unacknowledged black poor outside the funeral of Dr. Martin Luther King as, "following the casket on its mule-drawn cart," this "pitiable crowd of nobodies" spontaneously "began to sing a song the dead man had loved." The song testifies to the love of these poor for *their* Martin, but the invited dignitaries only follow "eagerly in genial mime" without inner voices of responsiveness. As the music fades from the air, Meridian hears the other, unloving voices of individuals, white and black, who converse loudly, trivially, ostentatiously. Soon "the call for Coca-Colas" replaces the poor people's song, and "there was a feeling of relief in the air, of liberation, that was repulsive." In response, Meridian turns "in shame, as if to the dead man himself," but she hears only "a skinny black boy tapping on an imaginary drum" pronounce an epitaph, not for King but in defense of this desolate American carnival. "We don't go on over death the way whiteys do," he tells a "white couple who hung guiltily to every word."

After witnessing this tradition-sundering act of self-parody, Meridian drops out of sight and hearing. Walker's break sends readers to their own inner space, and the next words are the sound of Meridian's voice, years later, filling a new page. The time is about 1975, the place Chicokema, the occasion her pursuit of the revolutionary question in her continuing conversation with Truman. Because hers is a life of commitment, Meridian pursues the relation among ideas, emotions, and actions with an impersonal, troubled seriousness foreign to Truman. Because Truman has long since abandoned politics for a hypocritical artistic career, to him "the discussion was academic, so he could state his points neatly." Nevertheless, Meridian suspends her disbelief and treats him fraternally as a serious person capable of an evolving dialogue.

"I mean, I think that all of us who want the black and poor to have equal opportunities and goods in life will have to ask ourselves how we stand on killing, even if no one else ever does. Otherwise we will never know—in advance of our fighting—how much we' are willing to give up."

"Suppose you found out, without a doubt, that you could murder other people in a just cause, what would you do? Would you set about murdering them?"

"Never alone," said Meridian. "Besides, revolution would not begin, do you think, with an act of murder—wars might begin in that way—but with teaching."

"Oh yes, *teaching*," said Truman, scornfully.

Like a jazz musician trying out a new melody, Meridian develops improvisationally those ideas arrived at earlier in her solitary mind. To her, politics and teaching are variations on the African-American pattern of call-and-response. Action, like speech, is dialogue. But ideas seem to enter Truman like the current from a life-support machine. "Revolution," he tells her, "was the theme of the sixties," although she is at that moment living a life of undramatic but palpable revolution. Because she is willing to learn from any corner, she takes Truman more seriously than he takes himself. "But don't you think the basic questions raised by King and Malcolm and the rest still exist? Don't you think people, somewhere deep inside, are still attempting to deal with them?"

Meridian's words are a confession of faith backed up by her life, but Truman holds his ground rigidly, if honestly. "No," he replies, and his response recalls Walter Cronkite's official refrain during the 1960s and 1970s. *That's the way it is,* July so and so, nineteen hundred and such and such he would say every night as if to soothe the citizenry against the chaotic facts of war and riot alluded to in the previous half-an-hour of news. At this point of apparent standoff between Meridian and Truman, Walker fills in the memory gap with an account of one of Meridian's political acts of change. Rather than comply with recent federal desegregation laws, the Chicokema town fathers close down the public pool and retreat to "private swimming pools in their own back yards." Consequently, each spring and fall a black child usually drowns in water drained off from the reservoir into the adjacent low-lying black neighborhood. The afflicted community grieves passively, apolitically until Meridian leads them into the town meeting. In silence she leaves the body of a bloated decomposing child next to the mayor's gavel.

The people promise to "name the next girl child they had after her," but Meridian seizes the moment and instead makes "them promise they would learn, as their smallest resistance to the murder of their children, to use the vote." Like Meridian's contemporaries, the people fear they will be laughed at "because that is not radical." Characteristically, Walker and Meridian withhold news of the outcome until we have witnessed the prior experience that enabled Meridian to speak and act with the people. Later, we are told matter-of-factly that these people, like those in Miss Jane Pittman's quarters, act on their own behalf. No more poor black children drown in this way in this town for the simplest and most effective of reasons: black votes joined to black voices.

In the meantime Meridian overcomes Truman's glib responses with a thoughtful, meditative silence. In the interval before they resume talking, Walker invites us to come along as silent companions as she follows Meridian's earlier quest for a loving political voice. Two months after Martin Luther King's assassination, Meridian begins going to black churches. Each time she chooses a different one, because she is not looking for any single true black church but instead those diverse dwellings where black people make church and find the way home in Ralph Ellison's sense of fusing love and democracy. In one such place Meridian answers unexpectedly the novel's persisting question: "Will you kill for the Revolution?" She does not change the question but interprets its terms according to a fuller context than that imagined by the revolutionaries who framed the question in the North some years before. To do so she follows the lead of a congregation that adapts the traditional music and ritual of black Christianity to its immediate needs and experience.

As she hears the people sing, Meridian recognizes an old "once quite familiar song," but when the words fail to come back to her, she "soon realized it was the *melody* of the song she remembered, not the words because these words sounded quite new to her." She is right, the congregation finds new words for the old melodies and also makes up new songs Meridian does not associate with church. The melody is martial, she realizes, and in response, "found herself quoting Margaret Walker's 'For My People' ":

> Let the martial songs be written,
> let the dirges disappear.

The unsought, unexpected connection startles Meridian into an apprehension of what is happening to these people whose souls she thinks hold no surprises. Disoriented, she hears the young minister begin to preach in a voice and cadence "so dramatically like that of Martin Luther King's that at first Meridian thought his intention was to dupe or to mock." So far her response lacks a center of gravity. Unfamiliar with the experience prompting the songs and now the sermon, she distrusts the young minister's relation to Martin Luther King: She is amazed that a contemporary could have an unself-conscious, intimate, kinship with King in this remote place far from talk of revolution. In an act of tolerance she stifles an impulse "to laugh bitterly" at what she thinks is "the pompous imitative preacher," and enters the flow of his voice. To her surprise, his voice bears witness to the potential wholeness in his people's personal and political lives. Moreover, the congregation's response tells her that he does speak for them, that his voice is also theirs.

Caught up in the flow of call-and-response, Meridian's inner voice picks up the rhythm. Her repetitive "he told" communicates his (and her) conviction that words and deeds are kin. For the minister does not aim his criticism only at white folks; he demands that the individuals in his congregation work harder to meet their responsibilities to each other. Meridian changes her mind because the call-and-response between the minister and his congregation builds on Martin Luther King's work. Don't go to Vietnam, he tells the young men; don't let your young children fight your battles, he tells the parents. And "it struck Meridian that he was deliberately imitating King, that he and all his congregation *knew* he was consciously keeping that voice alive" as a force for change. And as Meridian listens more and more responsively, she hears "not his voice at all, but rather the voice of millions who could no longer speak." Then, hearing the voices around her, Meridian revises her idea, for these people speak repeatedly through the varied intonation of the different *ah-mens* they utter in response to the preacher's calls to action. The congregation speaks unsentimentally, militantly, and their voices reach Meridian with "a firm tone of 'We are fed up.' "

They have cause to be fed up. One of their own has been murdered, martyred in the struggle for justice like Jimmy Aaron in *The Autobiography of Miss Jane Pittman*. Along with the other worshippers, Meridian yields to the grief of the boy's father, a "red-eyed man" so devastated he wonders to what extent love led to his son's violent death. Formerly, he "had thought that somehow, the power of his love alone (and how rare even he knew it was!) would save his son. But his love—selfless, open, a kissing, touching love—had only made his son strong enough to resist everything that was not love." Convinced of "his own great value, he had set out to change the ways of the world his father feared." To his father's puzzlement, he embraced struggle and revolution. Now, the grieving father "did not allow closeness" even by his people who long to "open themselves totally to someone else's personal loss, if it was allowed them to do so." He cannot bear so intimate a response, but his faith in the people remains, and, when asked, he appears and speaks on *occasions* like the anniversary of his son's death. Aware of his continuing part in their struggle, the people know the red-eyed man cannot grieve alone and remain true to his love for his son and his son's love for him and the people. So the red-eyed man's three painful, somehow adequate and eloquent words—"My son died"—arouse the people. Their response flows into the work going on more determinedly than ever because of the unspeakable murder and brutality inflicted on the best and strongest among them. As a willing potential participant, Meridian bears witness to the practical healing power of the people's song and ceremony: "*And* then there rose the sweet music that received its inimitable *soul* from just such inarticulate grief as this, *and* a passing of the collection plate with the money going to the church's prison fund, *and* the preacher urged all those within his hearing to vote for black candidates on the twenty-third. *And* the service was over" (my italics). She is now a participant and, therefore, her voice is faithful to the inner rhythms of their story. Here culture, especially music, humanizes politics—those small actions that intensify and change the lives of the people and their children. In this black church the deepest, most abiding human responses of love and grief express the meaning of revolution in African-American experience.

Now, in a miniature of the novel's crazy quilt collage, the fragments Meridian witnesses come together. Lingering in church, she puts into inner words the promise she has heard the people make with their amens and their music. " 'Look' they were saying, 'we are slow to awaken to the notion that we are only as other women and men, and even slower to move in anger, but we are gathering ourselves to fight for and protect what your son fought for on behalf of us. If you will let us weave your story and your son's life and death into what we already know—into the songs, the sermons, the brother and sister—we will soon be so angry we cannot help but move.' " As she imagines the people's voice, the words include her in the community of struggle. " 'Understand this,' they were saying, 'the church' (and Meridian knew they did not mean simply 'church,' as in Baptist, Methodist or whatnot, but rather communal spirit, togetherness, righteous convergence), 'the music, the form of worship that has always sustained us, the kind of ritual you share with us, these are the ways to transformation that we know. We want to take this with us as far as we can.' " In this shared voice Meridian hears the people's awareness of each other and of her as if they have waited knowing always what she has just come to understand: namely, that "the years in America had created them One Life."

This context reveals an intrinsic community and a community in flux, and because of this, Meridian is able to address the question posed without music by her contemporaries: "Will you kill for the Revolution?" But she answers in relation to the condition of love and struggle she has just witnessed and participated in, and so she roots the word and idea of "revolution" in the particular flow of the people's experience. True to her personality, her answer is not absolute, rigid, or final but fluid, promissory, and evolving. And her response moves in harmony with the simultaneously traditional and contemporary landscape she travels through and briefly rests in: "Under a large tree beside the road, crowded now with the cars returning from church, she made a promise to the red-eyed man herself: that yes, indeed she *would* kill before she allowed anyone to murder his son again." True to her slowly evolving self, Meridian continues to work out the relationship between personal and political responsibility. Despite "the new capacity to do anything, including kill, for our freedom—beyond sporadic acts of violence," she recognizes that "I am not yet at the point of being able to kill anyone myself, nor—except for the false urgings that come to me in periods of grief and rage—will I ever be." For her, scrupulosity is a condition of being. From time to time she comforts her soul with her cherished identity as someone who walks behind the "real" revolutionaries, those who do the "correct thing" and "kill when killing is necessary." But she balances the "correct thing" with the "right thing." When those who have killed cannot sing yet yearn desperately for music, she will come forward "and sing from memory songs they will need once more to hear." Thus, overcoming the false notes in her own soul, Meridian imagines revolutionary politics as work of the spirit and music as a recuperative political act. She becomes a mediating voice between revolution and the traditions true revolutionaries seek to empower through just and radical changes in the body politic. "For it is the song of the people, *transformed by the experience of each generation,* that holds them together, and if any part of it is lost the people suffer and are without soul" (my italics). Music, as the people in the church have shown her, is both a healing balm and a companion to action in these days and in days to come as it was in the days of slavery and also the Civil Rights movement of the 1950s and 1960s. Rounded in song, the mouth of the people becomes a figure for the restored hoop of the nation.

These questions of politics and identity, culture and revolution continue to engage Meridian according to the flow of her experience. Encountering a "starving child" or "a grown person who could neither read nor write," she renews her silent promise to kill for the sake of justice. But that promise moves away from murder, simple or complex, and toward her presence in the nation as a revolutionary citizen. In her rage at the injustice of particular lives, she feels "of a resolute and relatively fearless character, which, sufficient in its calm acceptance of its own purpose, could bring the mightiest country to its knees." Clearly, her sense of potential power is more extravagant than that proclaimed by her militant contemporaries in the 1960s. Surely, too, she is "a little crazy"; she needs to be, and this passionate overflow of self, if experienced many times over by many different individuals, might be the beginning of a second American revolution. For while Truman Held makes "a statue of Crispus Attucks [the first American to die in the Revolution] for the Bicentennial," in a partly cynical, wholly self-serving gesture, and Anne-Marion writes pretty poetry and, like the others in her former group, does "nothing revolutionary," Meridian redefines the meaning of equality and the inalienable rights in her daily work and life. Hers is the spirit of public happiness John Adams believed led to the success of the original American Revolution, reexpressed in a politics of, by, and for the black poor of the South two hundred years later. As Walker's novel stands in contrast to Truman's statue as a work of art in the context of the Bicentennial, so too, Meridian brings to the original American revolutionary impulse a politics of nourishment and nurturing—what Walker calls a *womanist* sensibility.

VII

During his stay with Meridian, Truman gradually hears her meditative internal voice and begins to listen for his own. He changes his thinking more because of an inner dialogue than because of any words spoken between them. He goes South still hoping to resolve his life and end the story in the old way by marrying Meridian. But in his presence she keeps on with her healing life of satisfying work and in that context offers him friendship based on doing things together in a spirit of equality. Appropriately, now the pattern of call-and-response shifts from rhetoric to action. Meridian asks nothing from Truman, but in response to his new silent openness, she takes him along on her voter registration work. With him at her side, she visits a family belonging to the poorest of the black poor. The mother is dying; the father rolls old slimy newspapers into logs he sells to white folks "for a nickel apiece and to colored for only three pennies." Meridian tries to persuade the man (and his wife) to register, but without polemics or ideology, for she sees that action as true and meaningful only in the context of particular lives. For Meridian, voting habituates the exercise of voice. "It may be useless," she tells the man who, struggling to survive, calls voting a waste of time, a needless risk "if we don't own nothing." In response, Meridian disagrees gently and changes the terms of the dialogue: "Maybe it can be the beginning of the use of your voice. You have to get used to using your voice, you know. You start on simple things and move on." But the man rejects her call and bids her go elsewhere, to people with fewer urgencies, whose right to life, liberty, and the pursuit of happiness is more assured. Go among your contemporaries, he might have said, and his meaning is not lost on Meridian. True to her earlier affirmation of teaching as a spoken and unspoken dialogue rather than "a handing down of answers," she understands that in the act of expressing another position, the man uses his voice to tell her about the "simple things" at the core of his life.

"Okay," Meridian says, and walks away in undiscouraged, easy silence. Her timing and instinct combine with her values in an act of respect that is the most abiding form of democratic leadership. And Truman follows willingly. He does not protest nor assert his manly presence by arguing with the man. Meridian's voice and motion assure the man of her sincerity so strongly that when she and Truman return shortly with two bags of food, he accepts them for his son and ailing wife. He and Meridian communicate from respect as if each were saying to the other: You meet your responsibilities, and I'll meet mine. So it is no surprise when, after the man's wife dies, he shows up with *his* gifts: "six rabbits already skinned and ten newspaper logs." That's for the groceries he might have said but doesn't and from respect, because his gifts are from his hands. With no prodding, no exchange of words, the man testifies to the reciprocal power of his voice and Meridian's in another way. He performs a political act—"under the words WILL YOU BE BRAVE ENOUGH TO VOTE in Meridian's yellow pad he wrote his name in large black letters." He signs up not for Meridian but to enlarge the struggle he carries on in his life. Made in the spirit of mutual, offhand eloquence, the man's commitment is his and not dependent on Meridian's personal presence. Convinced by his experience, including his encounter with Meridian, that "the years in America had created them One Life," the man acts on the authority of experience: his signature is his voice.

Despite other successes, Walker resists turning *Meridian* into a series of small triumphs for voter registration. Instead, she touches realities that are beyond the power of change, conditions that illuminate almost unspeakable corners of the human heart. Meridian and Truman, she writes in acknowledgment of an intense mutual fate, "must go to the prison. And so they must. And so they must see the child who murdered her child, nothing new." The repetitions roll and break like waves, which, as they are about to flatten out, throw up a sudden spume of fear. The girl's voice penetrates Meridian and Truman so deeply that, when she asks "who, in the hell, are you?" they fall back on words of identification that they think shield their identities. "People who ask people to vote," they answer in an inadequate mutual voice. But the girl sees through their mask of fact: "If you all can't give me back my heart (she says suddenly, with venom), go the fuck away." They do, they have to, they go away with nothing, not words, not friendship, not even Meridian's burning lines of verse as consolation. There is no politics to compensate for this "fucking heart of stone," as Meridian names the soul behind the girl's insane but undeniably human voice. And there is little comfort, for the girl is not entirely an anomaly in the world of *Meridian*. Her murder of her child recalls the brutal murder of Truman and Lynne's six-year-old daughter, Camara, and also Meridian's former urges to kill her baby son. Deep in their separate selves Meridian and Truman are bonded by what they have seen and heard and suffered together. Truman feels *shame* but is not able to identify his emotion with his and Lynne's murdered daughter nor with his and Meridian's aborted baby of whose existence he has no conscious knowledge. Meridian writes a poem of forgiveness for Truman, for everyone, not least herself, and as she sleeps "that night with Truman's arms around her," his "dreams [escape] from his lips to make a moaning, crying song." Truman's involuntary song foretells his evolving sensibility; soon he begins "to experience moments with Meridian when he felt intensely maternal."

At the end of *Meridian* everything whirls with the motion of change. Meridian and Truman "settle accounts," and at some indeterminate later time Truman declares a brotherly love for his wife, Lynne. "I don't want to do anything but provide for you and be your friend." Perhaps sensing the pain his absence of desire may cause her, he asks a genuine, unrhetorical question: "Can you accept that?" Still, Truman pursues the past with Meridian. "I want your love the way I had it a long time ago," he tells her and in his turn accepts painfully her declaration that "my love for you changed." She has, she claims, set him *free,* and, therefore, she feels free to issue a warning that implies that true friendship between them should influence his inner voice as well as his actions and speech. "You are *not* free, however, to think I am a fool." The remark underscores Meridian's determination to be a serious person in every facet of her experience. Her struggle toward a qualified, continually vulnerable wholeness involves benevolence toward the existence of others, a willingness to see them through their eyes as well as hers. Benevolence now seems Meridian's test for those she is intimate with in her work and her life. For his part, Truman first learns to read Anne-Marion's message to Meridian about the Sojourner tree's newly manifested life. Then, by "the soft wool of her newly grown hair," he understands that Meridian, too, is, in part, "new, sure and ready, even eager, for the world."

As always, Meridian and Truman talk, and at first Truman's spoken words continue to be less genuine than his inner voice. "Your ambivalence," he tells her in a language akin to the *retrick* of the long-head boy in *The Autobiography of Miss Jane Pittman,* "will always be deplored by people who consider themselves revolutionists, and your unorthodox behavior will cause traditionalists to gnash their teeth." Although Truman's feelings have changed, he still speaks words he has been taught to speak and thinks he is supposed to speak. He fails to distinguish his loneliness from Meridian's solitude. For her, true solitude is a sign of potential community; she and those like her "will one day gather at the river. We will watch the evening sun go down. And in the darkness maybe we will know the truth." Her words, the last *spoken* in the novel, are at once prophetic and elemental, metaphysical and sensuous. She includes Truman in her company of solitary silent souls; at least she invites him to join these still marching saints. But she does not stay for an answer because she knows his spoken words lag behind the readiness of his inner voice. Instead, she hugs him freely, naturally—"long, lingeringly (her nose and lips rooting about at his neck, *causing him to laugh)*" (my italics). Then she leaves quickly, in the ascent, the prime of her life—"walking as if hurrying to catch up with someone"—herself maybe and maybe the whole revolving world. She leaves keeping faith with the possibility that she will wear the crazy quilt of her world as Hurston's Janie Crawford draped the net of the horizon around her shoulders.

Lovingly, she leaves Truman in her place to do what is now *their* work. She leaves her sleeping bag behind as a nest to shelter him while his evolving self prepares to act differently toward the world. She knows his loneliness is cause for fear, but she also knows that their conversation has gone as far as it can now. So she leaves him to respond to her inner vision, to that interior dialogue to which she contributes even when not physically present. Her words and parting hug call his inner voice. Free to feel and to cry, Truman takes silent, solitary possession of the gifts she has given him. He identifies the house as his, realizes that the people will come to milk his cow, and that they "would wait patiently for him to *perform,* to take them along the next *guideless* step. Perhaps he would" (my italics). In a spirit of moral contingency and integrity reminiscent of Meridian, Truman senses that among these poor people politics follows from personal worthiness and dignity. He senses, too, that political acts are best performed by a self somehow at once in flux and on the way to completion—a revolutionary self.

Truman's thoughts lead to the resumption of his inner dialogue with Meridian. He *hears* the words of her poem, not as she once wrote them down but as if she were speaking to him now. He feels the room turn with the revolving motion of the world. Like Meridian in her time of dissolution, he yields to a spell of dizziness. As a reflex, he fits his body into Meridian's sleeping bag and puts her cap on his head. Located in her former place, Truman imagines the process of self-discovery and restoration extending to others in his generation. "He had a vision of Anne-Marion herself, arriving,

lost, someday, at the door, which would remain open"; he makes no pretense
of leading her. Rather, his thoughts return to Meridian, and in careful,
disciplined, specific, far-reaching words his newly immediate, complex inner
voice communicates the spirit of change for which Meridian and now he,
Truman, stand. He "wondered if Meridian knew that the sentence of bearing
the conflict in her own soul which she had imposed on herself—and lived
through—must now be borne in terror by all the rest of them."

Truman and Walker avoid stitching Meridian's story into a legend. It
would be easy for him (and us) to read the images identified with Meridian—
her cap, her hair, her frail yet strong stature, her power to lead people—as
signs of another African-American woman from the days of the underground
railroad and the Civil War. In her struggle Meridian becomes one of those
black women she remembers from childhood stories as "always imitating
Harriet Tubman—escaping to become something unheard of." With her contemporaries, Meridian functions as exemplary general on a 1970s underground
railroad of politics and personality. But the extrinsic journey is in reverse,
from the North to the South, because in Meridian's time the South offers the
surest passage from slavery to freedom. Although, unlike Harriet Tubman,
Meridian issues no commands, her presence and interior voice call others to
become passengers on a journey as terrible and necessary as the escapes led
by General Tubman. And in the unlegendary historical present, Truman's
words place his dialogue with Meridian on a new plane.

The signs of presence and aura of voice that Meridian leaves all around
the house lead Truman to wonder about her from the vantage point of his
finally open mind. The *sentence* that he bears in his soul and Walker writes
down now in collaboration with *him* testifies to his potential. Already he experiences the conflict Meridian has endured for her own sake, her people's
sake, and, especially, her contemporaries' sake. And he begins to be aware
that her silent dialogue as well as her speech has given him and the others
she touches the time and space they need to rejoin what Michael Harper calls
the "dark struggle to be human" ("Eve [Rachel]"). The sentence written and
passed by Walker and accepted by Meridian and now Truman calls the rest
of us to bear the conflict between restraint and indulgence, pain and pleasure,
love and hate, life and death as a condition of personal revolution and a
prologue to political action. With its allusion to the intervening years of loss
as well as gain, Walker's *sentence* intensifies Invisible Man's 1950s question:
"Who knows but that, on the lower frequencies, I speak for you?" For black
(*and all*) citizens to know that "the years in America [have] created them One
Life" (*Meridian*) carries with it the sentence of participation. To discover
and create and tell our stories, as Meridian does, using her voice in speech,

in silence, in writing, is the essence of the revolutionary task explored in *Meridian*. She and Walker remind us that sometimes the voices of authority we need to overcome to listen to our best selves are creations of our own diminished hearts.

Of all the words thought and felt, spoken and written in *Meridian,* those Meridian speaks simply, quietly, humbly, to the impoverished black man best embody a loving political voice. "You have to get used to using your voice, you know. You start on simple things and move on." In her crazy quilt collage of a novel Alice Walker and her characters offer readers a beginning of the restoration of the reciprocal sense of language and experience that is essential if America is to resume a revolutionary course. Walker's call is subtle but not easily ignored, over time, on those "lower frequencies" of consciousness where, heard or unheard, our inner voices live and speak.

TAMAR KATZ

"Show Me How to Do Like You": Didacticism and Epistolary Form *in* The Color Purple

Show me how to do like you
Show me how to do it.
—STEVIE WONDER

Beginning with its epigraph, Alice Walker marks off *The Color Purple's* territory and purpose: it is a novel that intends to teach its readers, and it is also a novel about how that instruction might take place. *The Color Purple's* central character, Celie, serves as an example of the ideal learning process. Poor, oppressed, miserable, she learns to shed the yoke of patriarchal oppression in its many forms—in marriage, in love, in economics, in religion. As readers we are, in a sense, to learn from Celie how it is done by seeing it done.

The Color Purple is an epistolary novel: a series of letters from Celie to God, Nettie to Celie, Celie to Nettie, and finally Celie to God, the stars, trees, sky, peoples, Everything. Through its epistolary structure *The Color Purple* establishes two juxtaposed structures of instruction—direct address, or persuasion, and indirect: the use of the example or the document. The relation between these two structures inside the boundaries of the novel echoes and reenacts the inherently destabilized project of the novel as a whole, indeed of any overtly didactic fiction. *The Color Purple* must adopt a stance toward its readers that combines the strength of persuasive address with the authority traditionally ceded to nonpersuasive, "disinterested" writing. And by making explicit the problems of address in, and within, the novel's formal structure,

---

© 1988 by Tamar Katz. Published for the first time in this volume.

185

Walker brings to light not just this epistemological dilemma underlying didactic fiction, but the specific dilemma of the marginal writer.

Walker thematicizes the issue of instruction most clearly in a section of
the novel found by many readers, ironically, to be jarring and disjunctive:
Nettie's letters from Africa. These letters, however, set up a model of teaching
and learning that provides a foil for the central plot of Celie's education.

Throughout *The Color Purple,* Nettie is associated with teaching. Her
stepfather, early on, claims he wants to "make a schoolteacher out of her,"
and after Celie is kept home from school, Nettie teaches her about Christopher
Columbus and his boats "the Neater, the Peter, and the Santomareater." Later,
when Nettie joins Corrine and Samuel in missionary work, she speaks explicitly of their life together as a process of instruction:

> Although I work for Corrine and Samuel and look after the
> children, I don't feel like a maid. I guess this is because they teach
> me, and I teach the children and there's no beginning or end to
> teaching and learning and working—it all runs together.

But *The Color Purple* associates Nettie with a purely formal kind of
instruction, one that is drastically undercut throughout. Nettie's stepfather's
claim that he wants to make her a teacher masks his real intention; he wishes
to keep her at home in order to rape her as he has raped Celie. As models
of primer understanding and rote memory, Nettie's lessons to Celie about
Columbus bear only the most ironic relation to the conditions of Celie's life.
And Nettie's entire story of her missionary work with the Olinka takes the
form of a gradual disenchantment with the formal Christian ideals she was
taught and must herself teach. Corrine comes to distrust her and treat her
with less than the Christian charity she has preached. The Olinka are not
interested in being taught by missionaries—they feel no need for this instruction. As Samuel notes bitterly, "it isn't resentment, exactly. It really is indif-
ference. Sometimes I feel our position is like that of flies on an elephant's
hide." Ultimately, the education the missionaries offer—an education in the
name of a white, male God whose existence the novel itself finally denies—is
powerless to help the Olinka defend themselves against the invasion of the
road and the rubber plantation.

The model of education associated with Nettie in *The Color Purple* has
a parallel in a form of instruction directed at Celie continuously. Other
characters try to improve her, in the most direct way. "You got to fight them,
Celie," Mr. ———'s sister says. "You got to fight them for yourself." Nettie's
very first letter repeats this theme: "You got to fight and get away from Albert.
He ain't no good." But such direct instruction is rarely effective in

the novel, and often furthers white or patriarchal systems of oppression—as in the missionary imposition of the impractical Mother Hubbard dress, or Darlene's attempts to teach Celie to speak "standard" English. And of course the most insidious direct instruction of all opens the entire novel: "You better not never tell nobody but God. It'd kill your mammy."

But for all these failed, misguided, or insidious models of instruction, *The Color Purple* remains, above all, a type of *Bildungsroman*—a novel about the instruction of Celie and her coming to consciousness. Accordingly, I wish to turn away from the novel's internal thematicization of instruction, and toward an investigation of the same issues as they occur in its formal structure. For through epistolary form, *The Color Purple* also presents an alternative model of instruction, a model based not on direct address, but indirect, not on the didactic lecture, but the didactic example. This model, on its own and in its intersection and juxtaposition with direct address, makes clear the patterns in which Celie and the reader learn.

We can trace the literary roots of *The Color Purple*'s instructional model to a form traditionally allied with the didactic—the epistolary novel as the genre flowered in eighteenth-century England—and in particular to the work of Samuel Richardson. Richardson came to write epistolary fiction with the explicit intent to teach; before either *Pamela* or *Clarissa,* he published, in 1741, a letter manual. This volume provided exemplary letters for all manner of relevant topics. Richardson elucidated what he felt to be its edifying purpose in its full title:

> *Letters Written to and for Particular Friends on the Most Important Occasions Directing not only the Requisite Style and Forms to be Observed in Writing FAMILIAR LETTERS; But How to Think and Act Justly and Prudently in the Common Concerns of Human Life.*

The didactic potential of this letter manual calls attention to a similar potential in the epistolary novel as a closely related form. And one source of didactic power for both was their proximity to real life. For epistolary novels especially, the connection to a nonfictional form reinforced their moral power and relevance to their readers' lives.

But if the epistolary novel has often been used for didactic purposes, it possesses as well certain problems inherent in its structure, problems that have to be struggled with in any attempt at conclusive didactic effect. As Terry Eagleton points out in *The Rape of Clarissa,* epistolary fiction tends in two opposite directions at once—toward structural openness and doctrinal closure. Since the form leaves no room for an authorial voice to make its moral points independently, it must rely on more indirect means. Richardson recognized this problem as well: "It is impossible that readers the most attentive, can always enter into the views of the writer of a piece, written, as hoped, to Nature and the moment." For Richardson, the answer (or the attempt at one) lay in the constant revising of his work according to comments sent him by friends and critics.

But, just as epistolary fiction dramatizes the acts of writing and reading, it also dramatizes this very dilemma of uncertain reception—both within epistolary structure (on the level of the characters as readers) as well as without (on the level of a work's author and public).

As distinguished from autobiography or diary fiction, epistolary fiction focuses specifically on the relation of letter writer to letter reader. The problems usually get cast from the reverse of Richardson's perspective: not how to ensure your meaning is taken correctly, but how to ensure the letter you're reading is reliable. Since both the style and content of letters are shaped by the expectation of a particular reader, every letter is not simply a true record of feeling, but a directed, persuasive action. (Novels of seduction like *Clarissa* unfold the perils of just such a situation.) The problem, worded from either perspective, inside or outside the novel's frame, is essentially the same. In Richardson's *Pamela*—and still further in *The Color Purple*—epistolary structure not only poses the problem but offers its own attempt at a solution.

Richardson offers in *Pamela* a possible test for the truth of any epistolary message. Mr. B——, who has been making repeated attempts on Pamela's virtue, forces her to surrender her copies of the letters in which she has reported to her parents the story of his advances and her distress. While B—— has never believed Pamela's protestations of virtue *to him,* he is moved to belief by the incontrovertible evidence of her letters. Her letters, in fact, can be treated as *evidence* because they are not directed to him, and thus they are not an attempt to persuade him.

It has been suggested that as readers of epistolary fiction we are placed in the position of B——, not as the recipient of a novel's letters, but as voyeurs. However, in specifically didactic epistolary fiction, I would argue, this schema is simultaneously both true and untrue. The reader of didactic fiction occupies a double stance. He or she *is* the recipient of a directed message—a novel in this case, not a letter. But the peculiarity of epistolary fiction (and this accounts perhaps for its particular affinity with the didactic) is that it summons the documentary authority vested in a letter directed to someone other than the reader.

And now, to return to *The Color Purple,* I think it might become clearer how Richardson and the epistolary tradition (with certain changes rung on it serve Walker in both the instruction of Celie and the instruction of the reader.

The Color Purple highlights the doubleness of the reader's stance in the significant manner in which it truncates traditional epistolary form. For Walker has given us a series of letters that almost never reach their addressees, a series of letter writers with absent, unhearing, or impotent readers. Celie writes to a God who is either "sleep" or nonexistent (at least in the form in which she addresses him). Nettie writes letters that, at first, don't reach Celie, then reach her all at once (and so end up serving as a related tale, but not, in effect, as direct communication). Celie's letters to Nettie are returned to her unopened. In fact, most of the novel's epistolary exchanges are nonfunctional in the traditionally understood sense of communication between writer and reader. Walker emphasizes, even ironizes, this lack of function, as both Celie and Nettie exhort their readers to act in impossible or idealized ways. "I am fourteen years old," Celie writes in her opening letter to God. "I have always been a good girl. Maybe you can give me a sign letting me know what is happening to me." And we recall that Nettie's first letter to Celie begins, "You've got to fight and get away from Albert." These letters serve only to remind us that the expected connection of writer to reader has failed to take place.

These letters lack their expected functions and qualities in other ways as well. Celie's letters to God, for instance, are oddly incorporeal. In a literary genre traditionally obsessed with the privacy necessary for letter writing, and the material conditions necessary for that privacy—the locked room, the hiding place, the constant threat of violation hovering over both—*The Color Purple* presents us with a letter writer who possesses neither the time nor the privacy to write, and whose own letters are never hidden or uncovered.

Nettie's letters to Celie follow a more conventional plot pattern—Mr. —— intercepts them and hides them. Yet in this too, traditional plot functions are cut short and bear little narrative fruit. Although Mr. —— hides Nettie's letters, he does not bother to read or even to open all of them. And Celie's discovery of the hidden letters does not bring about any significant action (she just hates Mr. —— more than she did before). What this particular twist on epistolary convention does effect, however, is a repositioning of Celie that is especially interesting in light of all the missing addressees in the novel. When Celie reads Nettie's letters, she reads them as Mr. —— (or Mr. B——, in *Pamela*) would have read them. She "overhears" correspondence directed at herself. She must split herself, act as addressee and voyeur simultaneously. And in this, as a reader of a miniature epistolary novel embedded in the larger epistolary novel that is *The Color Purple*, Celie stands in for the reader of didactic epistolary fiction in general.

(It would be possible, though I don't intend to pursue it much further here, to extend this model of intercepted documents or overheard discourse to Walker's thematic representation of the way in which Celie and the other characters in the novel learn and come to consciousness [*within* the frame of the letters]. They all witness scenes: Celie watches Sofia with Harpo, Shug with Mr. ———; Nettie observes the Olinka among themselves and with the roadbuilders. It remains unclear from whom, exactly, Mr. ——— learns—quite possibly he does so from sending Celie the rest of her sister's letters, thus enabling her to continue "overhearing" her own correspondence.)

A reader of *The Color Purple,* then, learns (or receives instruction) by assuming Celie's ambivalent position within the novel, outside it. He or she learns by watching Celie as a double example. Celie exists as a form of "documentary" proof from whom we can draw edifying conclusions, convincing us as an example of woman's oppression and liberation because she does not direct her confidences to us. In fact, even the direction of her letters adds to her authority as an example. We trust Celie because of her "innocence," as Henry Louis Gates, Jr. has put it. This innocence exists not only in her ignorance of her own pregnancy and in her use of the vernacular; it is established the moment she addresses her initial plea to God. And Celie also exists as an example of how we should behave—and learn—as readers. In her reading of Nettie's letters, and in her reading of other characters as examples around her, she shows us how to learn from both written and social documents.

I have spoken so far mostly of Celie as an addressee or a voyeur—the recipient and interpreter of messages. But as Gates points out, the progress of *The Color Purple* can easily be seen as the process of Celie's writing herself into being and consciousness, of her growing power and control as a writer. And it is to Celie's role as writer that I now wish to turn, in the context of some of the problems of direction and reliability already mapped out. Celie, in her innocence and in the context of her address to God, is an ostensibly reliable reporter of events. Her stepfather further confirms her authority for an outside reader by preempting the possibility of taking the cynical view—claiming it for himself and imposing it on Mr. ———. "She near twenty," he says. "And another thing—she tell lies." This claim for Celie's unreliability—and particularly the danger that she might attempt to convince *us*—undercuts its own position. Her stepfather's statement, we can clearly see, in *its* discursive context, intends to persuade and to mislead. And this claim, when juxtaposed to the opening injunction, "You better not never tell nobody but God," strengthens the truth value of Celie's story, when and because it is told to God.

The idea of Celie's absolute reliability, however, is at odds in more subtle ways with her development as a writer. While we take Celie's written words to be essentially "true," in the way an uncovered document might be true, we also watch the character Celie as she gains control over the reporting of actions. The idea of an absolute division between the two becomes increasingly difficult to maintain. The collapse of this division (which Gates discusses at length) occurs in Walker's use and revision of free indirect discourse, especially as it comes to her through Zora Neale Hurston's *Their Eyes Were Watching God*. With Celie's *written* free indirect discourse, it becomes impossible to sort out whether we're reading the actual reported words of another character (that is, whether we're seeing discourse of a documentary nature), because all words are but ultimately written by Celie.

It is possible to discuss this collapse of division in terms of showing and telling. Such a collapse, when translated into these terms, demonstrates the added relevance of *The Color Purple*'s epigraph to its project. The Stevie Wonder quote, "Show me how to do like you. Show me how to do it," aptly summarizes not only this central theme of the novel, but its inherent self-contradiction—one that exists as two separate poles at once collapsed and distinct. The Wonder quote parallels a hypothetical reader's request for an ideal, reliable source of instruction (a showing—a document or example, in the terms the novel establishes). Both Celie and Walker would seem to move toward a model of instruction that operates simply by showing, by the authority of the example. But both character and author present their examples in the shape of their own words; they both *tell* whatever they show.

Barbara Johnson, in her article "Thresholds of Difference: Structures of Address in Zora Neale Hurston," discusses a related issue as it occurs in Hurston's work. She shows how the enactment of this paradox has special resonance in black women's writing, where the status of the example is a particularly problematic one. The question of difference between writer and literary (or anthropological) example holds a special charge because it underlines and undercuts the traditional division of whites/men as writers, and blacks/women as written about.

The breakdown of this division in Hurston's work appears most clearly and parallels *The Color Purple* most strongly in *Mules and Men*. Here Hurston sets out to "report" black folktales much as Walker in a sense "reports" Celie and Nettie's letters, or as Celie herself "reports" dialogue. The same slide that we have seen between Celie as addressee and Celie as voyeur, or between Celie/Walker as reporter of evidence and Celie/Walker as shaper of a message, occurs in Hurston's introduction. Johnson explains:

Hurston began as an outsider, a scientific narrative voice that refers to "these people" in the third person, as a group whose inner lives are difficult to penetrate. Then, suddenly, she leaps into the picture she has just painted, including herself in a "we" that addresses a "you"—the white reader, the new implied outsider. The structure of address changes from description to direct address. From that point on it is impossible to tell whether Hurston the narrator is *describing* a strategy or *employing* one.

Hurston's rhetorical stance throughout *Mules and Men* (and elsewhere in her writings, as Johnson shows) highlights and enacts the peculiarly marginal and shifting position of the black woman writer. The "outsider" role in which Hurston begins—the scientific reporter—is traditionally that of a white male, traditionally that of the insider who establishes the black object of study as a "they." Hurston here reverses the terms—turns the insider into an outsider and turns the black object of study into a black subject—the "we" of the passage. In so doing, she not only reverses the terms, she problematizes and undermines the opposition on which they are built.

The Color Purple enacts the same destabilization. Walker's subject matter (that is, her object) is the life of a black woman—so far traditional subject-object divisions remain intact. But Walker questions the otherness of that object (Celie) by maintaining her in the position of a readable document or example, while simultaneously repositioning her in the roles of both author and reader.

As a black, female writer, Alice Walker is herself dangerously subject to a shift in position—but in reverse. While Celie is made to slide from example to author, Walker, like Hurston, can often be seen to slip all too readily from author to example. Hurston, at the time of the Harlem Renaissance, sometimes became what Langston Hughes described as "a perfect book of entertainment." Walker, in the hands of the mass media of the 1980s, often slips back to the status of example herself. In interviews, articles, calendars, Walker is treated as exemplary—not just as a black feminist writer but as *the* black feminist writer. This is true to a large extent because, as Trudier Harris acutely observes, "the media, by its very racist nature, seems able to focus on only one black writer at a time." This societal reinscription of Walker back into her "place"—as exemplar and object—ironically alerts us again to the formal and epistemological issues raised in *The Color Purple,* and their political implications. For while Celie can be said to shift from example to author (from object to subject), she also embodies—as does Walker—the ever-present political threat of this transition's reversal. What Walker risks creating, and becoming, is an exemplary subject. The dangers inherent in this position are made clear once again in the novel's epigraph: Showing someone how to do *like you* is equivalent to showing them how to do *it.* The example, ever again, reasserts its nature as object.

The Color Purple enacts this problem on all its levels—structural and thematic. What the novel intends to teach us on a thematic level—the nature of patriarchal oppression, the nature of learning and enlightenment—relies on Celie, and in part Walker, as examples. But what *The Color Purple* also intends both to teach and show us through its epistolary structure, is the constant, and inevitable, transgression and reassertion of the boundaries and risks of what we know as the example.

MARIANNE HIRSCH

Clytemnestra's Children: Writing (Out) the Mother's Anger

I am angry nearly every day of my life,
but I have learned not to show it; and I still
try to hope not to feel it, though it may take
me another forty years to do it.
— LOUISA MAY ALCOTT, *Little Women*

She need sit no longer
at the back of my mind
the lonely sucking of her thumb
a giant stopper in my throat.
— ALICE WALKER, "One
Child of One's Own"

Anger, Marilyn Frye has said, is an "instrument of cartography." To be angry is to claim a place, to assert a right to expression and to discourse, a right to intelligibility. "By determining where, with whom, about what and in what circumstances one can get angry . . . , one can map others' concepts of who and what one is" (*The Politics of Reality: Essays in Feminist Theory*). If we see anger as a particularly pointed assertion and articulation of subjectivity, we can use it as such an instrument of cartography to map the subjectivity of those who are denied it by culture and discourse. I come to the study of anger out of the desire to define the topography of maternal subjectivity generally absent from literary and theoretical representation. Anger, as I will argue, stands in a paradoxical relation to the maternal as culture has defined it. In fact, the term "maternal anger" is itself something of an oxymoron.

My title signals both my approach and its inherent difficulties. In its reference to *Les Enfants de Jocaste* (1980)—Christiane Olivier's critique of the male bias of psychoanalytic theory—the first part of my title "Clytemnestra's Children" announces a psychoanalytic point of departure. And the name of Clytemnestra, substituted for the name of Jocasta, further insists upon classical foundations. My subtitle also promises a certain kind of context: the colon and especially the parenthesis—"writing (out)"—which allow for a double reading, place the paper within a contemporary theoretical framework, which, like the psychoanalytic and the classical paradigms within which I have now situated myself, carries with it assumptions about the maternal that may actually complicate rather than facilitate the exploration of the topic. And yet this approach is as inevitable as it is problematic; it has a chance of being fruitful precisely because it takes us through classic texts to fundamental assumptions and, I hope, beyond them.

A brief look at Olivier's book may illustrate the difficulties of such an exploration. Both Sophocles and Freud, Olivier maintains, focus on Oedipus, the son in love with the mother, murderer of his father. But where is Jocasta in the story of Oedipus? Where is the account of her desire, the assessment of her guilt? Why, as Oedipus has more and more come to occupy a central place in our cultural mythology and in our psychic topography, has Jocasta been ignored and forgotten? Olivier insists on reminding us that inasmuch as we are identified with Oedipus, we too are the sons and daughters of Jocasta.

Olivier's book is meant to break the silence surrounding women in psychoanalytic theory, to inscribe the female referent into a system in which woman has been no more than a fantasy constructing the subjectivity of man. Her promising beginning, however, does not lead Olivier to achieve her goal, for, even though she breaks one silence surrounding women, she maintains another. Her book is not about Jocaste, but about her *enfants,* more specifically about her *filles.* As she revises psychoanalysis to include the female story of development, Olivier concentrates on the little girl, compared to the little boy, both in relation to a mother who remains just as much an other, just as absent, and just as silent as Jocasta does in the story of Oedipus. If woman ceases to be the object in Olivier's analysis, she does so only in the role of daughter; when she becomes a mother, her subjectivity disappears from the purview of classical drama and psychoanalytic theory, even in its feminist revisions.

The change from "les enfants de Jocaste" to "les enfants de Clytemnestre" shifts the emphasis to the topic of anger, but does not in itself succeed in breaking the mother's silence. For if the children of Jocasta conspire in the continued absence of the mother from the story of development, the children of Clytemnestra actively murder the mother into silence. Luce Irigaray sees the murder of Clytemnestra as the originary moment of civilization under paternal law, more archaic than the Freudian founding murder of the father by his sons in the primitive horde (*Le corps-à-corps avec la mère*). The children of Clytemnestra respond with extreme and violent anger (at the mother and in the name of the father) to the mother's own rage (at the father and, paradoxically, in the name of her children as well as in her own name). Thereby, as Irigaray puts it, they insure the mother's exclusion from culture and the symbolic order. Maternal anger, threatening and endangering, must be made illegitimate, must be erased from discourse, an erasure which reaches also to other dimensions of maternal subjectivity.

The purpose of this paper is to begin to define the shapes of maternal subjectivity by using, as an "instrument of cartography" one of its articulations—maternal anger. But if I approach maternal anger through psychoanalytic and classical texts, I remain subject to the dilemma illustrated by Olivier and by the story of Clytemnestra: I have to begin with Clytemnestra's children, and not with Clytemnestra; I have to speak as a daughter. Can the topography of maternal anger be mapped in traditional classical and psychoanalytic narratives or do these texts limit us to the expressions and projections of fathers, husbands and children? Can we perhaps find the strictly maternal articulations of anger in the work of contemporary women writers? In addressing both of these questions, I recognize that, in privileging anger, I represent maternal subjectivity from one particular vantage point, a vantage point that is unavoidable perhaps since anger may well be what defines subjectivity whenever the subjective is denied speech.

I

I begin, then, with Freud's by now overly familiar narrative, which states that "a powerful tendency to aggressiveness is always present beside a powerful love, and the more passionately a child loves its object the more sensitive does it become to disappointments and frustrations from that object; and in the end the love must succumb to the accumulated hostility. . . . It is the special nature of the mother-child relationship that leads, with equal inevitability, to the destruction of the child's love" ("Femininity"). For Freud, anger between child and mother, anger directed specifically at the mother, fundamentally underlies the sequence of individual maturation. It is only by positing the daughter's hostility and resentment at the mother that Freud can motivate the girl's shift in libidinal attachment from mother to father, a shift he considers fundamental. We can see, in his late essays on "Femininity" and "Female Sexuality," how he strains to find sufficient grounding for this hostility.

Freud's plot is clearly overdetermined; the girl comes to hate her mother for every possible reason. Unlike the boy, the girl is unable to modulate the ambivalence that colors any powerful attachment; her relation with her mother, Freud maintains, consists of an unresolved and immature mixture of affection and anger for the rest of her life. Yet her entrance into maturity and adulthood, her establishment of the "feminine situation" as Freud calls it, does depend on her abandonment of the attachment to her mother, on her acceptance of the father as object of desire, and her replacement of the wish for a penis with the wish for a baby.

This shift from mother to father, certainly the most dubious in Freud's system, needs to be overdetermined. When he tries to look at the subsequent period of female development, adulthood, Freud's narrative becomes even more fragmentary. A woman of thirty, Freud tells us, is psychically rigid and unchangeable, depleted by the work of becoming-woman. For her, he maintains, "there are no paths open to further development" ("Femininity"). Moreover, as Freud says, "one gets an impression that a man's love and a woman's are a phase apart psychologically" ("Femininity"): the woman's emotional fulfillment, unlike the man's, comes not from her relationship with her husband but from the attachment to her children (actually, Freud privileges the son here), through whom she vicariously gains access to her own earliest moments of infantile plenitude.

Freud's narrative, even if we take it entirely on his terms, contains a profound paradox, one that he does not and cannot see. On the one hand, he insists that female fulfillment lies in the relation between mother and child; on the other, he posits a necessary and hostile rupture of that relation by the child. What he fails to look at is how the mother herself experiences the rupture on which he insists. If the story of individual development, as Freud tells it, rests on a process of separation from the mother, then the mother's part in that process remains absent from theoretical and narrative representation.

When the Freudian plot of female development is revised, first by the early female analysts (especially Melanie Klein and Helene Deutsch) and later by feminist theorists (especially Nancy Chodorow, Dorothy Dinnerstein, Jane Flax, and Luce Irigaray), its two main features remain constant: a woman's greatest attachment and most fulfilling emotional relationship is still said to be with her children, and those children, these theories still insist, must break from her through anger and hostility. But, for feminist theory, this rupture is much less radical than it is for Freud. The girl's attachments are more triangular, more split between mother and father: Helene Deutsch speaks of the girl's "bi-sexual oscillation between father and mother." This feminist attenuation of the Freudian plot, however, does not alter its presentation of a mother who is overly invested in her child, powerless in the world, a constraining rather than an enabling force in the girl's development, and an inadequate and disappointing object of identification. I would maintain, then, that feminist theorizing, for the most part, still presents the adult woman's position in the terms outlined by Freud.

Although feminist psychoanalytic theorists are now beginning to speak of the absence of the mother as subject from psychoanalysis, Julia Kristeva, Luce Irigaray, Nancy Chodorow, Carol Gilligan, Susan Suleiman, Barbara Johnson, myself, and others have, at this point, only begun to write the developmental story from a maternal perspective. These efforts at revision still take the form of a critique of existing theories which have silenced the mother's experience. It is questionable whether, in the terms in which it argues, psychoanalytic feminist writing can go beyond this critique. And, I would argue, this goes for feminist theory more generally, inasmuch as it has adopted a psychoanalytic framework. In all psychoanalytic writing, the child is the subject—the mother is, in Kristeva's terms, in the position of the "abject" who threatens a tenuous boundary between the not-yet-subject and the not-yet-object; she remains the object who enables or impedes the child's development (see especially *The Powers of Horror: An Essay on Abjection*). The mother's experience can only be named inasmuch as it is a response to the child's: as the story of the mother's participation in the child's process of separation. Yet, as such, this maternal story, even when feminist theory tries to write it, does not begin to grant the mother agency, initiative, or subjectivity.

What would happen if we were to try to tell this untold tale, staying within the terms of psychoanalytic discourse? How can we invest with speech the silence that defines maternal experience? There is, as Linda Orr has pointed out, a strange liaison between silence and anger: silence makes us uncomfortable because we tend to suspect that it conceals anger, as in "Are you mad at me?" Faced with the mother's silence, we posit her anger. This projected angry mother would react to the child's so-called "inevitable" hostility with anger of her own, would feel wronged when, after years of nurturing and care, she is left behind. And then we would see that should she rebel, should she express her own feelings about an enforced and inevitable separation, she would cease to be maternal. For the essence of the maternal in psychoanalytic writing lies in the service to the interests of the child. And to be angry is to assert one's own self, not to subordinate it to the development of another's self. A mother cannot articulate anger *as a mother*: she must step out of a culturally circumscribed role which commands mothers to be caring and nurturing to others, even at the expense of themselves.

Moreover, to be angry is to create a space of separation, to isolate oneself temporarily; such breaks in connection, such disruptions of relationship, again challenge the role that not only psychoanalysis, but culture itself assigns to the mother. Our culture's conjunction of anger and aggression, that is, of feeling and behavior, moreover, makes the mother's anger doubly threatening and precludes the expression and perhaps even the experience of it. We are haunted by the specter of Medea, the woman who turns her anger at her husband into violence against her children. Furthermore, our cultural separation between care and anger, care and self-interest, makes it as impossible for the mother to integrate anger into her activity of mothering, as for the mother to care for herself even as she nurtures her children. Unconscious desires for the mother's unconditional love, unconscious beliefs in her omnipotence and potential destructiveness, beliefs present even in feminist writings about motherhood, (we need only to think of Olivier here) create irrational, pervasive fears of the mother's aggressive power. These fears and needs may well be responsible for the inability to theorize an anger that can co-exist with love and that does not turn into aggression.

Even as feminist theorizing, based in psychoanalysis, urges feminists to shift their political allegiance back from father to mother, even as it urges us to sympathize with our mothers' position in patriarchy, it is still, as Chodorow and Contratto have pointed out in "The Fantasy of the Perfect Mother" (in *Rethinking the Family*, edited by B. Thorne and M. Yalom), written from the child's primary process perspective: permeated with desires for the mother's approval, with fear of her power, and with anger and resentment at her powerlessness.

But to tell this part of the psychoanalytic narrative is still to assume that the child's development necessitates a rupture from the mother, that the mother is overly invested in her child and is devastated by the break, that attachment is profoundly endangered by the expression of anger, that maternal subjectivity exists exclusively in response to the child's. The psychoanalytic plot has not only silenced the mother's response to separation; it also allows us only a narrow space in which to fill in what is missing. Investing maternal silence with anger further isolates the mother and mythologizes her destructive power. Suggesting that we posit anger as the essence of an untold maternal experience, and implying, at the same time, that anger is the antithesis of the maternal, psychoanalytic theory actually facilitates separation, placing those who theorize into the position of the child and placing the mother into a position of otherness.

II

I move from psychoanalytic to literary texts in the search for a fuller narrative of maternal anger, and a fuller representation of maternal subjectivity. Is the literary plot of individual development, unlike the psychoanalytic story, capable of including the mother's point of view, not only her own part in the mother-child interaction, but her own subjectivity, not exclusively determined by her child's? Can the mother write/tell her own version of this story, can she write/tell the anger that is surely part, and surely not all of it? Or does she co-conspire in her own silence, afraid to reveal her story to her child? In an effort to explore the parameters of female authorship, I go to the work of women writers for the mother's own story of separation, told in her own voice. Doing so, I imagine a plot which would include, without polarizing, anger and love, attachment and separation. But I turn to female authorship with caution. For the psychoanalytic and classical paradigms I have been discussing convincingly demonstrate the depths of cultural fears, internalized by children and by mothers. Mothers also are the children of Clytemnestra. Yet, I believe that mother's experiences may be quite different from our images, and that maternal anger may take a shape we will remain incapable of imagining as long as maternal subjectivity is denied speech, and as long as we persist in perceiving as children.

To find this different story I shall look at one text, a short story by Alice Walker, entitled "Everyday Use," read in conjunction with Walker's famous essay "In Search of Our Mothers' Gardens" written at the same period, and an essay written five years later, "*One* Child of One's Own." The choice of the texts of a black woman writer written in the 1970s is a deliberate one. For the black woman, doubly oppressed by a white patriarchal culture, anger has more pointed implications. For the particular generation of black writers to which Walker belongs, moreover, the issue of separation from parents, home and past is a vital one—it has political as well as psychological dimensions. The redefinition of the past involved in the liberation movement of the sixties constitutes an important preoccupation in the writings of Walker, Toni Cade Bambara, Toni Morrison, Gloria Naylor, and Paule Marshall, writers who, as Valerie Smith has argued, use maternal narrative voices as figures for their own ambivalence about the radical activism of the 1960s. In their essays and their fictions, these writers situate themselves in the problematic position of daughter-writers in relation to a revered, largely oral maternal past. They belong to a generation whose writing is obsessed with issues of continuity and separation, connection and disconnection from two pasts, often in conflict with one another—the immediate past of their mothers, who have made a particular, perhaps questionable, adjustment to the dominant white American culture, and the more distant heritage of their African ancestors, which these younger black writers began to reclaim, often at the expense of their allegiance to their own immediate families. Walker's story, located in a black Southern community in the 1960s, reminds us that the analysis of psychological and literary representations of maternal experience and of the poetics of anger need to be grounded in specific cultural, political and historical contexts. And Walker's "ambiguously non-hegemonic" posture, as Margaret Homans has called it, her position both inside the cultural paradigms defined through classical and psychoanalytic texts, and outside of them, enables her to question the validity of these paradigms in a very particular way.

"Everyday Use" is unusual for the maternal perspective it offers: it is the first-person narration of an older black mother awaiting the return of her daughter, Dee. After moving away from their poor rural home to the city, Dee has become successful by breaking with a familial past she has come to view as oppressive. Also waiting for Dee is a sister—Maggie—in every sense her opposite. Shy, homely, nervous, ashamed, Maggie is the daughter who made no break but remained at home. As the story begins, we get a very definite sense of the articulate strength and rich quality of the narrator-mother's voice, a voice all the more remarkable because its possessor assures us that she does not have a quick tongue, that she is uneducated and virtually illiterate, and that she mistrusts words, books, and knowledge. Whereas some critics have viewed the mother's voice as a narrative incongruity or a conceptual flaw in the story, for me this self-disavowing voice *is* the story. What interests me in particular is the process by which the mother's voice evolves to the point of "everyday use"—to the point of being able to articulate both her love and her anger. Tracing the emergence of the mother's voice could shed some light on the connections between oral and written traditions, between maternal and daughterly voices and between anger and writing.

The misunderstandings that mark the reunion between mother and daughter in the story revolve around Dee's relation to her familial past, a past she has rejected by leaving and by Africanizing her name, but which she now wants to reclaim as fashionable "heritage." She admires the wooden benches, the traditional butter churn, the old quilts she had refused as backward when she went to college, but now wants to own for purposes of interior decoration. For her, heritage is something to be displayed on the coffee table and on the wall; for her sister Maggie, on the other hand, who had been promised the quilts made by her grandmother and aunt out of pieces of old clothing, the past is a living reality in which she participates both by planning to use the quilts on her bed, and by learning how to quilt herself. The rich image of the quilt, a patchwork of fragmentary and material representations of the past's survival into the present, delineates these daughters' relation to their matriarchal heritage. The daughter who has left her maternal heritage can only reconnect with it intellectually and aesthetically, in ignorance of its daily reality. The daughter who has remained home knows the reality of the past, but is scared of present and future. The mother who has been abandoned and betrayed by one daughter ends up fostering and protecting the other more needy one who has remained loyal to her.

The mother-narrator reports Dee's appearance and that of the man who is accompanying her, in a tolerant voice marked by understated humor and subtle irony. Yet, as the story progresses, the two visitors come to look more and more foreign, less and less in touch with the reality of her world. Still she remains calm, open-minded and curious:

> "Well," I say. "Dee."
> "No, Mama," she says. "Not 'Dee,' Wangero Leewanika Kemanjo!"
> "What happened to 'Dee?' " I wanted to know.
> "She's dead," Wangero said. "I couldn't bear it any longer, being named after the people who oppress me."
> "You know as well as me you was named after your Aunt Dicie. . . ."
> "But who was *she* named after?" asked Wangero.
> "I guess after Grandma Dee," I said.
> "And who was she named after?" asked Wangero.
> "Her mother," I said, and saw Wangero was getting tired.

The mother quietly goes along with Wangero, with the longhaired Hakim-a-Barber, with all of Dee's requests. Reporting the visit, she presents herself as passive and totally accepting: she quietly takes all of Dee's abuse. Yet her narrating voice demonstrates a different strength, her ability to take pleasure in her daughter's difference without conceding any of her own choices and values. Through irony she is able to modulate her reactions and communicate to the reader/to herself, the distance she insists on maintaining from Dee's reality, without visibly rejecting her. Even as she experiences her daughter's strangeness as uncomfortable, she notices and notes every detail about her and is able to delight in her perception of it. Whereas the mother as character is passive, immobile, almost pathetic, the mother as narrator is funny, active, in control. It is the power of this mother-narrator which underscores the acquiescence and defeat of the mother-character, an acquiescence which reveals her consent to her own erasure through much of the story.

The confrontation between mother and daughter occurs over Maggie's modest resigned concession of the quilts to Dee. " 'She can have them, Mama,' she [Maggie] said, like someone used to never winning anything, of having anything reserved for her. 'I can 'member Grandma Dee without the quilts.' " Confronted with the necessity of making a choice, the mother chooses Maggie and rejects Dee, and the way in which she asserts her choice, her sudden freedom to act, her sudden transformation from passive object to agent in the narrative constitutes the crux of the story. It is Maggie's statement that releases the mother's anger and thereby also her love, propelling this woman who only moments before felt too heavy to get up from her chair into a rapid series of actions: "When I looked at her like that something hit me in the top of my head and ran down to the soles of my feet. Just like when I'm in church and the spirit of God touches me and I get happy and shout. I did something I never had done before: hugged Maggie to me, then dragged her into the room, snatched the quilts out of Miss Wangero's hands and dumped them into Maggie's lap. Maggie just sat there on my bed with her mouth open." What is it that provokes this almost religious illumination, freeing the mother to act, to speak out, and, I would argue, eventually to tell her tale?

As we go back over the story, we see that the almost violent abruptness in this scene—snatching, hugging, dragging, dumping—has been present in the mother's voice, if not in her actions, since the story's beginning. The mother's surface serenity barely succeeds in disguising her profound agitation as she waits. Thus, Dee's arrival is preceded by an imaginary meeting on a TV talk show, in which Dee hugs a much slimmer and more verbal mother and pins an orchid to her dress. As she fantasizes this happy reconciliation, the mother immediately adds an alternate, much angrier version in parentheses: "(A pleasant surprise of course: what would they do if parent and child came on the show only to curse out and insult each other?)." As she describes herself, the contrast to the imaginary TV mother comes into focus: she is big-boned, rough, manly, she can kill hogs and knock out bull calves, and she can eat their innards. Unlike the TV mother and unlike Dee, she cannot look a white man in the eye, or speak with a witty tongue. She cannot be the mother Dee wants her to be.

Other reminiscences add to the atmosphere of expectation, gradually making it more disturbing. Maggie's pathetic gestures and appearance are, we find out, the result of a fire that burned down their old house, a fire in which she was severely injured. As the mother recalls Dee's behavior during the fire, she becomes more visibly angry: "Why don't you dance around the ashes? I'd wanted to ask her. She had hated that house so much. I used to think she hated Maggie too." A greater and greater distance develops in the course of these thoughts between Dee, on the one hand, and the mother and Maggie on the other. Dee's education appears aggressive, her attitude almost violent: "She used to read to us without pity; forcing words, lies, other folks' habits, whole lives upon us, sitting trapped and ignorant underneath her voice. She washed us in a river of make-believe, burned us with a lot of knowledge we didn't necessarily need to know." The mother recalls Dee's verbal aggression, her "scalding humor that erupted like bubbles in lye," and recalls also her own anger, always contained, "Often I fought off the temptation to shake her." Her reflections end with the speculation that "when Dee sees it (their new house), she will want to tear it down."

Contrary to her own self-assessment, the mother-narrator has succeeded in establishing, through subtle manipulation of imagery and irony, the quality of the rift between her world and her daughter's and has suggested that under the serene surface of the yard, lurks anger and simmering violence. References to slaughtered pigs, burned-down houses, hurtful looks, and violent alien words paint feelings and gestures of mutual aggression, even as the mother calmly sits and waits for her daughter's return.

Dee's appearance is in itself felt as aggressive: the loud colors of her dress hurt the mother's eyes. Her first action is to pull out a camera and to snap pictures of mother, sister, cow and house. Her thoughtless comments, her distance from their lives, only confirm the initial impression. Dee dominates the conversation and controls the plot of the meeting. The mother, however, remains tolerant and interested. Although she turns a rather vicious humor against Hakim-a-Barber, "the barber," as she calls him to the reader, she maintains the connection with Dee, until she is confronted with the necessity of making a choice between the conflicting needs of her two children. I would argue that when the mother hears Maggie's resigned acquiescence, she sees it as a betrayal of the grandmother and aunt from whom Maggie learned to quilt. As Valerie Smith has suggested in "Writing Revolution," the mother sees in Maggie's angerless fear an image of her own passive acceptance of Dee's aggression, her own suppressed anger. And then she claims her authority and expresses her anger openly, asserting her value and the value of her life against the rejection of her daughter. Ironically, of course, her action connects her only more firmly to the angry and assertive Dee.

The transformation Maggie undergoes in the story—from the frightened attempt to hide, to her inarticulate angry sucking in of the breath, to her short concession speech and finally her *real* smile—charts her competitive relationship with her sister, as well as her own relation to her past and her mother. For if the mother has been angry with the powerful Dee all along, she has also been enraged at the powerless pathetic Maggie, calling her a "lame animal," describing her "dopey hangdog look." As with Dee, however, her helpless anger at Maggie has not prevented her from noticing every detail of her appearance, from guessing and understanding her minutest feelings. And this sympathy enables her to identify with Maggie's acquiescence and to find it unacceptable.

Initially, Maggie's helplessness, combined with Dee's contempt, have paralyzed, incapacitated the mother to the point where she was absolutely unable to speak out. Finally freed by Dee's excessive demand and Maggie's passive acquiescence to acknowledge her anger at both daughters, the one who leaves and the one who clings, the mother can develop into someone who resembles much more closely the narrator who manipulates so brilliantly the ironies of this tale. If the story ends in a scene of separation from Dee, it is one provoked by the mother herself, the mother who remains behind, content with her own life, with its quiet stasis. That separation is eased, of course, by Maggie's presence, by Maggie's unconditional acceptance of the female heritage the mother can hand down to her, and by the visibly empowering effect that the gift of the quilts, and her acceptance into the female community of quilters, have on her: "Maggie smiled; maybe at the sunglasses. But a real smile, not scared." Dee goes with Hakim-a-Barber to the powerful male world (both white and black) of books and television shows in which she has always felt comfortable. As she puts on her sunglasses, she comes to look at the world through their different perspective. Maggie, even if she marries John Thomas, will remain home, loyal to her mother and her maternal past. It is important to note that the triangle in this story is not with father (he's totally absent) or husband, but between two sisters and their mother. The male world is there only by implication—in the claims it makes on the daughters, in the separations it effects from the mother.

Walker wrote this story at the same time as her influential essay on black women's creativity, "In Search of Our Mothers' Gardens." In the essay, Walker connects black women's artistic creativity very firmly to a maternal past; although the creative spirit of the mothers was thwarted by oppression and abuse, much can be learned from their hidden spirituality. Their artistic expression took unconventional forms: storytelling, quilt-making, gardening, singing. Her own voice as a writer, Walker maintains, derives from her mother whose oral stories she can translate into writing, whose manner of telling them she has absorbed, whose gardening she admires. In the essay Walker insists on the connection between her maternal heritage and her identity as a writer, but unlike the story, the essay is written entirely in the voice of the daughter who finds her own voice as she revises the story of two mothers—her own and her adopted literary mother, Virginia Woolf.

"Everyday Use" constitutes an interesting, though oblique, comment and fictional illustration of the essay. The mother's remarkable voice, we assume, derives from the generation of Walker's mother—she tells us in the essay that she often writes about characters who are older. If we assume that Walker imagines a mother, her mother, confronted with two daughters whose relation to their common past is vastly different, we wonder where, in the story, Walker would situate *herself*—with Dee, the verbal city daughter, or with Maggie, the scared rural daughter? Clearly, Walker and her generation of women writers need to find a position between Maggie's (staying home and not changing) and Dee's (leaving home and rejecting it or turning it into artifact). In writing the mother's anger, is not Walker trying to understand, to empathize with the maternal response to her own distance and closeness, her own rejection and acceptance of her maternal heritage? For Walker's *writing* itself constitutes a form of distance, a distance she modulates and reduces by writing about the past, by using it as a way back to establishing closeness. In so doing, Walker has granted *the mother* a voice with which to tell that story, but has also made *herself* vulnerable to becoming the object of maternal anger, to being rejected in the persona of the bad daughter Dee, even while she is nurtured in the persona of the good daughter Maggie. Yet in her dedication, "for your grandmama," we see that Walker addresses her own daughter in the story, placing herself in the position of link between grandmother and granddaughter, in the position of mother and daughter both. This particular doubleness of the narrative voice is the key to its unusual and seemingly incongruous quality—it is the product both of mother and daughter, both of oral and written tradition, both of internal authenticity and external projection, both of extraliterary and of literary strength, both of anger and love.

As she writes the story of maternal anger, Walker imagines a mother who is tolerant and generous, even as she is angry; a mother who can feel and express her anger without doing devastating damage; a mother who is able to combine anger with attentive love; but a mother whose power is limited by her circumstances, who knows that one child needs her more than the other. Although Walker's story is the result of the daughter-writer's attempt to imagine the mother's story, *and* the result of the mother-writer's attempt to articulate her experience of motherhood and daughterhood, it is not free from the fearful projections of maternal anger we have seen before.

Anger in this story does ultimately create a rift between mother and daughter: the effects on Dee are suggested only in the distancing gesture of putting on her sunglasses and covering her face. If Dee loses as much in power as Maggie gains by the mother's choice, we can begin to understand why the maternal voice in the story is a creation of the daughter's imagination and of her guilt. We can begin to understand why the mother herself would hesitate to write her own version of this story as long as her child can read it, why the mother continues to conspire to perpetuate her own silence and why Walker must, at each point, act as a daughter and as a mother both. Walker's story does not and ultimately cannot resolve the differences between the three female voices and positions it explores—there are, after all, only two old hand-made quilts and, as some women in the family leave home, their capacity to reproduce their traditions by producing more quilts is lost. At a moment of radical social change, and in an economy of scarcity, divisions and the anger they evoke, can find no easy resolution.

Walker's later essay, "*One* Child of One's Own: A Meaningful Digression within the Work(s)," represents a further elaboration of her position in relation to anger and the maternal. The obvious reference to Woolf, as well as Walker's allusions to Tillie Olsen's *Silences,* and to George Eliot, Jane Austen, the Brontës, Sylvia Plath as well as to Nella Larsen, Lorraine Hansberry, and Zora Neale Hurston, seems to underscore a commonality between black women writers and white when it comes to the cultural opposition between writing and motherhood. Walker, in this essay, writes in the voice of a young black mother who traces her progress through the white patriarchal and feminist world of the sixties and seventies. She articulates her own maternal voice through a radical break from her own nonwriting mother who, as a representative of "women's folly," counsels her to have more than one child. Angrily, Walker rejects her mother's voice and, in a strong alliance with her own daughter, she boldly sets *herself* up as the mother, exploring, in great detail, the insights that a *maternal* perspective on the world offers her. That perspective is filled with anger: at "women's folly" which has imprisoned previous generations of black women, at the white pediatrician who won't make a housecall, at the white feminist who erases the words and fears the bodies of black women, at the black women who identify with their men and therefore abandon their responsibilities to women across the world. Her ability to write her anger forcefully makes it possible to strengthen the voice she has adopted; it enables her to see that in "the racism and sexism of an advanced capitalist society" which would "deny [her] the untrampled blossoming of [her] existence" her child is "only the very least of her obstacles in her chosen work."

III

In my reading of this essay, I puzzled for a long while over this particular formulation which seemed to reveal the existence of a great deal of unacknowledged anger at her daughter Rebecca. The suppression of her anger at her child emerged with greater clarity as I thought over other details of the essay: the speaker's memories of her own harassed mother as she tried to get five children ready for church, her own memories of the unpleasantness of pregnancy and the excruciating pain of childbirth, her discomfort with the changes in her body caused by pregnancy and birth, her fear that having a child had changed her irrevocably, that it would prevent her from writing, and, most powerful, perhaps, her actual experience of the child as "a giant stopper in [my] throat." I concluded that not only was Walker's speaker unable to write as a mother without separating in anger from her own mother and her "women's folly," that is, without making the break that Freud's classic psychoanalytic plot demands of daughters, but that she also adhered to a pervasive cultural taboo: her anger can never be openly and directly aimed *at* her child, its very existence must be repressed.

A question by Mary Helen Washington has prompted me to attempt to rethink this conclusion and to add this coda to my essay. When I read this paper in the fall of 1986 at the Boston Area Colloquium on Feminist Theory at Northeastern University, Washington asked why I focused my analysis on only one aspect of Walker's essay, her anger at her mother and her possible anger at her daughter, thereby ignoring "what the essay was really about," her anger at white feminists. Was I in fact ignoring "what the essay was really about" or was there another question I should have asked: why the particular conjunction of these two themes in this essay? Why frame an essay about black women's anger at white feminists with suggestions for the optimal reproductive choices open to women writers? And why interrupt her discussion of ways to resolve the opposition of writing and motherhood with an analysis of the absence of black voices and bodies from the important monuments of the (white) feminist movement?

Rereading the essay with these questions in mind reveals meaningful repressions in the psychoanalytic feminist methodology I have been using in this paper. Specifically, it glosses over the political dimensions of the anger expressed in Walker's essay and to the relationship between motherhood and politics. Is it significant, for example, that the speaker conceived a child so that her husband might be able to avoid being drafted before he turned 26, so that they might not have to move to Canada? Is it important that her pregnancy was dominated by feelings of rage against the Vietnam war, by feelings of anxiety, depression, and violence? Is it important that her writing constituted the only possible protection against her violent anger? "When I didn't write I thought of making bombs and throwing them. Of shooting racists. Of doing away—as painlessly and neatly as possible . . . —with myself.

Writing saved me from the inconvenience of violence." The essay documents how Walker's speaker moves from the depression that comes with the suppression of anger to the forceful expression that makes anger into an effective political force. And that move, that transformation is intimately connected to her motherhood.

In an essay entitled "The Politics of Anger: On Silence, Ressentiment and Political Speech" (*Socialist Review* 11 [1981]), Peter Lyman asserts that "anger becomes a political resource only when it is collective." In isolation, anger is privatized and neutralized, unrecognizable. This is the problem with an exclusively psychological approach to anger, Lyman suggests, and he envisions a psychology more attuned to the historical reality of our century: "A psychology of suffering would have to understand guilt, anxiety, depression, or hysteria as suppressed social relations. Psychology without this sense of social relations 'mythologizes' human suffering, treating it as essentially individual and as a problem of 'personality.' Psychology serves the interests of the hegemony when it strips human experience of its collective and active character, and conceals oppression by blaming the victims for their symptoms." Throughout her essay, Walker explores the possibilities of turning her anger into a political force by finding the collective that would recognize its legitimacy. This search constitutes a complex and tortuous process of identity-formation. And throughout this process, throughout what she refers to as her pilgrimage, the speaker finds it necessary to separate in anger from the groups she encounters and with whom she tries to bond. She finds she has to reject her maternal ancestry, the representatives of "women's folly," even while she feels the pain of that rejection. She rejects the feminists who are incapable of seeing her as both black and a woman, and she rejects the black women and men who are incapable of seeing her as both a woman and black. How, in the face of her ensuing isolation does Walker's speaker manage to avoid the internalization of her anger and its resultant depression?

It might now be possible to suggest that what allows her instead to speak her anger is her unquestioned alliance with her child. Walker's is a journey of forever changing allegiances, charting a heterogenous, shifting and often self-contradictory identity. In conceiving of identity in this manner, we move beyond a Freudian model of a family romance in which the developing individual shifts her cathexes from mother, to father, to husband, and then to her own child. If we confront, beyond the family, the claims of racial, class, linguistic, ethnic, gender, and cultural affiliations and assimilations, and the clash between culturally dominant and subordinated groups, and if we grant, to members of each of these groups, the right to subjectivity and the access to the symbolic, we need to develop a more complicated model of identity and self-consciousness. Such a model would have to reflect a more tortuous process of adopting, and continually refining and redefining a sense of selfhood. That sense of selfhood would have to balance the personal with the political, subjective experience with a cognitive process of identification with various group-identities. It would have to include a consciousness of oppression and political struggle.

If Walker is tracing in this essay the process of identity as a process of shifting affiliation, she may be suggesting that in the course of such a process one bond would need to remain unproblematic and thereby consistently empowering. "I began to see," Walker's voice suggests," that her birth and the difficulties it provided us, joined me to a body of experience and a depth of commitment to my own life hard to comprehend otherwise." It is perhaps this sense of commitment and self-regard that makes it possible for the speaker to develop the sense of righteousness, self-protection, and self-assertion that is the precondition of a forcefully political anger. And the alliance with Rebecca may well give her both a personal sense of affirmation and a collective sense of identity. "It is not my child who has purged my face from history and herstory and left mystory just that, a mystery; my child loves my face and would have it on every page, if she could, as I have loved my own parents' faces above all the others, and have refused to let them be denied, or myself to let them go."

The speaker's refusal or inability to acknowledge her anger at her child may well corroborate a pervasive cultural taboo to which all women, whether white or black, are subject, as I suggested above. Yet, clearly, more is at stake here. Taking Marilyn Frye's suggestion and viewing Walker's anger as an "instrument of cartography" which could help us to chart who, in this essay, she represents herself as being, we can now begin to appreciate difference— the specificity of her situation as a black, woman writer, writing at a particular moment of feminist consciousness. We can see her anger, her various forms of anger, as strategies of self-assertion. And the self she asserts may be multiple in its adherences and divided in its alliances, but, Walker seems to suggest, it cannot be an isolated one: "We are together, my child and I. Mother and child, yes, but *sisters* really, against whatever denies us what we are." Such a formulation suggests, as well, that this model of identity as process is not, for Walker, an antihumanist, postmodern one of an alienated subject divided in language and against itself. If my reading is valid, Walker asserts the need for affiliation, bonding, and connection, as well as a sense of affirmation, as basic to the process of identity.

After finding in Walker's essay a model of identity and a form of anger that moves beyond a privatized psychology to political significance, I find I cannot close my reading here, but have to place it, once again, under analytic scrutiny. I find that this reading also leaves something unsaid. In particular, I am still bothered by what I have referred to here as the speaker's unquestioned, unproblematic bond with her child and by the place of the child in the essay. "*One* Child of One's Own"—the possessive in the title is in itself disturbing. And so is, finally, the erasure of the child, as person, from the entire body of the essay. Although at times Rebecca feels like a barrier to writing, "a giant stopper in my mouth," she is most often presented as an asset, as the child who "by the age of seven, at the latest, is one's friend, and can be told of the fears one has, that she can by listening to one . . . help allay." When the daughter becomes "the sister" in political struggle, I worry that she disappears as daughter, as child, as person. As she loves her mother's face and would have it on every page, I worry that her own face disappears from the pages of the essay. Could this perhaps be the form that the speaker's unacknowledged anger at Rebecca takes—the form of erasure? Does anger, in getting diverted from the personal and psychological to the political, erase love and recognition of the individual child?

In answer to these questions, I can only suggest that Walker's speaker makes, in the essay, not a definitive but a provisional bond with her child, a bond motivated at the time by pragmatism and need—by the child's dependence on her and, conversely, by her need for one bond that will allow her to call the other allegiances in her life into question. In another context, other bonds may remain unquestioned and this one may emerge as problematic. Of all the relationships in her life, it makes eminent sense at that moment to choose this one as the one that provides the background for all the others. Yet in suppressing her anger at her child, Walker runs the risk of idealizing motherhood, of idealizing her child, and thereby of erasing her. She runs the risk of simply reversing an all too familiar relationship, that is, of turning the child into an adoring nurturing "maternal" figure, the object who enables the growth of her subjectivity. Most importantly, perhaps, through this gap in her text, she runs the risk of going backwards, from the political back to the personal and psychological.

Teresa de Lauretis has suggested that in feminist analysis the personal and the political must be allowed to coexist, in tension, without being collapsed ("Feminist Studies/Critical Studies: Issues, Terms, Contexts," in *Feminist Studies/Critical Studies*). Walker's painful, fractured, and self-contradictory essay provides an opportunity to understand how difficult and tenuous that coexistence is and perhaps has to be. Reading Walker, feminist readers—black and white, mothers and daughters—can begin to define the contours of maternal anger in such a way as to demystify its power without weakening its force. Doing so, we can begin to claim a place for mothers and for women. In that place we can begin to imagine the conjunction of anger and love, to describe more than one dimension of maternal subjectivity. We can explore the historical, economic, and political circumstances that have profound effects on familial interactions, contextualizing the relationship of love and anger, anger and aggression, subjectivity and anger, and sorting out issues of desire, competition, and identification. We can begin to map the topography of a subjectivity based not on autonomy but on a fundamental connectedness. Doing so, we can perhaps cease to be Clytemnestra's children and free ourselves to listen to the loving and angry voices of our mothers, and to articulate our own anger as well as our love.

BELL HOOKS

Writing the Subject:
Reading The Color Purple

*T*he *Color Purple* broadens the scope of literary discourse, asserting its primacy in the realm of academic thought while simultaneously stirring the reflective consciousness of a mass audience. Unlike most novels by any writer it is read across race, class, gender, and cultural boundaries. It is truly a popular work—a book of the people—a work that has many different meanings for many different readers. Often the meanings are not interesting, contained as they are within a critical discourse that does not resist the urge to simplify, to overshadow, to make this work by a contemporary African-American writer mere sociological treatise on black life or radical feminist tract. To say even as some critics do that it is a modern day "slave narrative" or to simply place the work within the literary tradition of epistolary sentimental novels is also a way to contain, restrict, control. Categorizing in this way implies that the text neither demands nor challenges, rather, that it can be adequately and fully discussed within an accepted critical discourse, one that remains firmly within the boundaries of conservative academic aesthetic intentionality. While such discourse may illuminate aspects of the novel, it also obscures, suppresses, silences. Michel Foucault's comments on discourse in *The History of Sexuality* serve as a useful reminder that critical vision need not be fixed or static, that "discourse can be both an instrument and an effect of power, but also a hindrance, a stumbling block, a point of resistance and a starting point for an opposing strategy."

To critically approach *The Color Purple* from an oppositional perspective, it is useful to identify gaps—spaces between the text and conventional critical points of departure. That the novel's form is epistolary is most obvious, so

---

© 1988 by Bell Hooks. Published for the first time in this volume.

apparent even that it is possible to overlook the fact that it begins not with
a letter but an opening statement, a threatening command—speaker unidenti-
fied. "You better not never tell nobody but God. It'd kill your mammy."
Straightaway Celie's letter writing to God is placed in a context of domination; she is obeying orders. Her very first letter reveals that the secret that
can be told to no one but God has to do with sexuality, with sexual morality,
with a male parent's sexual abuse of a female child. In form and content the
declared subject carries traces of the sentimental novel with its focus on female
characters and most importantly the female as potential victim of exploitative
male sexual desire, but this serves only as a background for deviation, for
subversion.

Significantly, *The Color Purple* is a narrative of "sexual confession."
Statements like: "First he put his thing up against my hip and sort of wiggle
it around. Then he grabs hold my titties. Then he put his thing inside my
pussy." refer solely to sexual encounters. Throughout *The Color Purple*, sexuality is graphically and explicitly discussed. Though a key narrative pattern
in the novel, it is usually ignored. As readers approaching this novel in the
context of a white supremacist patriarchal society wherein black women have
been and continue to be stereotyped as sexually loose, a black woman writer
imagining a black female character who writes about sexuality in letters to
God, using graphic and explicit language, may not seem unusual or even interesting, particularly since graphic descriptions of sexual encounters conform to a current trend in women's writing. But this is most unlikely, as it
is the culture's fascination with sexual autobiography that has led to a burgeon-
ing of fiction and true-life stories focusing on sexual encounters. This trend
is especially evident in popular women-centered novels. Attracting mass au-
diences in similar ways as their nineteenth-century predecessors, these new
works captivate readers not by covert reference to sexual matters but by explicit exposure and revelation. They completely invert the values of the Victorian novel. While the nineteenth-century female protagonist as innocent had
no language with which to speak sexual desire, the contemporary heroine
in the woman-centered novel is not only the speaking sex, the desiring sex;
she is talking sex.

Celie's life is presented in reference to her sexual history. Rosalind
Coward's witty essay, "The True Story of How I Became My Own Person,"
in her collection *Female Desires,* warns against the reproduction of an ideology
where female identity is constructed solely in relationship to sexuality, where
sexual experience becomes the way in which a woman learns self-knowledge.

> There's a danger that such structures reproduce the Victorian
> ideology that sexuality is somehow outside social relationships.

The idea that a woman could become her own person just through sexual experiences and the discovery of sexual needs and dislikes again establishes sexual relations as somehow separate from social structures.

Walker reproduces this ideology in *The Color Purple*. Patriarchy is exposed and denounced as a social structure supporting and condoning male domination of women, specifically represented as black male domination of black females, yet it does not influence and control sexual desire and sexual expression. While Mr. ———, dominating male authority figure, can become enraged at the possibility that his wife will be present at a jukejoint, he has no difficulty accepting her sexual desire for another female. Homophobia does not exist in the novel. Celie's sexual desire for women and her sexual encounter with Shug is never a controversial issue even though it is the catalyst for her resistance to male domination, for her coming to power. Walker makes the powerful suggestion that sexual desire can disrupt and subvert oppressive social structure because it does not necessarily conform to social prescription, yet this realization is undermined by the refusal to acknowledge it as threatening—dangerous.

Sexual desire, initially evoked in the novel as a subversive transformative force, one that enables folk to break radically with convention (Mr. ——— passion for Shug transcends marriage vows; Celie's acceptance and fulfillment of her desire for a female leads her to reject heterosexuality; Shug's free-floating lust shared with many partners, each different from the other, challenges the notion of monogamous coupling) is suppressed and finally absent—a means to an end but not an end in itself. Celie may realize she desires women, express that longing in a passionate encounter with Shug, but just as the signifier lesbian does not exit to name and affirm her experience, no social reality exists so that she can express that desire in ongoing sexual practice. She is seduced and betrayed. Seduced by the promise of an erotic vocation wherein sexual fulfillment is deemed essential to self-recovery and self-realization, she must deny the primacy of this sexual awakening and the pain of sexual rejection.

Ironically, Shug's rejection serves as a catalyst enabling Celie and Albert to renew and transform their heterosexual bonding. Walker upholds the promise of an intact heterosexual bond with a relational scenario wherein the point of intimate connection between coupled male and female is not the acting out of mutual sexual desire for one another, but the displacement of that desire onto a shared object—in this case Shug. Given such a revised framework for the establishment of heterosexual bonds, sex between Shug and Celie does not threaten male-female bonding or affirm the possibility

that women can be fulfilled in a life that does not include intimate relationships with men. As Mariana Valverde emphasizes in *Sex, Power, and Pleasure:*

> Lesbianism is thus robbed of its radical potential because it is
> portrayed as compatible with heterosexuality, or rather as part of
> heterosexuality itself. The contradictions that our society creates
> between hetero- and homosexuality are wished away and social
> oppression is ignored.

Wedded by their mutual desire for Shug, their shared rejection, Celie and
Albert are joined in a sustained committed relationship. Reunited, they stand
together, "two old fools left over from love, keeping each other company under
the stars."

Shug, whose very name suggests that she has the power to generate
excitement without the ability to provide substantive nourishment, must also
give up sexual pleasure. Betrayed by the sexual desire that has been the source
of her power, Shug's lust for a young man is not depicted as an expression
of sexual liberation, of longing for a new and different sexual pleasure, instead
it is a disempowering force, one that exposes her vulnerability and weakness.
Placed within a stereotypical heterosexist framework wherein woman is denied
access to ongoing sexual pleasure which she seeks and initiates, as the novel
progresses Shug is depicted as an aging female seducer who fears the loss of
her ability to use sex as a means to attract and control men, as a way to power.
Until this turning point, sex has been for Shug a necessary and vital source
of pleasure. As object of intense sexual desire, she has had power to shape
and influence the actions of others but always in the direction of a higher good.

Ultimately, Walker constructs an ideal world of true love and commitment
where there is no erotic tension—where there is no sexual desire or sexual
pleasure. Just as the reader's perception of Shug is dramatically altered towards
the end of the novel, so is the way we see and understand Celie's sexual history;
her sexual confession changes when it is revealed that she has not been raped
by her real father. The tragedy and trauma of incest, so graphically and
poignantly portrayed, both in terms of the incest-rape and Celie's sexual
healing which begins when she tells Shug what happened, is trivialized as
the novel progresses. Presented in retrospect as though it was all an absurd
drama, the horror of Celie's early sexual experience and the pleasure of her
sexual awakening assume the quality of spectacle, of exaggerated show. A
curious tale told in part as a strategy to engage and excite the reader's imagination before attention is diverted towards more important revelations. Given
the fascination in this culture with sex and violence, with race and sex, with
sexual deviance, a fascination which is recognized and represented most often

in pornography, Walker's subject has immediate appeal. Readers are placed in the position of voyeurs who witness Celie's torment as victim of incest-rape, as victim of sexual violence in a sadistic master-slave relationship; who watch her sexual exploration of her body and experience vicarious pleasure at her sexual awakening as she experiences her first sexual encounter with Shug. Ironically, pornographic fiction consumed by a mass audience is a genre which has always included narratives describing women engaged in sexual acts with one another, observed by powerful others—usually men. Walker subverts this pattern. As readers we represent the powerful other. Her intent is not to titillate sexually, but to arouse disgust, outrage, and anger at male sexual exploitation of females and to encourage appreciation and acceptance of same-sex female sexual pleasure.

To achieve this end, which is fundamentally anti–male domination, Walker relies on similar narrative strategies and preoccupations as those utilized in the pornographic narrative. Annette Kuhn's essay on representation and sexuality which focuses on pornography's "Lawless seeing" points to the connection between pornographic fiction and other simple narratives:

> in pornographic stories, literary as well as visual, characters are never very strongly developed or psychologically rounded human beings. They perform function, they take on roles already fixed within the commonplace fantasies that porn constructs—the sexually active woman, the Peeping Tom, the plumber out on his rounds. In porn, characters are what they do, and given a minimal amount of familiarity with the genre, the reader needs little by way of explanation in order to understand what is going on. Pornography has a good deal in common with other simple forms of narrative, stories in which characters are no more than what they do and the reader has some general idea, as soon as the story begins, of who is going to do what to whom and with what outcome. . . . In many respects, pornographic stories work like fairy tales.

Characters are very much what they do in *The Color Purple*. Mr. ———— is brute, Lucious the rapist, Harpo the buffoon, Celie the sexual victim, Shug the sexual temptress. Many of the characters perform roles that correspond with racial stereotypes. The image of "the black male rapist" resonates in both racial and sexual stereotypes; Walker's characterization cannot be viewed in a vacuum, as though it does not participate in these discourses which have been primarily used to reinforce domination, both racial and sexual.

Pornography participates in and promotes a discourse that exploits and aesthetisizes domination. Kuhn asserts that pornography insists on sexual difference, that sexual violence in master-slave scenarios reduces this difference to relations of power. Feminists who focus almost exclusively on male violence against women as the central signifier of male domination also view sexual difference as solely a relation of power. Within pornography, Kuhn states, there is

> an obsession with the otherness of femininity, which in common with many forms of otherness seems to contain a threat to the onlooker. Curiosity turns to terror, investigation to torture, the final affirmation of the objecthood of the other. The feminine here represents a threat to the masculine, a threat which demands containment. Sexually violent pornography of this kind concretises this wish for containment in representations which address the spectator as masculine and place the masculine on the side of container of the threat. It insists that sexuality and power are inseparable.

Walker inverts this paradigm. Presuming a female spectator (women and specifically white women from privileged classes are the primary audience for women-centered novels), she constructs a fiction in which it is the masculine threat, represented by black masculinity, that must be contained, controlled, and ultimately transformed. Her most radical re-visioning of the oppressive patriarchal social order is her insistence on the transformation of Mr. ———. He moves from male oppressor to enlightened being, willingly surrendering his attachment to the phallocentric social order reinforced by the sexual oppression of women. His transformation begins when Celie threatens his existence, when her curse disempowers him. Since sexuality and power are so closely linked to politics of domination, Mr. ——— must be completely desexualized as part of the transformative process.

Unable to reconcile sexuality and power, Walker replaces the longing for sexual pleasure with an erotic metaphysic animated by a vision of the unity of all things, by the convergence of erotic and mystical experience. This is ritually enacted as Shug initiates Celie into a spiritual awakening wherein belief in God as white male authority figure, who gives orders and punishes, is supplanted by the vision of a loving God who wants believer to celebrate life, to experience pleasure, a God who is annoyed, "if you walk by the color purple in a field somewhere but don't notice it." In *The Color Purple* Christianity and patriarchy are oppressive social structures which promote anhedonia. Celie and Albert, as oppressed and oppressor, must as part of their personal transformation learn to feel pleasure and develop a capacity to experience happiness. Concurrently, Nettie and Samuel, laboring as missionaries in Africa, develop a critical consciousness that allows them to see the connections between

Western cultural imperialism and Christianity; and this enables them to see God in a new way. Nettie writes to Celie, "God is different to us now, after all these years in Africa, more spirit than even before, and more internal." Though critical of religious beliefs which reinforce sexist and racist domination, Shug insists on the primacy of a spiritual life, constructing a vision of spirituality which echoes the teachings of religious mystics who speak of healing alienation through recognition of the unity in all life.

Spiritual quest is connected with the effort of characters in *The Color Purple* to be more fully self-realized. This effort merges in an unproblematic way with a materialist ethic which links acquisition of goods with the capacity to experience emotional well-being. Traditionally mystical experience is informed by radical critique and renunciation of materialism. Walker positively links the two. Even though her pronounced critique of patriarchy includes an implicit indictment of perverse individualism which encourages exploitation (Albert is transformed in part by his rejection of isolation and self-sufficiency for connection and interdependency), Celie's shift from underclass victim to capitalist entrepreneur has only positive signification. Albert, in his role as oppressor, forces Celie and Harpo to work in the fields, exploiting their labor for his gain. Their exploitation as workers must cease before domination ends and transformation begins. Yet Celie's progression from exploited black woman, as woman, as sexual victim, is aided by her entrance into the economy as property owner, manager of a small business, storekeeper—in short, capitalist entrepreneur. No attention is accorded aspects of this enterprise that might reinforce domination: attention is focused on how useful Celie's pants are for family and friends; on the way Sofia as worker in her store will treat black customers with respect and consideration. Embedded in the construction of sexual difference as it is characterized in *The Color Purple* is the implicit assumption that women are innately less inclined to oppress and dominate than men; that women are not easily corrupted.

Rewarded with economic prosperity for her patient endurance of suffering, Celie never fully develops capacities for sustained self-assertion. Placed on a moral pedestal which allows no one to see her as a threat, she is always a potential victim. By contrast, Sofia's self-affirmation, her refusal to see herself as victim, is not rewarded. She is consistently punished. Sadly, as readers witness Celie's triumph, her successful effort to resist male domination which takes place solely in a private familial context, we also bear witness to Sofia's tragic fate, as she resists sexist and racist oppression in private and public spheres. Unlike Celie or Shug, she is regarded as a serious threat to the social order and is violently attacked, brutalized, and subdued. Always a revolutionary, Sofia has never been victimized or complicit in her own oppression.

Tortured and persecuted by the State, treated as though she is a political prisoner, Sofia's spirit is systematically crushed. Unlike Celie, she cannot easily escape and there is no love strong enough to engender her self-recovery. Her suffering cannot be easily mitigated, as it would require radical transformation of society. Given all the spectacular changes in *The Color Purple,* it is not without grave and serious import that the character who most radically challenges sexism and racism is a tragic figure who is only partially rescued—restored to only a semblance of sanity. Like the lobotomized Native American Indian in *One Flew Over the Cuckoo's Nest,* Sofia's courageous spirit evokes affirmation, even as her fate strikes fear and trepidation in the hearts and minds of those who would actively resist oppression.

Described as a large woman with a powerful presence, Sofia's vacant position in the kinship network is assumed by Squeak, a thin petite woman, who gains presence only when she acts to free Sofia, passively enduring rape to fulfill her mission. This rape of a black woman by a white man does not have grievous traumatic negative consequences, even though it acts to reinforce sexist domination of females and racist exploitation. Instead, it is a catalyst for positive change—Sofia's release, Squeak asserting her identity as Mary Agnes. Such a benevolent portrayal of the consequences of rape contrasts sharply with the images of black male rapists, images which highlight the violence and brutality of their acts. That the text graphically emphasizes the horror and pain of black male sexist exploitation of black females while de-emphasizing the horror and pain of racist exploitation of black women by white men that involves sexual violence is an unresolved contradiction if Walker's intent is to expose the evils of sexist domination. These contrasting depictions of rape dangerously risk reinforcing racist stereotypes that perpetuate the notion that black men are more capable of brutal sexist domination than other groups of men.

Throughout *The Color Purple* exposures of the evils of patriarchal domination are undercut by the suggestion that this form of domination is not necessarily linked to race and class exploitation. Celie and Albert are able to eradicate sexism in their relationship. The threat of masculine domination ceases when Albert forgoes phallic privilege and serves as a helpmate to Celie, assuming a "feminine" presence. However, the phallocentric social order which exists outside the domain of private relationships remains intact. As symbolic representation of masculine otherness, the phallus continues to assert a powerful presence via the making of pants that both women and men will wear. This is not a radical re-visioning of gender. It is a vision of inclusion that enables women to access power via symbolic phallic representation. As French feminist Antoinette Fougue reminds us:

> Inversion does not facilitate the passage to another kind of struc-
> ture. The difference between the sexes is not whether or not one
> does or doesn't have a penis, it is whether or not one is an integral
> part of a phallic masculine economy.

Within *The Color Purple* the economy Celie enters as entrepreneur and land-owner is almost completely divorced from structures of domination. Immersed in the ethics of a narcissistic new-age spiritualism wherein economic prosperity indicates that one is chosen—blessed, Celie never reflects critically on the changes in her status. She writes to Nettie, "I am so happy. I got love. I got work. I got money, friends and time."

Indeed the magic of *The Color Purple* is that it is so much a book of our times, imaginatively evoking the promise of a world in which one can have it all; a world in which sexual exploitation can be easily overcome; a world of unlimited access to material well-being; a world where the evils of racism are tempered by the positive gestures of concerned and caring white folks; a world where sexual boundaries can be transgressed at will without negative consequences; a world where spiritual salvation is the lot of the elect. This illusory magic is sustained by Walker's literary technique, the skillful combining of social realism and fantasy, the fairy tale and the fictionalized autobiographical narrative.

As the fictive autobiography of an oppressed black woman's journey from sexual slavery to freedom, *The Color Purple* parodies those primary texts of autobiographical writing which have shaped and influenced the direction of African-American fiction—the "slave narrative." With the publication of slave autobiographies, oppressed African-American slaves moved from object to subject, from silence into speech, creating a revolutionary literature—one that changed the nature and direction of African-American history; that laid the groundwork for the development of a distinct African-American literary tradition. Slave autobiographies worked to convey as accurately as possible the true story of slavery as experienced and interpreted by slaves, without apology or exaggeration. The emphasis on truth had a twofold purpose, the presentation of reliable sources, and, most importantly, the creation of a radical discourse on slavery that served as a corrective and a challenge to the dominant culture's hegemonic perspective. Although Walker conceived of *The Color Purple* as a historical novel, her emphasis is less on historical accuracy and more on an insistence that history has more to do with the interpersonal details of everyday life at a given historical moment than with significant dates, events, or important persons. Relying on historical referents only insofar as they lend an aura of credibility to that which is improbable and even fantastic,

Walker mocks the notion of historical truth, suggesting that it is subordinate to myth, that the mythic has far more impact on consciousness. This is most evident in the letters from Africa. Historical documents, letters, journals, articles, provide autobiographical testimony of the experience and attitudes of nineteenth-century black missionaries in Africa, yet Walker is not as concerned with a correspondence between the basic historical fact that black missionaries did travel to Africa than providing the reader with a fictive account of those travels that is plausible. Walker uses the basic historical fact as a frame to enhance the social realism of her text while superimposing a decidedly contemporary perspective. Historical accuracy is altered to serve didactic purposes—to teach the reader history not as it was but as it should have been.

A revolutionary literature has as its central goal the education for critical consciousness, creating awareness of the forces that oppress and recognition of the way those forces might be transformed. One important aspect of the slave narrative as revolutionary text was the insistence that the plight of the individual narrator be linked to the oppressed plight of all black people so as to arouse support for organized political effort for social changes. Walker appropriates this form to legitimize and render authentic Celie's quest without reflecting this radical agenda. Celie's plight is not representative; it is not linked to collective effort to effect radical social change. While she is a victim of male domination, Shug is not. While she has allowed patriarchal ideology to inform her sense of self, Sofia has not. By de-emphasizing the collective plight of black people, or even black women, and focusing on the individual's quest for freedom as separate and distinct, Walker makes a crucial break with that revolutionary African-American literary tradition which informs her earlier work, placing this novel outside that framework. Parodying the slave narrative's focus on racial oppression, Walker's emphasis on sexual oppression acts to delegitimize the historical specificity and power of this form. Appropriating the slave narrative in this way, she invalidates both the historical context and the racial agenda. Furthermore, by linking this form to the sentimental novel as though they served similar functions, Walker strips the slave narrative of its revolutionary ideological intent and content, connecting it to Eurocentric bourgeois literary traditions in such a way as to suggest it was merely derivative and in no way distinct.

Slave narratives are a powerful record of the particular unique struggle of African-American people to write history—to make literature—to be a self-defining people. Unlike Celie, the slave who recorded her or his story was not following the oppressors' orders, was not working within a context of domination. Fundamentally, this writing was a challenge, a resistance affirming that the movement of the oppressed from silence into speech is a liberatory gesture. Literacy is upheld in the slave narrative as essential to the practice of freedom. Celie writes not as a gesture of affirmation or liberation but as a gesture of shame. Nettie recalls, "I remember one time you said your life made you feel so ashamed you couldn't even talk about it to God. You had to write it." Writing then is not a process which enables Celie to make herself subject, it allows distance, objectification. She does not understand writing as an act of power, or self-legitimation. She is empowered not by the written word but by the spoken word—by telling her story to Shug. Later, after she has made the shift from object to subject she ceases to write to God and addresses Nettie, which is an act of self-affirmation.

Taken at face value, Celie's letter writing appears to be a simple matter-of-fact gesture when it is really one of the most fantastical happenings in *The Color Purple*. Oppressed, exploited as laborer in the field, as worker in the domestic household, as sexual servant, Celie finds time to write—this is truly incredible. There is no description of Celie with pen in hand, no discussion of where and when she writes. She must remain invisible so as not to expose this essential contradiction—that as dehumanized object she projects a self in the act of writing even as she records her inability to be self-defining. Celie as writer is a fiction. Walker, as writing subject, oversees her creation, constructing a narrative that purports to be a space where the voice of an oppressed black female can be heard even though the valorization of writing and the use of the epistolary form suppress and silence that voice.

Writing in a manner that reads as though she is speaking, talking in the voice of a black folk idiom, Celie, as poor and exploited black female, appears to enter a discourse from which she has been excluded—the act of writing, the production of story as commodity. In actuality, her voice remains that of appropriated other—interpreted—translated—represented as authentic unspoiled innocent. Walker provides Celie a writing self, one that serves as a perfect foil for her creator. Continually asserting her authorial presence in *The Color Purple*, she speaks through characters sharing her thoughts and values. Masquerading as just plain folks, Celie, Nettie, Shug, and Albert are the mediums for the presentation of her didactic voice. Through fictive recognition and acknowledgement, Walker pays tribute to the impact of black folk experience as a force that channels and shapes her imaginative work, yet her insistent authorial presence detracts from this representation.

Traces of traditional African-American folk expression as manifest in language and modes of story-telling are evident in Celie's letters, though they cannot be fully voiced and expressed in the epistolary form. There they are contained and subsumed. Commenting on the use of the epistolary form in *Seduction and Betrayal: Women and Literature*, Elizabeth Hardwick suggests,

> A letter is not a dialogue or even an omniscient exposition. It is
> a fabric of surfaces, a mask, a form as well suited to affectations
> as to the affection. The letter is, by its natural shape, self-justifying;
> it is one's own evidence, deposition, a self-serving testimony. In
> a letter the writer holds all the cards, controls everything.

That Celie and Nettie's letters are basically self-serving is evident when it is revealed that there has never been a true correspondence. And if readers are to assume that Celie is barely able to read and write as her letters suggest, she would not have been able to comprehend Nettie's words. Not only is the inner life of the characters modified by the use of the epistolary form, but the absence of correspondence restricts information, and enables the letters to serve both the interest of the writers, and the interests of an embedded didactic narrative. Functioning as a screen, the letters keep the reader at a distance, creating the illusion of intimacy where there is none. The reader is always voyeur, outsider looking in, passively awaiting the latest news.

Celie and Nettie's letters testify, we as readers bear witness. They are an explanation of being, which asserts that understanding the self is the precondition for transformation, for radical change. Narrating aspects of their personal history, they engage in an ongoing process of demythologizing that makes new awareness and change possible. They recollect to recover and restore. They seek to affirm and sustain the initial bond of care and connection experienced with one another in their oppressive male-dominated family. Since the mother is bonded with the father, supporting and protecting his interests, mothers and daughters within this fictive patriarchy suffer a wound of separation and abandonment; they have no context for unity. Mothers prove their allegiance to fathers by betraying daughters; it is only a vision of sisterhood that makes woman bonding possible. By eschewing the identity of Mother, black women in *The Color Purple,* like Shug and Sofia, rebelliously place themselves outside the context of patriarchal family norms, revisioning mothering so that it becomes a task any willing female can perform, irrespective of whether or not she has given birth. Displacing motherhood as central signifier for female being, and emphasizing sisterhood, Walker posits a relational basis for self-definition that valorizes and affirms woman bonding. It is the recognition of self in the other, of unity, and not self in relationship to the production of children that enables women to connect with one another.

The values expressed in woman bonding—mutuality, respect, shared power, and unconditional love—become guiding principles shaping the new community in *The Color Purple* which includes everyone, women and men, family and kin. Reconstructed black males, Harpo and Albert are active participants expanding the circle of care. Together this extended kin network affirms the primacy of a revitalized spirituality in which everything that exists is informed by godliness, in which love as a force that affirms connection and intersubjective communion makes an erotic metaphysic possible. Forgiveness and compassion enable individuals who were estranged and alienated to nurture one another's growth. The message conveyed in the novel that relationships no matter how seriously impaired can be restored is compelling. Distinct from the promise of a happy ending, it allows for the recognition of conflict and pain, for the possibility of reconciliation.

Radical didactic messages add depth and complexity to *The Color Purple* without resolving the contradictions between radicalism—the vision of revolutionary transformation, and conservatism—the perpetuation of bourgeois ideology. When the novel concludes, Celie has everything her oppressor has wanted and more—relationships with chosen loved ones; land ownership; material wealth; control over the labor of others. She is happy. In a *Newsweek* interview, Walker makes the revealing statement, "I liberated Celie from her own history. I wanted her to be happy." Happiness is not subject to re-vision, radicalization. The terms are familiar, absence of conflict, pain, and struggle; a fantasy of every desire fulfilled. Given these terms, Walker creates a fiction wherein an oppressed black woman can experience self-recovery without a dialectical process; without collective political effort; without radical change in society. To make Celie happy she creates a fiction where struggle—the arduous and painful process by which the oppressed work for liberation—has no place. This fantasy of change without effort is a dangerous one for both oppressed and oppressor. It is a brand of false consciousness that keeps everyone in place and oppressive structures intact. It is just this distortion of reality that Walker warns against in her essay "If the Present Looks Like the Past":

> In any case, the duty of the writer is not to be tricked, seduced, or goaded into verifying by imitation or even rebuttal other people's fantasies. In an oppressive society it may well be that all fantasies indulged in by the oppressor are destructive to the oppressed. To become involved in them in any way at all is, at the very least, to lose time defining yourself.

For oppressed and oppressor the process of liberation—individual self-realization and revolutionary transformation of society—requires confrontation with reality, the letting go of fantasy. Speaking of his loathing for fantasy Gabriel García Márquez explains:

> I believe the imagination is just an instrument for producing reality

and that the source of creation is always, in the last instance, reality. Fantasy, in the sense of pure and simple Walt Disney-style invention without any basis in reality is the most loathsome thing of all. . . . Children don't like fantasy either. What they do like is imagination. The difference between the one and the other is the same as between a human being and a ventriloquist's dummy.

The tragedy embedded in the various happy endings in *The Color Purple* can be located at that point where fantasy triumphs over imagination, where creative power is suppressed. While this diminishes the overall aesthetic power of *The Color Purple,* it does not render meaningless those crucial moments in the text where the imagination works to liberate, to challenge, to make the new—real and possible. These moments affirm the integrity of artistic vision, restore and renew.

Chronology

1944   Alice Walker is born on February 9, in Eatonton, Georgia, to Willie Lee and Minnie Tallulah (Grant) Walker. She is the eighth and last child born into this sharecropping family.

1952   Walker loses sight in one eye as the result of an accident with a BB gun. Unsightly scar tissue grows over the eye, and she is warned that she may lose sight in the other as well. Walker grows up unable to look people in the eye, and self-conscious of her affliction.

1958   The scar tissue on her eye is removed.

1961–65   Walker attends Spelman College in Atlanta, Georgia. Spelman is an elite college for black women. After two years she transfers to Sarah Lawrence, receiving her degree in 1965. During this time she undergoes an abortion, and travels to Africa for a summer, both of which inspire her to write poetry. She gives the poems to Muriel Rukeyser.

1965–67   After graduating from Sarah Lawrence, Walker moves to New York's lower east side to work for the welfare department. Soon after, she moves to Mississippi to work in the Civil Rights movement. In 1966 she is a Breadloaf Writer's Conference Scholar, and in 1967 she receives both a Merrill Writing Fellowship and a McDowell Colony Fellowship.

1967   On March 17, Walker marries Melvyn Roseman Levanthal, a Civil Rights lawyer; they later have one daughter, Rebecca.

1968   *Once,* Walker's first book of poems (written in the aftermath of her abortion during college) is published. Walker is a writer-in-residence and teacher of black studies at Jackson State

University, Mississippi. The following year she teaches at Tougalou College.

1970   *The Third Life of Grange Copeland,* Walker's first novel, is published.

1971   Walker receives a Radcliffe Institute Fellowship. In 1972 she teaches literature at Wellesley College and the University of Massachusetts, while still on the Radcliffe Fellowship.

1973   *Revolutionary Petunias* (poems) is published, and Walker is awarded a National Book Award for this volume. She also receives the Lillian Smith Award from the Southern Regional Council. *In Love and Trouble,* a collection of stories, is published.

1974   Receives the Rosenthal Foundation Award from the American Academy of Arts and Letters for *In Love and Trouble.* A book for children, *Langston Huges: American Poet,* is published.

1975   Becomes contributing editor to *Ms. Magazine.*

1976   Walker and Levanthal divorce. *Meridian,* Walker's second novel, is published.

1977   Walker receives a Guggenheim Fellowship, as well as her second McDowell Colony Fellowship.

1979   Edited *I Love Myself When I Am Laughing . . . : A Zora Neale Hurston Reader* and *Good Night, Willie Lee, I'll See You in the Morning* (poems). During this time she moves out to California to write *The Color Purple.*

1981   *You Can't Keep a Good Woman Down,* a collection of stories, is published.

1982   *The Color Purple* is released, receiving a nomination for a National Book Critics Circle Award. Walker is named a distinguished writer in Afro-American Studies at Berkeley. In the spring, she teaches literature at Brandeis University, as the Fannie Hurst Professor of Literature.

1983   Walker is awarded the Pulitzer Prize for *The Color Purple. In Search of Our Mothers' Gardens,* a book of "womanist" prose, is published.

1984   Publishes *Horses Make a Landscape More Beautiful* (poems).

1988   *Living by the Word,* a volume of essays, is published.

Contributors

HAROLD BLOOM, Sterling Professor of the Humanities at Yale University, is the author of *The Anxiety of Influence*, *Poetry and Repression*, and many other volumes of literary criticism. His forthcoming study, *Freud: Transference and Authority*, attempts a full-scale reading of all of Freud's major writings. A MacArthur Prize Fellow, he is general editor of five series of literary criticism published by Chelsea House. In 1987–88, he served as Charles Eliot Norton Professor of Poetry at Harvard University.

PETER ERICKSON teaches English at Williams College. He is the author of *Patriarchal Structures in Shakespeare's Drama*.

THADIOUS M. DAVIS is Professor of English at the University of North Carolina at Chapel Hill and has written widely on Southern and Afro-American literature.

BARBARA CHRISTIAN is Professor of Afro-American Studies at the University of California at Berkeley. Her books include *Black Woman Novelists* and a *Teaching Guide to Black Foremothers*.

KEITH BYERMAN teaches English at the University of Texas at Austin and is the author of *Fingering the Jagged Grain*.

MAE G. HENDERSON is Associate Professor in the African-American World Studies Program and the Department of English at the University of Iowa. She is coeditor of the five-volume *Antislavery Newspapers and Periodicals: An Annotated Index of Letters 1817–1871* and the author of a forthcoming monograph on black expatriate writers.

SUSAN WILLIS, author of *Specifications*, teaches at Duke University.

W. LAWRENCE HOGUE has published articles in *Black American Literature Studies* and *MELUS* and is the author of *Discourse and The Other: The*

Production of The Afro-American Text. He is currently completing a book, *Ethnicity, Modernism, Post-modernism: A Critique of the Grand Narrative,* that examines the effectiveness of ethnic and racial American writers' literary and ideological models or narratives in engaging modern and post-modern experiences.

DIANNE F. SADOFF is Associate Professor of English at Colby College and the author of *Monsters of Affection.*

DEBORAH E. McDOWELL is Associate Professor of English at the University of Virginia.

JOHN F. CALLAHAN is Professor of English at Lewis and Clark College. He is the author of a study of F. Scott Fitzgerald and, most recently, *In the African-American Grain.*

TAMAR KATZ teaches English at Cornell University.

MARIANNE HIRSCH, a member of the Department of French and Italian at Dartmouth College, is completing a study of maternal anger in literature.

BELL HOOKS (Gloria Watkins) is the author of *Ain't I a Woman: Black Women and Feminism* and *Black Feminist Theory: From Margin to Center.* She teaches English and Afro-American literature at Yale University.

Bibliography

Baker, Houston A., Jr., and Charlotte Pierce-Baker. "Patches: Quilts and Community in Alice Walker's 'Everyday Use.'" *The Southern Review* 21 (1985): 706–20.

Christian, Barbara. "The Contrary Black Women of Alice Walker." *Black Scholar* 12, no. 2 (March–April 1981): 21–30, 70–71.

———. "No More Buried Lives: The Theme of Lesbianism in Lorde, Naylor, Shange, Walker." *Feminist Issues* 5, no. 1 (Spring 1985): 3–20.

———. "Novels for Everyday Use: The Novels of Alice Walker." In *Black Women Novelists,* 180–238. Westport, Conn.:Greenwood, 1980.

Coles, Robert. "To Try Men's Souls." *The New Yorker,* 27 February 1971, 104–6.

Cooke, Michael G. "Alice Walker: The Centering Self." In *Afro-American Literature in the Twentieth Century,* 157–76. New Haven: Yale University Press, 1984.

DuPlessis, Rachel Blau. *Writing beyond the Ending: Narrative Strategies of Twentieth Century Women Writers.* Bloomington: Indiana University Press, 1985.

Early, G. *"The Color Purple* as Everybody's Protest Art." *Antioch Review* 44 (1986): 261–75.

Ensslen, Klaus. "Collective Experience and Individual Responsibility: Alice Walker's *The Third Life of Grange Copeland.*" In *The Afro-American Novel Since 1960,* edited by Peter Bruck and Wolfgang Karrer, 189–218. Amsterdam: B. R. Gruner Publishing, 1982.

Fifer, Elizabeth. "The Dialect and Letters of *The Color Purple.*" In *Contemporary American Women Writers: Narrative Strategies,* edited by Catherine Rainwater and William J. Scheick, 155–65. Lexington: The University Press of Kentucky, 1985.

Finn, J. "Alice Walker and Flight 007." *Christianity and Crisis,* 31 October 1983, 397–98.

Fontenot, Chester J. "Alice Walker: 'The Diary of an African Nun' and DuBois' Double Consciousness." In *Sturdy Black Bridges: Visions of Black Women in Literature,* edited by Roseann P. Bell, Bettye J. Parker, and Beverly Guy-Sheftall, 150–56. Garden City, N.Y.: Doubleday (Anchor), 1979.

Fowler, Carolyn. "Solid at the Core." *Freedomways* 14 (1974): 59–62.

Froula, Christine. "The Daughter's Seduction: Sexual Violence and Literary History." *Signs* 11 (1986): 621–45.

Gaston, Karen C. "Women in the Lives of Grange Copeland." *CLA Journal* 24 (1981): 276–86.

Halio, Jay L. "First and Last Things." *The Southern Review* n.s. 9 (1973): 455–67.

Hallenbrand, Harold. "Speech after Silence: Alice Walker's *The Third Life of Grange Copeland*." *Black American Literature Forum* 20 (1986): 113–28.

Harris, Trudier. "Folklore in the Fiction of Alice Walker: A Perpetuation of Historical and Literary Traditions." *Black American Literature Forum* 11 (1977): 3–8.

———. "On *The Color Purple*, Stereotypes and Silence." *Black American Literature Forum* 18 (1984): 155–61.

———. "Tiptoeing Through Taboo: Incest in 'The Child Who Favored Daughter.' " *Modern Fiction Studies* 28 (1982): 495–505.

———. "Violence in *The Third Life of Grange Copeland*." *CLA Journal* 19 (1975): 238–47.

Heirs, John T. "Creation Theology in Alice Walker's *The Color Purple*." *Notes on Contemporary Literature* 14, no. 4 (September 1984): 2-3.

Lenhart, Georgann. "Inspired Purple?" *Notes on Contemporary Literature* 14, no. 3 (May 1984): 2-3.

McDowell, Deborah E. "The Self in Bloom: Alice Walker's *Meridian*." *CLA Journal* 19 (1981): 262–75.

McGowen, Martha J. "Atonement and Release in Alice Walker's *Meridian*." *Critique* 23 (1981): 25–35.

Meese, Elizabeth A. "Defiance: The Body (of) Writing/The Writing (of) the Body." In *Crossing the Double-Cross: The Practice of Feminist Criticism*. Chapel Hill: University of North Carolina Press, 1986.

Nowak, Hanna. "Alice Walker: Poetry Celebrating Life." In *A Salzburg Miscellany: English and American Studies 1964–1984,* I: 111–25. Salzburg: Inst. für Anglistik & Amerikanistik, Universität Salzburg, 1984.

Parker-Smith, Bettye J. "Alice Walker's Women: In Search of Some Peace of Mind." In *Black Women Writers,* edited by Mari Evans. Garden City, N.Y.: Doubleday (Anchor), 1984.

Pinckney, Darryl. "Black Victims, Black Villains." *The New York Review of Books* 29 January 1987, 17–20.

Pryse, Marjorie. "Zora Neale Hurston, Alice Walker, and the Ancient Power of Black Women." In *Conjuring: Black Women, Fiction, and the Literary Tradition,* edited by Marjorie Pryse and Hortense Spillers, 1–24. Bloomington: Indiana University Press, 1985.

Shelon, F. W. "Alienation and Integration in Alice Walker's *The Color Purple*." *CLA Journal* 28 (1985): 382–92.

Stade, George. "Womanist Fiction and Male Characters." *Partisan Review* 52 (1985): 265–70.

Stein, Kara F. "Meridian: Alice Walker's Critique of Revolution." *Black American Literature Forum* 20 (1986): 129–41.

Steinem, Gloria. "Do You Know This Woman? She Knows You: A Profile of Alice Walker." *Ms.,* June 1982, 35f.

Tate, Claudia. "Alice Walker." In *Black Women Writers at Work,* edited by Claudia Tate, 175–87. New York: Continuum, 1983.

Turner, Darwin. "A Spectrum of Blackness." *Parnassus: Poetry in Review* 4, no. 2 (Spring–Summer 1976): 202–18.

Washington, Mary Helen. "An Essay on Alice Walker." In *Sturdy Black Bridges: Visions of Black Women in Literature,* edited by Roseann P. Bell, Bettye J. Parker, and Beverly Guy-Sheftall, 133–49. Garden City, N.Y.: Doubleday (Anchor), 1979.

―――. "I Sign My Mother's Name: Alice Walker, Dorothy West, Paule Marshall." In *Mothering the Mind: Twelve Studies of Writers and Their Silent Partners,* edited by Ruth Perry and Martine Watson Brownley, 142–63. New York: Holmes & Meier, 1984.

Watkins, Mel. "Sexism, Racism, and Black Women Writers." *The New York Times Book Review,* 15 June 1986, 1, 35–37.

―――. "Some Letters Went to God." *The New York Times Book Review,* 25 July 1982, 7.

Williams, D. S. *"The Color Purple." Christianity and Crisis,* 14 July, 1986, 230–32.

Winchell, Mark Royden. "Fetching the Doctor: Shamanistic Housecalls in Alice Walker's 'Strong Horse Tea.' " *Mississippi Folklore Register* 25, no. 2 (Fall 1981): 97–101.

Acknowledgments

" 'Cast Out Alone/to Heal/ and Re-create/Ourselves': Family-Based Identity in the Work of Alice Walker" by Peter Erickson from *CLA Journal* 23, no. 1 (September 1979), copyright ©1980 by the College Language Association. Reprinted with permission.

"Walker's Celebration of Self in Southern Generations" (originally titled "Alice Walker's Celebration of Self in Southern Generations") by Thadious M. Davis from *The Southern Quarterly* 21, no. 4 (Summer 1985), copyright © 1983 by the University of Southern Mississippi. Reprinted with permission of the publisher.

"The Black Woman Artist as Wayward" (originally titled "Alice Walker: The Black Woman Artist as Wayward") by Barbara Christian from *Black Women Writers* (1950–1980), edited by Mari Evans, copyright © 1983 by Mari Evans. Reprinted with permission.

"Walker's Blues" (originally titled "Women's Blues: The Fictions of Tony Cade Bambara and Alice Walker") by Keith E. Byerman from *Fingering the Jagged Grain: Tradition and Form in Recent Black Fiction* by Keith E. Byerman, copyright © 1985 by the Univeristy of Georgia Press. Reprinted with permission of the University of Georgia Press.

"*The Color Purple*: Revisions and Redefinitions" (originally titled "Alice Walker's *The Color Purple*: Revisions and Redefinitions" by Mae G. Henderson, a revision of an article first published in *Sage: A Scholarly Journal on Black Women* 2, no. 1 (Spring 1985), copyright © 1985. Reprinted with permission of the publisher and author.

"Walker's Women" (originally titled "Alice Walker's Women") by Susan Willis from *New Orleans Review* 12, no. 1 (Spring 1985), copyright © 1985 by Loyola University, New Orleans. Reprinted with permission of the *New Orleans Review*.

237

"Discourse of the Other: *The Third Life of Grange Copeland*" (originally titled "History, the Feminist Discourse, and Alice Walker's *The Third Life of George Copeland*") by W. Lawrence Hogue from *MELUS* 12, no. 2 (Summer 1985), copyright © 1985 by W. Lawrence Hogue. Reprinted with permission.

"Black Matrilineage: The Case of Alice Walker and Zora Neale Hurston" by Dianne F. Sadoff from *Signs: Journal of Women in Culture and Society* 11, no. 1 (Autumn 1985), copyright © 1985 by The University of Chicago. Reprinted with permission of The University of Chicago Press and the author.

"(The Changing Same): Generational Connections and Black Novelists" by Deborah E. McDowell from *New Literary History* 18, no. 2 (Winter 1987), copyright © 1987 by *New Literary History*. Reprinted with permission of The Johns Hopkins University Press.

"The Hoop of Language: Politics and the Restoration of Voice in *Meridian*" by John F. Callahan from *In the African-American Grain: The Pursuit of Voice in Twentieth-Century Black Fiction,* copyright © 1987 by the Board of Trustees of the University of Illinois. Reprinted with permission of the University of Illinois Press and the author.

" 'Show Me How to Do Like You': Didacticism and Epistolary Form in *The Color Purple*" by Tamar Katz, copyright © 1988 by Tamar Katz. Printed with permission.

Excerpts from "Do I Do" by Stevie Wonder, copyright © 1982 by Jobete Music Co., Inc., and Black Bull Music, Inc. Reprinted with permission.

"Clytemnestra's Children: Writing (Out) the Mother's Anger" by Marianne Hirsch, copyright © 1988 by Marianne Hirsch. Printed with permission. A shorter version of this essay appeared as "Maternal Anger: Silent Themes and Meaningful Digressions in Psychoanalytic Feminism" in *Minnesota Review* n.s. 29 (Fall 1987).

"Writing the Subject: Reading *The Color Purple*" by Bell Hooks, copyright © 1988 by Bell Hooks. Printed with permission.

Index